Travel North Black Girl
A 3,000 Mile Journey in Search of Love, Peace, and Home

Olivia Hill

FIRST EDITION

Hardback ISBN: 978-1-942337-26-3
Paperback ISBN: 978-1-942337-27-0
e-ISBN: 978-1-942337-28-7
Library of Congress Control Number: forthcoming

Travel North Black Girl is published by:
Woodneath Press
8900 NE Flintlock Rd.
Kansas City, MO 64157
A program of The Story Center at Mid-Continent Public Library.

For information please direct emails to:
woodneathpress@mymcpl.org or visit our website:
www.mymcpl.org/story-center/publishing/woodneath-press

Cover design by Klara Maisch, Olivia Hill, & Lori Garcia
Cover design consultation by Amber Noll
Book layout and typography by Dave Burns, with Lori Garcia
Set in Garamond

Printed in the United States of America

Dedication

This book is dedicated to my friend I lost too young, Bernice Martin.

And my best and truest friend, Nancy Brazee.

Remember when we became friends?

You had no words then. So I painted some on the air with my voice for us!

Bold letters: **Black, Red, and Green.**

It was enough then for us to share and be protected under.

Until you caught your own voice. After the dream catcher sifted the mean and painful words and only left the peaceful, loving, and strong ones.

Author's Note

Thank you, first and foremost, in taking the chance on my story. Before you dive in, I wanted to clarify that this is a creative nonfiction. Although the stories are true, the names and some details has been changed to respect individual's privacy. I have no intent to cause pain or harm to any individual in this book. I intend only to recount events that impacted my life, as I recall them. This memoir is set in the '60s up to the early '80s. References to indigenous groups or reflections on Black culture attempt to stay true to the time period and may not reflect my current viewpoint or what is politically correct today.

Second, I know you will see my grandmother, often called mom, referenced many times in my narrative. She took and raised me at the age of two. She also taught us (my siblings and I) to call her mom. In Black communities, having a grandparent raise a child was common, making this quite normal to me. When my biological mother came into my life, I celebrated calling her mom too, but reference her as mother in this narrative. You will also find that I rarely refer to my siblings by their names. This partly was to protect them but to also protect myself psychologically. I needed the distance to write some of the darkest moments of my past.

Last, you will hear the dialect of my people in this journey. The mixture of African language, Southern accent, and Gullah influence are interwoven into the voice of my grandmother and relatives. This is not broken English. This is the legacy of the Black experience in our tongue.

Enjoy the journey ahead,

Olivia Hill

For my people, there was a basic desire that drove them north—freedom. The magnetic forces of the North pulled me, like my ancestors. What was I to answer?

Chapter One

1982.

Newlyweds.

We stood on the dock; seagulls screamed complaints in the sky above our heads. "Rough roads behind, sharp rocks ahead." I listened to the warnings of the gulls fill the air with haggard cries. If only I had known this was an omen of what was to come later that day.

The gulls' screams were no match for my own tortured thoughts. I was terrified of *this* unknown, of everything that lay ahead. The sky was beautifully clear, bright but cold, and everything around me seemed to go about life in an orderly manner. I had just survived a ferry trip from Whittier to Cordova, and I was steeling myself for the next and last ferry to the village. I was in turmoil over whether I belonged in this new world. These feelings kept me on high alert and activated my survival skill, fear which almost always triggered anger. I searched for something that would ground me.

I had very little firsthand knowledge about where I was going, or the people. The question folded in my mind. *How will the villagers react to me being Black: would my skin and hair be a curiosity; would they want to know about where I grew up or how I might see our world differently; or, on the contrary, would my dark skin automatically tell them what they needed to know? To treat me with suspicion and disdain.* My husband was Jewish, but for all other purposes, he would be seen as a white man and a teacher.

I must be out of my mind! Going to this place … isolated, not knowing anyone! My thoughts churned. *If this man bails on me … what the hell. Am I a project?* That's how it was put to me by his cousin's girlfriend before we got married, that he liked taking on social causes. *I don't know, I don't know … what the hell! What is wrong with you?* I tried to get a hold of myself, to stay calm. *He's a good man, and he married you because he's in love with you. Right …? You're not alone … You're in this together.* The thoughts gave me no peace. *What if one of us got hurt … could we get to a hospital in time? I could freakin' die out here; nobody would even know it! I might never see home again?*

It felt odd to think of home as a place I'd miss and might not ever go back to. To feel this fear of isolation, when there was not one friend that I'd left behind. Isolation was something I knew well from the family I grew up in, so that should have prepared me for being in the bush. Yet I didn't feel prepared. This dilemma might have simply been an issue of the devil you know is better than the one you don't.

I watched my husband on the dock looking out at the water, up at the sky, then back to his watch impatiently. I walked behind him and took his hand, pressing my body up against his back. I needed to hide myself safely in his center, to find the strength to do this, to not betray my fears.

"What? What are you doing, oh … are you cold?" He pulled away, turned to face me, took my hands and rubbed them a few times, then stuck them in my own pockets. I forgot his rules: no open displays of affection, no hand holding, no cutesy nuzzling or kissing. He had his own dark corners to contend with. A family that didn't show one another affection. The type that didn't attend to one another's hurt feelings with acts of affection or mistakes with meaningful guidance or discipline. Maybe that's what drew us together; two wounded creatures with the ability to see the invisible bruises. Seth had been ignored as a child. Ignored when he was bullied and tormented by the kids in the non-Jewish neighborhood of his childhood. Ignored when one of the most unspeakable acts that could happen to a child, happened to him.

His mother was a broken, wealthy heiress. Seth's father was a rough man that grew up in poverty and married his mother in order to secure himself a wealthy future. A marriage his father honored by cheating. She nursed Seth with the same indifference by locking herself away in her room, crying for years because of her failed marriage. They dealt with the needs of their children by throwing money at them for any problems that might arise. If that didn't work, yelling would suffice.

I remember when Seth told me he had a Jamaican nanny and I laughed. Then asked all the questions that came from my inability to conceive what that even looked like. I thought, *How did a woman let a stranger live in their home and pay them to hug, kiss, feed, change, soothe, and comfort their child when they were just down the hall?* My experience of being raised by someone other than my parent brought me to a simple conclusion: family did that job with no pay with the exception of welfare if they could get it. It didn't matter if they were ill-equipped to parent or not, they got the job. Kindness or mistreatment, it would be family that administered it. But Seth loved his Jamaican nanny. He spoke of her kindness, even in her sternness and straightforward ways that were built into her Jamaican-ness. He talked lovingly about her, as if she was the only one that had ever cared for him.

When Seth was in his preteens, he spent as much time as he could hanging out at friends' houses and wandering about neighborhoods. There were little restrictions or consequences when he broke rules. Little was demanded of him. It didn't matter when he ate dinner, as long as he showed up, even if he left right after. Seth told me once that he went a week without taking a bath, and no one in his family even noticed. He said it was like he didn't even exist. We grew up as polar opposites but the damage to us was the same.

As his parents' divorce dominated his life and his family disintegrated, the nanny was the exception to everything that had happened to him up to that point. She was the consistent rule. She gave value to his life every time she scolded him for not eating or washing. She cheered him on during his moments of achievements and held him to her expectations when he didn't do his best. "Seth, no child I'm raisin' walk 'round not clean, you too handsome for dirt to cover up that handsomeness. Now get washin' and good, or I'll get it done. You need to eat proper food, I'm cooking this fo' you, what you wantin'? I'll make your favorite, you be home on time, you hear me now? Too handsome to be actin' ugly."

He'd smile sometimes at the thought of her. I couldn't help but wonder if I was just a brown outer package that reminded him of her, or was there a deeper, more valuable similarity between her and I that drew him to me? Of course, she and I shared being straight talkers. I said what had to be said, especially in the defense of others, and we both loved to cook. That need to make people feel good with food and see them well-fed, I think is automatic to those that come from lesser means. It's hard to think that you could be the shadow of someone else's memory. *I hope that I'm enough, that what he sees is truly me.*

I stood hovering, but not touching him, trying to respect his rule. I was reminded of the rules that were forced on me by my grandmother; specifically, the one that demanded you not draw attention to yourself.

At that moment on the dock, I couldn't focus on rules, his or the ones that were always screaming in my head. I was freaking out inside, and my body trembled with fear. I just needed an anchor or something reassuring to grind out my worries. My husband's way of showing me love was different to what I experienced as a child. I needed acknowledgment and he acknowledged me. He asked me questions and shared stories about a world I had never experienced. It made me believe I was important, and someone wanted. He told me I was smart, smart enough to go to college, when I saw myself as anything but. I saw myself as rather unremarkable with the exception of plain old common sense.

I was proud that he thought I was an exceptional cook and could keep a clean house at twenty-two. My husband, six years older than me, joked that the women he dated before me couldn't even boil water. I was attracted to the fact he was educated; "booksmart," my grandmother would call it. He was handsome, even by Black folks' standards. Seth cared about teaching poor Black and Brown kids who grew up like me in the inner city. Where schools that moved you from grade to grade without being able to read were common. Where Black and Brown teachers didn't care any more than the white teachers. I watched Seth pour hours of extra work and money into wanting those kids' lives to be better through education. Whatever shortcomings he was showing me now, I was willing to accept, because I believed he wanted my life to be better too.

The dock seemed overrun with seagulls and their cries. "Why are these damn gulls so loud? What are they doing?" I blurted out, annoyed, trying to distract myself from the fear. "Where's the boat?"

The sound of a small plane flying in the distance caught my attention. The engine sounds crept into my thoughts, wreaking havoc. I watched, puzzled, as this tiny plane moved closer, landing in front of us. Seth motioned at the plane and me, but his voice was drowned out by the voice of my father in my head. "Hmph! God meant fo' us ta fly, he'd gave us wings. I ain't fallin' out no sky when I got a solid ground to stand on … won't make me no grease spot on the ground." He would say this when we saw planes fly overhead. I had been conditioned to fear, and such fear had been knitted in me since I was a child. Yet flying for the first time would be a minuscule endeavor compared to this feeling that was always with me, no matter the situation. It was similar to that feeling when someone is quietly standing behind you on the edge of a cliff or following you at a distance down a dark street. But this feeling follows me wherever I go, because it's inside.

Six Flags Over Mid-America was its official name, but for us, it was Disney World. Kids in my Kansas City neighborhood talked about Six Flags like it was some far away exotic island, not three hours and forty-five minutes away. It might as well have been light years away, especially if you were Black and financially challenged. Being Black in KC meant being confined like a rat in a maze with invisible boundary lines. That made for some serious big fish tales about the rides at Six Flags: so high you were in the clouds, or speeds so fast objects flew past you like a psychedelic rainbow. Of course, this was being told by kids that hadn't even been there. I believed the wild stories and was terrified at the thought of those rides. I feared falling miles to the ground, but at the same time, trembled with a weird excitement, anticipating seeing it all and riding the biggest beast. I didn't know if I would be brave enough to ride these terrifying monsters, but at the same time staying home was never an option, no matter the fear.

Going to Six Flags was a big deal for everybody in my neighborhood. Inner-city summer programs and Black church youth groups had bake sales, fish fries, and car washes—sometimes for a few years running—to raise enough money for such a trip. Families that couldn't afford a reduced fare played street ball, hide and seek, or just ran through yard sprinklers, trying to stay cool for the summer. My siblings and I were always a part of that latter group with the exception of one summer in 1972, when I took the biggest trip of my young life, leaving the confines of my neighborhood, house, and grandmother to go to Six Flags. This was the second year since their opening in April 1971, but Black folks didn't see this as coming in second or last. For us, this was the real opening, and we were going to be there.

"You know, the first year is all about workin' out the kinks, all them folks going first are the test dummies making sure everything is alright for us. So, see you really goin' during the official opening year!" That's the way we dealt with poverty and injustice.

My grandmother had a completely different attitude regarding the whole Six Flags trip and us leaving her sight. It was clear she didn't like being put in a position of having to make the decision for us to go. So, she tried her soft approach first, "Johnnymae, honey, I just don't have that kinda money right now … now if I had known earlier in the year maybe I could've done somethin'."

Everyone in the family both respected and feared my grandmother, being the eldest matriarch in the family. But they knew to be prepared if they were going to present or propose anything to her different from her preconceived ideas. Cousin Johnnymae didn't fail in doing her homework. "That's okay!" she told my grandmother, "The church is providing scholarships. I'm on the committee and we've been fundraising for over a year. We can apply for scholarships, and it will cover everything except spending money."

Round one was over. Now, round two would be my grandmother's most powerful weapon, trying to convince and manipulate us not to want to go. "Y'all, wanna go out there around all them people? Ya know it's gonna be ninety degrees in the shade. Another thing, I heard them rides are dangerous too … you know y'all don't wanna be ridin' them things! They goin' up in the air and comin' down a hundred miles per hour and if somethin' goes wrong, well I won't be there ta fix it. You can barely ride in the car without gettin' sick or bein' scared ta death. Well, what you want ta do? Vern, you want to stay home with Momma?" Everyone was quiet, but I was yelling in my head, *Heck no, I don't want to stay home with you!* I knew this was just her trick to divide and conquer, but it wasn't going to work.

"I think it could be fun! Cousin Johnnymae said there's animals and games and other stuff too," I said. My older sisters agreed, they thought it would be fun. My brother was not even in the equation, because he was a boy. Not to say our grandma didn't give him hell or control every decision in his life, it just seemed he got to do more, in spite of the tongue lashings. My sisters sometimes won because they were older, but only on rare occasions. And never a place or choice that my grandmother didn't approve. Being the youngest, I was a pawn to be used and manipulated for everyone's purpose. So, cousin Johnnymae got us the scholarships and this meant it was time for round three!

"I'm gettin' about tired of hearin' what Johnnymae gotta say. She ain't got no kids, and I'm sorry for her, but tryin' ta run my house, she betta think again! I know one thang, if you go you bet not get your tails out there and embarrass me askin' for everythang and anything you see! Don't be runnin' all over the place like you're a pack of animals. They waitin' ta see you don't have any home trainin' … every one of them, looking ta find the littlest thing ta say you don't. And for God's sake, stay together and watch out for each other. Act like you care 'bout one another!" My grandmother's lecture of dos and don'ts went on for weeks, until we finally left.

I worried the whole time about getting car sick. I was a skinny and sickly kid, burdened with constant stomach aches, allergies, and breathing problems. I would get sick just going on a car ride with my step-grandfather. My grandmother's lectures played in my head constantly as I thought about what she might do if I got sick on the bus. So, I willed myself not to.

Our small group was made up of my three siblings, eleven of cousin Johnnymae's youth group, and three other adults from her church stood in front of a mammoth-sized bus. There on the side of the bus was painted a gray animal running full gait. My sister told me that the picture was of a Greyhound dog and that's why the bus company was named Greyhound. I stared with a look of shock at the boney dog painted on the side of the bus. That dog was nothing like the dogs we kept. We had hunting dogs and mixed shepherd mutts that were thick and strong from table scraps mixed with dog food when we could afford it. This dog looked starved to death and ran as if its life depended on it.

The driver heaved each bag into an opening under the bus. I stared at him and cinched my cracked vinyl powder-blue Pan Am shoulder bag, belonging to my grandmother. "Come on, hand it here," the pink flush face of the driver spoke, but never made eye contact. "You'll get it back when you get there." My cousin Johnnymae nudged me from behind, but I refused to release my bag. She was much older than I, around my father's age and more like an aunt than a cousin.

With a point of her finger, we all headed onto the bus. As I stepped up the big stairs, I held the metal rail, pulling myself up into this great ship, bound for a place I'd never been.

I stood there a moment and looked down the row of seats. Slowly moving forward with both arms stretched out, I touched every seat all the way to the center of the bus, where the line stopped after all the teens filled up the back. The seats were blue and gray. They felt like mama's velvet chair, a chair Mrs. Lockhart (the woman grandma cleaned and cooked for) gave to her. We children were never allowed to sit on that chair, but I sneaked once or twice when nobody was home. My grandmother sat on it occasionally, reminiscing about her relationship with Mrs. Lockhart. I looked at that chair every day, taking its place in front of our window, in our house, throne-like. Its cushions demanded to be fluffed daily, while I had to sit on the hard, dirty thread-bare carpet. But sometimes when mom wasn't looking and I was in my place on the floor watching TV, I would rub it. I moved my hand back and forth over the short, soft velvet fibers feeling them shift under my fingers and watching the color go from dark to light, light to dark.

We drove for hours.

I sat mostly quiet, watching telephone poles and corn fields go by. I listened to the teens laugh and tease each other. I played a game in my head, trying to guess who liked my sisters and who my brother was showing off for. I wondered about the people that lived in the houses and on the farms we passed by. I watched kids on open land play and chase each other with a dog in tow. Cows and horses meandered about fields of green. I tried to see myself there.

I wanted to think about Six Flags, but I couldn't imagine it exactly. I could see roller coasters and huge Ferris wheels turning in the sky, but I didn't want to feel myself there. I hoped there was something and someone for me, waiting.

Finally, after a long bus ride, we arrived. Wow! We stepped off the bus to a billion people and kids, and as many buses and cars covered the parking lot. My brother and two sisters had made friends quickly on the ride there and immediately asked if they could check out the place with their newfound friends. "Stay together in groups," instructed cousin Johnnymae, "and meet here in two hours." Everyone huddled together to plan what they wanted to ride first. Unanimously, it would be the roller coaster, and then the Ferris wheel. I didn't want to do either. Everyone took off in different directions leaving me alone in Six Flags Over Mid-America. Everyone on the bus was older than me. I had turned twelve just five months ago and was allowed to come by default. If I didn't go, they couldn't go either. It amazed me how they jumped right in the middle of this swarm of people, unafraid, and swam against the current.

In this case, without looking back, my sister yelled for me to go with cousin Johnnymae, and they would come back later for me. I went and sat down on a bench at the meeting spot; I didn't see where cousin Johnnymae went or any of the other adults.

The sun was beating down on my parted scalp. Oil and sweat melted deep into the two thick braids on either side of my head. I could feel a familiar lump burn in my throat, which felt the size of a golf ball. It filled with each salty tear I swallowed and anger that tried to well up. I looked around again, and no one. I breathed in the hot air and returned it several times until the lump was swallowed. I could hear the screams of laughter and fear in the voice of the riders in the distance. I imagine my siblings flying down the tracks of the roller coaster with arms up screaming and smiling, the same as the people in the commercials. I wondered if they were on the big Ferris wheel turning just above the trees in the distance.

My eyes went everywhere. I sat there conjuring up every feeling in my imagination to know what it might be like on each ride. I closed my eyes and felt my mouth open to each scream as I listened for them. I licked the air with the smells of popcorn, hotdogs, and sugary cotton candy that went past me. Up to then, I'd never thought about what I liked or what I didn't really like before, because everything was always decided for me. I realized then that I liked leaving home and riding on a bus past cows, horses, and fields of grass. I liked watching people as I sat on the bench, no one to say, "Stop staring, it's not polite." I could watch those people and how they moved, talked, and cried over nothing, but got whatever they wanted.

"Not if they had my grandmother," I laughed a little out loud to my-self. I liked that most people didn't see me and after a while no one noticed me. I didn't like being lonely, but I was good at it. I didn't like kids making ugly faces at me when they passed. I didn't like being afraid of big things or big rides, but I loved imagining I knew how to ride them all, all by myself. I sat there waiting while the world passed, and I rode my imagination.

Johnnymae found me there about an hour and a half later.

"Where's everybody? You been on any rides yet?"

"No, ma'am, I stayed here. They went that way," I pointed.

I remember my cousin's face when she found me on the bench: confusion, pity, and sadness pressed into her dark round face. She walked me over to a little stand, selling drinks and food. We passed a vendor on the way that had windmills that glinted in the sun—red, green, gold, and blue. Just as we were about to pass the stall, a hot breath of wind blew and sent them spinning all at once. We both jumped and then burst into laughter. My whole body shook with unrestrained and uncensored pleasure, watching her laughing at us.

When we got to the stand, she pulled out an envelope that had "Food" written on the side and fingered through the limp, faded money my grand-mother had given her. Johnnymae handed me a five-dollar bill, and I bought a hotdog, popcorn, and a large soda pop. Having me count my change, she added what was left back into the envelope and placed it in her shoulder bag. I held my drink and popcorn, and my cousin carried my hotdog. Sipping the soda pop and nuzzling the corn, I balanced without dropping a single corn kernel on the way back to the meeting place. We were about to reach the windmill stall when Johnnymae exclaimed, "What color do you like?"

My eyes stretched almost as big as my mouth. She reached into her bag and pulled out, not my grandmother's envelope, but her wallet and handed the man a crisp ten-dollar bill. My cousin bought me a sky-blue windmill and candy with her own money. I smiled so big it hurt. We walked back but I walked close to her now, while the people watched me blowing my windmill and drinking soda pop all the way to the bench.

My siblings ran over to our check-in spot and asked for their money to buy food. They received their money and a reprimand for leaving me. Taking the money apologetically, they flew in different directions to find out how much they could buy with it. They sat on a nearby picnic bench and ate their undictated choices. I watched them all, my brother and sisters, laughing and eating, jumping and talking, happy in this beautiful unfamiliar landscape while my windmill turned quickly in the breeze of the shade. Cousin Johnnymae soon stood up and announced, "You have three more hours to go on rides, but be back here fifteen minutes before that time is up."

Johnnymae also instructed them to take me along and allow me to ride whatever I wanted. They were not to leave me by myself. Having no children, Johnnymae was kind and patient, the way people without kids are nice and not worn down yet. But now, even she moved away from us to talk with the other adults on the trip and looked to my sisters to relinquish her duties. Her mothering of me had its limits and she made it clear with a look that it had come to an end.

My middle sister quickly walked away with friends, leaving my eldest sister and I together. My eldest sister, dark and willowy, looked down at me, sitting on the bench. She held out her delicate long fingers and I took her hand. She asked me what I wanted to ride. In front of us was a merry-go-round, "That! That's what I want to ride," I exclaimed.

My sister smiled, but didn't laugh at me, possibly remembering the childhood memory of my five-year-old tears when our father could not afford to let me ride. The painted horses were familiar and gentle, like mythical beasts from fairytales read to me. The movies I watched had happy little white girls on merry-go-rounds. The horses rounded the corners, over and over again, as I had always imagined them, running wild. We climbed up, and I ran to sit on a white stallion with bright yellow, blue, and pink while my sister sat upon a horse of gold. Her smile grew big as the merry-go-round went faster. I laughed with excitement and a strange nervous fear from so much joy. We rode twice before she had me look for another ride.

We walked down the fairway when I stopped and asked, "What's that?"

"Bumper cars, you want to try?"

I climbed into the shiny primary-colored beetle. From her own beetle car, my sister laughed, showing the gap in her front teeth, my favorite feature of her face. With a jolt, the cars came alive and as cars slammed into me, she yelled instructions: "Go! Press the pedal and turn the wheel!"

Wham! I was hit on the left side. I spun and turned the wheel wildly to the left, then right, and pressed as hard as I could on the pedal. The car spun in a circle, round and round. I was hit over and over again, until I learned how to wham the other cars right back, all the while laughing out of control.

I would never go anywhere else like Six Flags as a child. The memory of that day is seared in my mind. Even more memorable was my grandmother allowing my siblings and I out of her sight and control. The whole family watched to see if she would give us freedom and possibly free herself from the fears that tormented her.

This small trip was more than the freedom children sought to be away from the watchful gaze of parents, in search of unbridled fun. This was the moment that planted a seed in my mind and showed me I could leave home. I could survive without my grandmother and an environment that attempted to condition me to believe survival was not possible on my own. If I wasn't completely aware of the importance of this trip yet, it did not matter. The event would be safely stored until needed, like the knowledge my ancestors held deep in their minds and souls.

Chapter Two

Reflecting on our last stop before heading to the village takes me back to our first stay in one of Alaska's most unique towns, Whittier. The superintendent for the village of Tatitlek lived in Whittier. My husband still had to sign his teaching contract to seal the deal of becoming an Alaskan bush teacher. So, Whittier-bound we were.

We wanted to arrive in Tatitlek at least a few weeks before school began with the purpose of settling in. At least that was my hope, seeing as I would be left to figure out our domestic life. In true form to the way things unfolded during our Alaska journey, faith would have to temper a lack of preparation. We mailed our belongings ahead to the village, as well as ordered food and other supplies. Getting these supplies was contingent on my husband signing his contract.

Getting to Whittier meant a drive from Fairbanks, through Anchorage, into Portage. There we would catch the train, taking us into Whittier. The day was gray with patchy rays of sun that shot through rain-swollen clouds. The wipers on the car squeaked across the windshield from the mist. The coast as we traveled the Seward Highway bared everything from its beauty to its scars. Mountains stood erect despite the gnawed-away areas made by dynamite for a highway to wrap around the side. The road wound along the coast and clung to the foot of the massive, jagged, black-faced monolith. Each mountain, a centurion stationed thousands of years ago, stood undisturbed by our insignificant crawling about. I could barely scale the height of the mountains with my eyes without feeling panic and elation. I saw a field of ghostly black tree trunks and branches, haunting every motorist that traveled by with tales of their death during the Great Alaskan Earthquake and Tsunami of 1964. The ocean was there too, to the right of me. It sloshed about its rocky vessel in the way a child carries a bowl filled to the brim with cereal and milk. There were scenic stops along the way where people resembling buoys bobbed side to side with hands over their eyes in search of whale pods and sea life in this great wet expanse. We did not stop until we pulled into a gravelly, clay-packed parking area near the train tracks. My husband checked the time for the train's arrival. We had fifteen minutes. Grabbing a couple of backpacks from the back seat, one suitcase, and a duffle bag from the trunk, we got out of the car and locked the doors. The car would have to stay there until our friends from Anchorage picked it up. I pulled my suitcase with tiny wheels across the rocky path, gripping tightly with two hands to keep it from toppling. We headed to where we would wait to board the train.

I stood there with my husband and a handful of others. We were surrounded by wilderness, and yet it was not lost on me that I was about to embark on another first in my life, riding a train. I was profoundly aware in these moments that my husband loved engaging total strangers in conversations about what he knew and likewise what knowledge they had.

"Yeah! Our first trip to Whittier … you, you been there already? Ohhhhh! You live there? So, anything to do there? You got to figure it's … got to be a little boring, right? I mean, I'm sure it's gorgeous, but you're frickin' trapped in there. Ahhh, okay! So, I read it was built by the military around the end of World War II! Man, they were making sure those little Russian guys weren't gettin' them … wasn't nobody gettin' past this mountain. Look at that thing!"

My husband stared towards the mountain a second and continued what he would call kibitzing for the whole fifteen minutes. The train pulled in and we boarded.

I had romanticized about riding a train my entire life. As a child, late at night, I'd listen to trains far off in the distance. Now I could finally feel for myself the sleepy rock of the train's car on the rails. I would hear the clacking sound as I held tight to my husband's arm while life moved past me, one frame at a time. Before now, trains were just a sound I heard coming into an open window or a prop used in old movies, like in one of my favorite movies as a child: *White Christmas* starring Bing Crosby, Danny Kaye, and Rosemary Clooney. It depicted romance and antics on a train, and I hoped my first trip would be as memorable.

I pondered the similarities in my romantic daydream. In the movie, the scene was set during a cold winter's day. My setting was a cold day as well, but without frosty breaths and a white blanket of snow. I would have to settle for being in the middle of fall with frigid rains and that wet dampness that chills to the bone. My husband would play Danny Kaye's part. Of course, my husband was much more handsome, humorous, and smart, but it seemed a logical choice with both sharing a Jewish heritage and Bing Crosby being too white. *I would be Rosemary Clooney? Hmmm, not so much.* I saw myself more suited for a Pam Grier type—tough and kicking ass!

The train pulled away. It jerked as it moved forward, then picked up speed until it evened out its pace. I listened to the wheels clacking along the tracks. I gazed out the window at the landscape gliding by as we headed towards the entrance of the Whittier Tunnel. I could see it as the train rounded a curve. My husband rattled off facts about the tunnel and drew me in for a moment.

"I know the locals call it the Whittier Tunnel, but it's really the Anton Anderson Memorial Tunnel, named after some army engineer that mapped it all out. Can you imagine! They blasted two and a half miles right through the middle of massive rock … Maynard Mountain. It's the longest tunnel through a mountain in North America."

My husband was still talking when we lurched into the hollowed-out, black mouth of the tunnel, swallowed by immeasurable darkness. I stretched my eyes as wide as I could to adjust to the dim murky yellow lighting in the train car. The bright white headlights glinted off the rock walls in flickers. Yet the light shared none of its illumination with the surrounding areas.

Whether from fear or from the reverence people give to unfamiliar spaces, there is a quieting that occurs among human beings in such conditions. We were experiencing it now. My husband even stopped talking. I looked down into my lap. I focused on a familiar thing, my hands. Occasionally, the sewn edge of my coat held my attention. Yet, I battled the thoughts that now played out in my mind. They were not romantic daydreams. Waves of panic came over me and the urge to jump up and run down the aisle screaming, "We're going to die! We're going to die," rose in my throat. I held tight while my grandmother's stern voice disrupted my internal hysteria. She always had an iron pride and unyielding expectation that now focused me. I was to maintain appearance for appearance's sake. I sat quietly, in fear … hands folded like a lady. With eyes closed, I pretended to rest.

After settling into Whittier, the evenings passed like most of our time spent at the Anchor Inn; slowly. It had been two weeks, and we still did not have the green light to go to the village. We followed the narrow halls of the Inn, going to and from our room. I couldn't help but think of myself as in some suspense movie, like the Bates Motel. A creepy feeling came over me when I walked through those tight, narrow halls. Someone could snatch me into a room, and the person walking in front of me wouldn't even know I was gone. The floors were uneven, and the dark wooden doorways made each entrance a black abyss. Muddled colors washed the dimly lit walls. Our room was tiny and old-fashioned with red carpet, ruffles, and faded floral wallpaper.

There was a small store inside the building where you could get toiletries, touristy knick-knacks, and videos to rent. The movie rentals were a prized commodity during the cold and dreary months of fall and winter. The owner was glad to buy up any movies that might come through Whittier. We had gone in several times during our extended stay, and the shop owner became friendly enough to ask if we were looking for anything special. He pointed to a small area in the corner away from everything. There we found a small display of porno, lit from above with dark blue curtains hung to block obvious view, peep-show style. I walked away from the area quickly, and my husband followed, slowly. The shop owner wanted to know if we had any videos of our own we might want to sell. He said, "Movies around here are like currency. If you have something good and entertaining, people will pay a good price."

We were hit with how expensive Alaska was when we saw the milk prices. A gallon of milk in Alaska ran at six to seven dollars. Down in the lower forty-eight, which is what Alaskans called the rest of America, they were paying one dollar and twenty-five cents to a dollar and seventy-five cents a gallon in some places. In Kansas City, we were paying a buck fifty, and I thought that was highway robbery. I knew how to live on the cheap with beans, greens, soup, and cornbread for weeks. But everything here was ten times more expensive. If you didn't have a good job, you'd better know how to hunt or subsist, or be prepared to leave or starve. We were shooting for the job, seeing as how we knew nothing about hunting.

The gift shop owner reminded me of the neighborhood hustlers I grew up with. They sold boosted goods on the corner, at the barber shop, or the beauty salon. The only exception was the fact that he had a store and would be considered legit. He was looking for copies of any popular movies: *Apocalypse Now, Mad Max, Alien, The Shining, and Star Wars.* One evening we went to return the movies we had rented, and the guy turned to my husband, speaking in a lowered voice.

"I can get a lot for porn, any kind! If you got anything you're done with, I'll buy it."

What? I thought, *So, did he think we were porn stars? Maybe my husband's New York/Jersey accent made him think that he fit some stereotype, or being a white man with a young Black woman gave him the idea we would be into porn or selling some homemade versions.* Gross and awkward, it made me feel dirty and exposed.

I moved away from them and tried to pretend not to hear him. I wandered around the store for a minute, then told my husband I was heading to the restaurant. I stopped in the gift shop only once more after that encounter to see if they had pain relievers for a headache. He took the opportunity to interrogate me with a barrage of questions:

I see you're not with your guy!
Where's he at?
So, you two are both from New York? ...
Is he a boyfriend?

This was accompanied by that feeling you get when a guy is laser beaming through your outer clothes, then your underwear, and your skin starts to hurt. I left without headache medicine and told my husband what happened. His responses made me doubt myself. "Yeah! I don't know, maybe you're being a little sensitive … he probably didn't mean anything … ahhh, he's just running his mouth."

The restaurant was on what would be the first floor of the building, but you had to climb a steep flight of encased stairs from the road to enter the restaurant and the rest of the inn as well. We were eating up what little funds we had budgeted for the hotel on Ms. Pac-Man and pumpkin pie, which became the height of my entertainment. My husband was entertained more by reading, talking, and working. Yet because of his lack of attention towards me, my job became vying for his attention in any way I could, and sex was what seemed to work.

We spent our days walking along the dock, watching the massive number of seagulls blanket the air with deafening cries. We watched the fishing boats coming and going on the dark blue water and the train moving through the black and green mountains surrounding us. Beautiful and tomb-like was the isolation. The cold rain fell most days, and those were the days I ate pie and fed Ms. Pac-Man. She ate my quarters like I ate that hotel pie, but she had no guilt or shame from her indulgence.

"Could you get me some more quarters, please? Do you have any more change?"

His lake blue eyes looked at me and he said in a Jewish Jersey accent, "What! You spent the whole ten dollars already?"

It was over: no more pie and no more Ms. Pac-Man.

Recreation money had dried up, and this forced us out of the hotel despite the miserable weather. We braved the wind, rain, and cold because our sanity now depended on it. We headed past the docks on one of our walks and followed the water as far as we could or dared to. The winds began to pick up, and icy cold rain mixed with seawater sheared any exposed skin.

I took notice of a large building I later came to know as the Buckner Building. Whipping my head side to side, trying to avoid needle-sharp rain, I saw it staring out at the sea and perhaps me.

"What is that?" I yelled, and my husband shrugged. It was some man-made military monstrosity erected for the human purpose of destruction, then abandoned to nature once it accomplished or failed its mission. I could feel the gaze from blackened windows, the massive gray concrete building intent on intimidating. The power of its size and unnaturalness in such a beautiful landscape made it even more ominous. I saw something move past several windows. Like tattered plastic waving in the wind, and then it was gone.

"Let's go back now!" I panicked, and we turned towards the Anchor Inn.

I was cold to the bone and frightened. There was something about things towering over me that had always made me shrink inside. I didn't understand the feeling that crawled along the back of my head, down my spine, and then took over my body, making me small. For as long as I could remember the feeling had been there, and it made my body tremble and my stomach hurt. Every part of me was affected and left me with no words. When I encountered these ominous things, my heart raced. My breath would suck in and out hard, trying to catch itself, and I would know to make myself small and hard to be seen.

There were giants everywhere in this place: the mountains, the buildings, the trees, and the ocean. They reminded me I was trapped here. As we walked quickly towards the hotel, in front of me was a pitch-black ellipse watching me, the train tunnel. It was the birth canal of the giant mountain that surrounded us and pressed us against the sea. It was the only way into Whittier except by water, and life was delivered twice a day: fishermen, hotel workers, whatever people who lived here needed, along with the occasional tourist.

The rain pounded my face, and a strange thought came: *What if I could run through the tunnel fast enough to make it to the other side before a train came?* I imagined that I would close my eyes to avoid the darkness of the tunnel. Running as fast as I could, I would open my eyes and be magically on the other side. We reached the stairwell of the Anchor Inn. I looked back towards the tunnel, like a guaranteed escape. I turned my gaze back to the stairs. I would ascend and go back to the little room. Warmer and a little safer, I'd wait.

The phone rang. It was my eldest sister Janice, ten years older than me. She was my mother's daughter, but not my father's.

"Hello," I said.

"Hey, this is Janice. What are y'all doing?"

"Nothing."

"I have someone that wants to speak to you."

"Who?"

"Your mother."

I couldn't speak, as if the dusty air from the basement had triggered my bronchitis. My mouth gaped open for a minute, and everything was silent. My sister Janice had started coming around us a few years before this call. I didn't remember anything about her prior to that, because I was a toddler when we were separated and hadn't laid eyes on her since.

When I saw her sitting in my grandmother's living room for the first time in years, I thought she was one of those Afro Sheen commercial models. And why would a model be sitting in my grandmother's house? But it wasn't a model, it was my oldest sister Janice. My grandmother always spoke fondly of my sister, how she loved her, and how my mother should've left my sister with her, and maybe she would've turned out better.

My grandmother let my sister and her husband come and take us roller skating or to a movie on the weekend sometimes. That was funny since we didn't know how to roller skate, and the time spent with them added up to them dropping us off at the rink and picking us up a few hours later to take us home. We sat there at the rink in the same spot she left us, watching people go around and around, skating and dancing to the music.

I later found out from one of my grandmother's therapy rants that my sister had been a prostitute, and she blamed my mother for it. My grandmother also had convinced herself that she wasn't a prostitute anymore since she was married. It's interesting how adults decide to believe what they want to believe because it makes it easier for them. The truth was that she dropped us off at the skating rink, so she could work. Even worse, her husband was her pimp. Her silence and being allowed to stay alive was bought with that marriage.

After seeing us on the regular for a year, Janice stopped coming to get us. I found out years later she had stopped because her husband started pressuring her to pull my other two sisters and me into his stable. The last time I was with her at their place, she was hell-bent on revenge. I guess she wanted payback for a whole list of things, including him beating her up all the time and maybe for what he wanted to do to us. So, she started poisoning him.

That day, she had made chili for us and dipped up our bowls from a large pot. It was the best chili I ever remember having. I can taste it every time I think of the spicy, slightly sweet and salty flavor, with the ground beef! I wanted more, but she told me no; the rest was for him. She pulled out a bottle from her pocket and added a special ingredient. It was the same kind of bottle I saw in our medicine cabinet with a skull and bones picture on the label. My grandmother used it on our cuts and scrapes, but she warned not to touch it because it could kill us if we drank it. It was the same red, orange-brown liquid, iodine. She poured the bottle in the chili, added some more hot sauce, stirred it around, dipped up a large bowl, and gave it to him. She told me to be quiet and get my things, she was taking us home. He was eating it when we left.

I didn't see my sister much after that until a few years had passed. When I did see her, it was with him. He looked different, bad, but alive. He had been a very attractive man: medium-brown skin, nicely built, and muscular yet trim. But when I saw him this time, he was swollen in his face, belly, and hands. His skin had darkened to an unnatural black.

It wasn't much longer after that, she finally got away from him. She told me she spent years feeding him that stuff. He wouldn't die, just got sick and ugly as hell. I was glad he didn't die at her hand for fear of what might have happened to her. When he eventually did die, I was ecstatic. It was satisfying to know he lived long enough to suffer for what he did to her and other young women, and especially for the secret that forced her into a marriage to keep her silent.

"Hey, are you there? Do you want to speak to her?" My sister's voice commanded me through the phone and back from a dazed state.

"Yes," I said with little thought about what it could mean.

"Ok, stay by the phone. I'll call you back."

My two other sisters, who were two and three years older than me, asked who was on the phone.

"Janice! She asked me if I wanted to talk to our mother?"

"What! For real?" My two sisters rushed over to me, standing by the phone smiling, excited, waiting for the phone to ring, and to hear the voice of our mother that none of us remembered.

The washing machine started banging and knocking hard with twisted clothes in the metal drum. We all jumped and spun around in fear. My eldest sister I lived with went to balance the clothes in the washer. The phone didn't ring and my two sisters returned to our chores of sorting and washing clothes, but I could not pull myself away from the amateurishly hung phone, barely attached to the exposed two-by-four on the basement wall. It was hung to save my grandmother from having to race up the stairs for a ringing phone when she was doing laundry. The teenagers of the house used it to sneak calls away from the ears and eyes of an always watching grandmother.

The phone rang. We all stared at it, frozen for a moment. Then one of my sisters said, "Answer it before someone else does." I heard a voice. It was not my sister Janice; this voice was deep and warm.

"Hello, hello," she said.

"Hi."

"How are you, baby, this is your mother, who is this? LaVern, my baby girl."

I heard my mother's voice. It was unfamiliar, but this time, I would be old enough to not forget it. Her voice had celebrity status as she, up to that point, was only a black and white cracked wedding photo in the bottom of a dresser drawer in our room. That day my mother called, I felt no hate. She was a light I wanted to walk right into, and I ran to my grandmother with the exciting news, "My mother called!"

That call changed my life forever. Unfortunately, my grandmother's hate for her was redirected to us kids. Her already controlling, criticizing, and punitive ways only intensified. My mother's renewed desire to gain custody or visitation rights was short-lived against my grandmother. It was like the Black Panthers against the establishment; it failed. My grandmother refused to honor any court order and threatened to kill us if we went with her. The night before we were to go to court, she called the three of us girls in front of her.

"What are you gonna tell that judge about your mama?" She'd start off and we'd look at each other, not understanding what she'd meant, or at least I didn't understand.

"Ma'am?" we said, looking at each other.

"You know what I mean, don't stand there lookin' stupid … as hard as I done work, killin' myself ta raise ya little niggas' … ya tell that judge ya want ta go with her, I'll kill ya where you stand, ya hear me? I'll find ya and kill e'ry one of ya."

I saw her hand ball into a knot.

"I've had about all I can take, I'm not takin' no more, now get out of my sight before I do somethin' ta you … I swear if I could kill you and bring you back, I'd kill you for a week."

From that point on, she left us with little choice. My middle sister and I chose to skip school to see my mother occasionally. My father's eldest daughter chose to stay loyal and obedient as a way to survive the brunt of my grandmother's brutality. This went on for the next four years, until I turned fifteen.

It was a dreary cold day, and my father's eldest daughter, almost four years older than I, met us at the door coming in from school. Her face was soft and wet from crying, full of fear.

"Mom knows you've been seeing our mother. She found the clothes."

My mother had bought my middle sister and I clothes for our birthdays. My birthday is in January, and my sister's is in February. We used to pretend we were twins because people thought we looked so much alike. The coats were beautiful, the most beautiful coats I'd ever owned. Most of our things came from the attics of the old white ladies my grandmother worked for, or Spartans, which was the Kmart of our day. When we went shopping for something nice for church or special occasions, we always went to JCPenney.

My middle sister and I rushed to our room to try and change our school clothes before she could get there. I knew my grandmother, just seeing bare skin was like a shark smelling blood and this could send her into a frenzy. The thought of having bare skin exposed and being beaten with a belt buckle or window stick was hell enough, so I was willing to do anything to save us from that.

My sister, in a panic, whispered, "You going to get undressed?"

I looked at her. "No! You undress, she not catching me with no clothes on."

We both laughed nervously until she entered our room with the clothes.

"Where'd ya get this mess? You'd bet not lie, I'll stump you ta death."

We said nothing.

"You hear me talking to you, you little lyin', sneakin' tramps?"

I then spoke, "Our mother."

"Yo' Momma? You startin' ta be just like her, little liar … I can't stand a liar. How'd ya get this mess? You been sneakin' over there behind my back?"

"No, ma'am, Daddy picked up the clothes from her."

I knew that this was only partly the truth, but for me, a bigger truth was that my dad had become something of a friend to my mom and her lover over the years. My mother told me it started one day when she saw him drive by her house. She lived only a few blocks from where my grandfather and my dad lived, but I never knew she was so close. He'd drive through sometimes with us in his beat-up old truck, she said. She'd yelled him down one day and bribed him to come by her house for beer in the hope he'd bring us kids. He did stop, but he never did bring us kids. Instead, he enjoyed many beers over the years and never let on to us that our mother existed.

I always knew my dad was afraid of my grandmother. Most of the time I felt sorry for him, because of the way she spoke to him. She'd even beat him in front of us. But keeping us from our mother, I couldn't forgive this. So, I asked Dad if he would pick me up from the school, so I could bring some clothes home that my counselor was giving out. I said a bunch of new clothes were donated to the school for Christmas. I hid them and we wore a piece at a time, thinking I could sell that story to my grandmother if she asked where we got them. My mistake was not telling her the same thing, but I was afraid and knew she would call the school to find out if that was true. If I could just wear them once, I thought, it would be worth it.

"You lie! Your daddy didn't bring this mess here. Now how'd you get it? I'm gonna beat yo' ass. I hate a liar, get them clothes off… you let me find my stick … I'ma try ta break your necks."

My sister stood for a minute shaking with fear. I looked out the window to the house next door that had the mulberries of my childhood. My grandmother now owned the house and had cleared away all the bushes, brambles, and mulberries. The clearing exposed a tunnel between the fence in the back of the house and an old dilapidated garage where vines rolled and connected the two. The vines made a circle, and dogs and other animals ran through from our side to the other, making a passageway.

"Let's climb out the window and run to our mother's house," I urged my sister.

She quickly responded, "No! She might catch us in the window."

I begged, "Come on, we can do it, you can go first, let's go before she comes back."

"No, I'm scared, you go," she whispered.

I dreamt of my escape many, many times through that hollow. It didn't come that time. I couldn't leave my sister to face my grandmother by herself.

Chapter Three

The superintendent, Nyal Worsham, made arrangements allowing us free lodging in Whittier's elementary school library for the remaining days before we left for the village. This meant we were once again sleeping in a sleeping bag. This time it was on a hard floor instead of the hard ground, which had been our bed the entire month it took us to get to Alaska, minus the bugs. It also meant finding space among stacks of books, desks, video equipment, shelving, and anything else that might be useful or obsolete in a classroom. Yes, we were in a storage room.

Nyal invited us to dinner to finally sign the teaching contracts. I was ecstatic that we were no longer going to be in limbo and broke. Because we were most definitely broke—and not "a few dollars in your pocket broke" neither—but busted. I was reminded of the many signs we saw in the windows of cars and repurposed school buses on the way to Alaska; "Alaska or Bust," they read. Well, we accomplished both. There was one caveat to our being penniless. We had budgeted enough to travel to the village and to buy (less than) a week's worth of food to survive on, once we arrived.

In front of us and obstructing the view of the mountain's sheer cliffs was Whittier's other obtrusive World War II building, the fourteen-story Begich Towers Incorporated, where Nyal Worsham lived. You would think that the beauty of Whittier's landscape with its big horseshoe of mountains opening to the ocean would inspire the building of something as magnificent as the land itself? Nope. The concrete monster, better known as the BTI, was home to all of Whittier's residents. Self-contained in the winter, the residents didn't have to leave for anything, ever! There was a store, school, post office, and restaurant to name a few conveniences, as well as subterranean tunnels that ran beneath, connecting it to the haunted-looking Buckner Building.

When we arrived at the superintendent's apartment on the upper level of the BTI, it was spacious compared to the dim room and dark mole-like halls of the hotel where we stayed. However, the BTI building also housed lots of wealthy oil men and their families. Thanks to the pipeline, it was a time of abundance for some. Nyal's apartment was modernly furnished, and it reminded me of a Frank Lloyd Wright house tucked away in the hills of California. It was a funny thought, since just prior to arriving in Alaska, I knew very little about architecture and nothing about Frank Lloyd Wright. All of that had changed when my husband and I got married in a Frank Lloyd Wright church in my hometown of Kansas City.

Of course, my husband shared with me everything he knew about Frank Lloyd Wright. To ensure I was properly educated, he checked out stacks of picture books from the local library in Kansas City in an attempt to push me through a crash course before our wedding. Architecture was pretty much rock houses, brick houses, or wooden houses with siding before my 101–Introduction taught by my husband. Maybe the reason that the superintendent's home reminded me of Wright's work had more to do with the view through Nyal's large panorama window which looked out to a waterfall. The rushing sound evoked a desire in me to step through the picture window and climb the cliffs despite my fear of heights.

We ate a modest meal of pizza and salad and talked about education and village politics. The politics seemed to be the holdup to our placement. In the end, my husband finally signed the contracts, and we could officially head to the village in two days. That was great in a long-term view, but I needed my husband to end the chit chat and address the real issue. How were we going to eat for those next two days? The last of our money was gone, used up on living in the Anchor Inn, workshops on living in the bush, and, yes, the pleasure of pie and Ms. Pac-Man. We had borrowed from my grandmother on so many occasions that I was embarrassed to ask again, but another call would be inevitable if we couldn't find another solution. I hated borrowing from her. She had gotten old and after years of working two or three jobs, all she had to show for it was SSI, the house she lived in, and the home next door to her that she couldn't or wouldn't rent. Yet, my grandmother lent us the money. Ironically, my husband was white, college educated, and came from wealth, but still his family refused to help.

Seth said he had a plan. He would ask for an advance on a paycheck that he hadn't done one stick of work for yet. I had my reservations about this idea. It was not the sort of thing you did based on how I grew up. No, I was raised with the "You don't work, you don't eat," rule of life. We were at the end of our visit and about to leave when he hadn't said a word about the advance. I felt it was now or nothing. I decided to take a chance and move the conversation in that direction to help my husband.

"When will he receive his first check?" I asked.

Nyal's answer left me with a downward look. "Oh, that's going to make things hard," I said under my breath. The superintendent then enlightened us that we needed to take at least a month's worth of supplies out to the bush. He reminded us that there were no stores in the village. Finally, he asked the winning question, "Do you have enough money to get supplies for the month till you get your check?"

The words leapt from my mouth like my great-grandmother spitting snuff: "No, sir." I spoke with respect, in the way I had been raised to speak to my elders and white folks. Yet, I had spent so many years rebelling against those two simple little phrases, "yes, ma'am" and "yes, sir."

My husband then spoke, "I was wondering if I could get an advance on my salary."

The superintendent was silent for a moment, and looked straight at me, then at my husband. "You have a salary, but you haven't made a paycheck yet," he spoke clearly and straight, and I felt a little ashamed. "I'm taking a big risk with the two of you … call my secretary and let her know how much you want to come out of your first check. I'll let her know you're going to call and I've okayed it. Did you get set up in the school? Good, that's not really allowed, so, don't go around sharing that information … Since it's just a few days, it should be alright … I think you're going to do a good job there."

We thanked Nyal profusely. My husband shook his hand, and I gave him the biggest hug and thanks. That was the last time I ever saw or spoke with Nyal Worsham. I've had my regrets over the years, and that was one of them—letting him down.

My grandmother kept remnants of beautiful upholstery cloth in that drawer with my mother's photo. She always threatened she would do something with the remnants of material, along with the other treasures not usable in their current condition, but too good to throw out. I saw the drawer as only extra space my sisters and I couldn't use. The inability to use all the space in the room gave me a feeling that maybe my living arrangement wasn't so permanent. Yet, living in this room and in this house was the only place I had a clear memory of life.

My father and mother separated when I was about two. My brother, the oldest, and us three girls went to live with my father's mother. When Janice was nine, she went to live with my grandmother on my mother's side, since she wasn't my father's child. Shortly afterward, my father's mother forced him to grant her full custody of us. Legally, I'm not sure, but nevertheless from then on we belonged to her. From the time I was a baby and up to about four, my father lived in the same house with us. When my grandmother remarried, her new husband didn't want my dad there. For a while my grandmother and her husband argued about it, going round and round, until she gave in and he won. So, my dad moved in with my biological grandfather permanently. We mostly saw him on the weekends or when my grandmother needed him to do something that her lazy husband didn't want to do. My step-grandfather demanded that he should be the only man in the household. But it turned out he had a far more sinister reason for getting rid of my father. That plan consisted of grooming three little girls and a boy, I being the youngest at the age of four, for sexual purposes. My grandmother, the only mother I knew, was complicit in what he did.

On one of my banishments to my room, I decided to explore the drawer. That's when I found it, the wedding picture at the very bottom under the heavy swatches of material. After that, I visited the drawer often, staring at the beautiful dark woman in white next to my father. I asked myself, "Could that be my mother, or the other woman he married and divorced?" She stared back at me as I traced my nose and hers to see if it was the same, followed by her almond eyes and full lips. Up until that point, I saw my face in my paternal grandmother's face, round and fair. That is, up until I found the photo. I had been brainwashed to accept my grandmother as my mother. A part of me wanted to belong to her—she was the only mother I knew. I did everything to love her and be her daughter. I lived for her to call me her baby, and on the rare occasion, stroke my face, let me sit on her lap, or laugh at some silly show she liked. It was a love rooted in codependency and control, the only kind I knew.

One day I went to the drawer and the picture was gone. I knew I couldn't ask what happened to it. How could I? My words would reveal my betrayal just by asking. She had crafted the perfect profile of our mother over the years—someone to be disdained; and a completely different one of herself—sacrificing. I had plenty of reasons to hate this one-dimensional woman in the photo. That she had abandoned me seemed reason enough.

"She left so she could run the streets and lay up with women, instead of takin' care of you all … She's the one that laid down and had a bunch of babies, not me.

"She didn't even have food in the house for you babies, but she and her friends ate up and drank up whatever was there, while my son was out workin'."

It was easy to hate that woman that didn't want me. The day I was born, my mother called my grandmother.

"You got another granddaughter, come and get it, 'cause I don't want her or your weak ass son." This is what I was told my mother said about me, and those words became the voice of my mother in my head. I think my grandmother's hatred for her came from how my mother treated her one and only child, my father. Her infant child, whom she single-handedly kept alive when doctors gave up and sent him home with her to die. She hated my mother because she seemed wild and free, unlike how she saw herself: responsible, disciplined, and in control. My grandmother saw honor in obligation, even if she deep down didn't want to do it.

Yet, there were times I heard her lament lovingly about my mother. "She was a pretty, dark girl. Your daddy and her went to school together ... she was smart as a whip ... That thang she live with—callin' herself a mother— was mean as a snake ta that girl. Beat her, wouldn't feed her, and always had a bunch of men hangin' around."

"She use'ta walk by our place when we live in Mrs. William's boardin' home. We didn't have but three rooms in the whole place. Me, your daddy, and grandpa shared a bath with the other tenets, but here she'd come on her way ta school, lookin' like she didn't have a comb, home, or food to eat. I started fixin' the child's hair, givin' her something ta eat—I couldn't get rid of her then. She could cook and clean well'nough and was willin' to learn anything I'd teach her ... I don't know what happen'd ta her ... 'cept for that mother of hers."

"When they got old 'nough ta-get married, I help't 'em get their first apartment, right below me, and furnished it too. She already had one baby by some old thang when she was just fourteen. Your daddy and her decided ta get married when she turn eighteen. Your father was four years older than her. Then! Here came you kids—one after 'nother. I'd come downstairs and they both still laid up with babies just cryin'. Then she start hangin' out with that trash she call friends. Bringin' 'em in the apartment when your daddy was gone ta-work ... dancin' and carryin' on. I went down there and told her what I thought. I put every one of 'em out of there. I was payin' the doggone rent! Told her if she kept it up, she could go with 'em. Then she come up on me like she tryin' ta flirt."

"I had to set her straight, 'You got the wrong one girl, I ain't about that mess. I don't know what kind of stuff you use' ta-doin' with your momma, but

I don't do that … Plus, you with my son!' I told her. 'My God, girl!' She had to be out of her mind … Your momma was layin' up with a woman when she went inta labor with you. I'm sorry ta-say-it, but the truth is the truth, ain't no sense in sugar coatin' it, you gonna find out sooner or later."

If my mother didn't want me, I didn't want her. The blood in my body would only flow one way, towards my father and grandmother. I did everything to find myself in them. Changed myself and anything my grandmother didn't like about me. I tried to walk, speak, and behave the way my grandmother wanted, but it didn't work.

The photo was gone. I knew my role. Don't piss Mom off. I trembled with anxiety and ripped the skin from my finger, just like my dad did.

"Mom, who is that in the picture with Daddy in the drawer?" I asked, despite the fear. Something always compelled me to seek the truth even if it would be easier to accept the lie. To go towards danger and fight even if the person was bigger than me and I knew I would lose.

"Just what I thought! You been goin' through my drawers … gettin' into what's none of your business. That's what you been doin'. You want ta-know? It's your ole no-good momma, but I 'spect you figure that out. You goin' to be just like her, ain't you? No matter what I do … go on, get on out of here before you make me mad … and stay out of my drawers."

My grandmother wanted me to hate the woman with the almond eyes: for neglect, abandonment, being a lesbian, hurting her son, and not being what she wanted. So, I did. She wanted me to love her instead, and I did that, too. I hated them both as much as I loved them. I learned that the truth would not be made clear to me, because they couldn't see the truth outside themselves. They would paint the picture they wanted to tell, and I would be the canvas.

We were prisoners in my grandmother's house. I hated that my grandmother's truth often came at you as hurled nasty bits and pieces, like a dog hurling off muck. The truth of my mother's sexual behavior came in that exact way. Even the sensitive subject of my mother not wanting me at birth was served up in the same fashion.

I learned my mother had spent time in jail for robbery, and the owner of the place was stabbed. My grandmother delivered to me the same searing-hot iron of truth. There was rarely a compassionate sit-down talk. Instead, conversations with my grandmother were always a soliloquy.

"I believe she did it! Went in there ta-rob that man and they stab him … that man just tryin' ta make a livin' … She did this to herself, just actin' like nothin', hangin' around 'em nasty people … She didn't have ta do that … What did she want for? Nothin'! Had a roof over her head, food, a husband that worked, I saw ta-that! She just wanted to drag me and my son down to her level … that who your momma is."

My mother told a different story.

"Yes! I was with some friends. I went out lookin' for work early that morning when I saw my girlfriend Bernice and some of her friends, and they gave me a ride … she'd just bought a used car and they were joy ridin'. I went out to look for a job, I had to do somethin'. I couldn't just keep sittin' in that house with no money comin' in … I didn't even have milk in the house for you babies. Your daddy was a good man, but he couldn't keep a job, and when he did, it barely kept a roof over our heads. He couldn't find much work other than washin' cars at Gene's used car lot or sweepin' up somewhere … and I wasn't going to ask that woman for another damn thing. She thought just because she helped on the rent she could come and go in our place like she owned it and us. She was always bustin' in on us early in the morning before we'd even got up, bitchin' about cleaning a handful of dishes left in the sink or clothes not put away … Hell, I had five kids! She thought she could run me, like she ran your daddy, the hell she would … I told her she better get her ass out of my apartment."

"They let me have a turn driving the car, and I was driving it when we got to the shop, and they went in to grab a soda pop … they come running back out two minutes later and I didn't see no soda pop. I thought maybe they had a problem with the shop owner, they got mad, and just walked out. I said, 'Hey! What's goin' on? Where's the pops?' They said, 'Come on, we gotta go.' So I drove off."

"I didn't find out until the police pulled us over and they took us to the station. Said we robbed the man at the shop and someone stabbed him … I didn't know nothin' about what they were doin'. I told them that

… Told them I was just out lookin' for work; I got five babies at home. My friends told the police that too *and* the judge! I didn't know they were going in there to rob the place. They said they just decided to do it right then. The judge, he didn't care. He was gonna make an example out of me along with the rest of them. Said he was going to teach me to choose better friends. I wasn't but twenty-four years old and had never been in jail before that. Damn baby, I lost my freedom and you babies, too."

I never knew if this was the final event that took us from our mother and her to prison. I heard many truths in the way my mother described my grandmother. Yet, my grandmother was not one to hold back telling us an awful truth. I have come to understand that the facts lay somewhere between these two women and I may never know the absolute story.

When I think of my grandmother and how many times she told the story of coming to get us, I remember it the way you remember a lullaby. It felt magical, like a fairytale, and the good witch saves the day. It lingered in my mind with the power and mystery of stories told by the elders. This story was my creation story, the story of coming to live with my grandmother. It sometimes took on a harsh tone or one that was sentimental, depending on her mood.

"It was bitter cold that day, snow up almost ta your waist. That's when that child called me. 'Grandma, we don't have food in the house,' she told me … She but a baby herself, about nine–ten years old. Your momma was gone all day … That's what your oldest sister said. If it was a lie, she told it. Then ask me if I'd come and feed y'all. I got on my clothes and waded out in that mess. When I got there, it was freezin' in that house, you all were runnin' around dirty, cryin' and your brother was sittin' on the floor playin' with a truck I think. You lyin' in your crib, not sayin' a word, just smilin' and lookin' at me when I went ta pick ya up. I bundle you all up and brought you on home with me. That was that, you been mine ever since."

Chapter Four

My perception of applying for a teaching job was rather simplistic. You fill out an application then you are interviewed for the job. Instead, the actual process could be compared to a North Pacific salmon run. The salmon run is when bright red orange and shimmering silver salmon fight their way upstream, against the rush of water and predators, to spawn. Starving and wounded, the fish spawn then swim aimlessly in small pools of water until they die.

During the summer and fall, the university in Fairbanks made living space available for teachers to register and view job openings, with most positions in rural areas. Much like the salmon run, a wave of teachers came from all over the country to shoal together at the university. Many of them trekked the long, dusty ALCAN Highway, navigating rough and unpaved roads like the salmon fought against the current. The teachers pooled together at the end of their arduous journey, packed in gill to gill, as the process of natural selection left both species worn, haggard, or dead in the water.

To travel to Fairbanks, we used our trusty guide and faithful companion, *The Milepost*. A comparison would be *The Negro Motorist Green Book,* which helped Black people travel during Jim Crow. Black folk needed *The Green Book* when they were traveling from state to state. The guide provided information on where they could find food, gas, and restrooms while avoiding life-or-death situations. At best, it was a miserable and frightening journey. *The Milepost* now told us where to eat, sleep, and pee, as well as how many miles there was to go.

"Badlands or Mount Rushmore?" my husband said. "We don't have time for both if we're going to make good time getting to the Canadian border."

I wasn't too particular about either one of them. The choice between seeing some rotten-sounding land or the big faces of white men carved into a beautiful mountain was not at the top of my vacation to-do list. We had caught news of a Native American protest in the area of the Black Hills and they felt strongly about the defacing of the land at Mount Rushmore. But, in true hubby fashion, he decided.

"Oh, come on, we're so close. I can't just *not* see at least one of them."

"What happened to getting to the border?" I said annoyed.

"Look, we're not far from the Badlands. Let's just go and then maybe if we have time, we'll just scoot right up this way and hit the border. I'm telling you, you're going to love it," he said, folding up the map.

When my husband first mentioned going to the Badlands, I didn't have a clue as to what in the world was a *bad* land. And why would you want to go? It conjured up for me some oozing, smelly cesspool of dead vegetation. It was nothing of the sort. When we arrived, the air blew by in hot, dry bellows. With each belch, it sent the silt of fine ocher to settle on my partially opened lips and wet tongue.

I stood gasping at this otherworldly land that stretched as far as the horizon. Some of the rock formations stood like people, weathered away over time. I felt akin to the clay layered forms baking in the heat. Fixated by its deathlike beauty, I remembered a similar heat when I was three and ran up behind my great-grandmother as she opened up her oven door. The oven heat had scorched my cheeks red. Now this massive oven felt intent on baking the rest of me.

The wind and sun continued to assault the land, working tirelessly to sculpt this masterpiece. I watched the heat waves dance in front of us and I could feel its spell. A spell it had incanted for tens of millions of years, its secrets now hidden in the sedimentary rock and on the wind that carried the red and brown ocher sand to claim more supple soils. Like dried bones coming to life, I looked out over the arid land that seemed to know my soul. In a silent reverence and peace, I listened in quiet as if waiting for the dead to speak.

"Man, there ain't shit out there." Seth announced. The silence was broken.

We headed to Wyoming on our way to the border. Making good time, we figured we could get through Wyoming quickly and into Montana. We'd hit the border and be camping in Canada before nightfall. As Murphy's Law would have it (and I've come to know a lot about this guy, Murphy) our car broke down in Wyoming. This was one of those times I was very aware of my being Black and my husband being Jewish. Our need for a *Negro and Jewish Motorist Green Book* felt imperative. We sputtered along in the middle of nowhere after exiting the highway. A weathered sign pointed the way to a mechanic's garage on a road that changed from paved to gravel, then dirt. The farther away from the highway we got, the deeper my sense of fear set in.

We pulled into an old building with pieces of cars strewed about. There was no one on-site, not a dog or house, just an open garage out in the middle of nowhere.

"I don't like this. Where is everybody?" I said anxiously, then made a joke. "Don't go out there, it's a trap for Jews and Blacks, they're waiting for you to get out of the car. They'll knock you in the head and bury you out back."

"Naw, I'm not worried, they won't know I'm a Jew … but you!" he said, smiling at me. We laughed as a man in dirty overalls appeared.

Like a scene from some gritty movie he spat and said, "What you need?" We stopped laughing and he didn't move from the shade of the garage.

"Having some problems with my car. I was hoping I could get someone to look at it," my husband said. He just stood there staring at us, wiping his hands, saying nothing. Now I was scared, especially when he turned and walked back in. *Oh shit*, I thought, *it's time to go.* But my husband began to follow him and disappeared into the shaded garage. *Oh my God, is he crazy? What the hell is he doing … should I wait or go in? Maybe I should honk … no just wait, but how long …* This was how it happened in those stories of backwoods, serial-killing racist white people. He was going to kill us and bury us in the junkyard, and no one would ever know.

It seemed like forever that they were out of sight. My thoughts raced. Just as I had convinced myself to get out of the car to see where my husband was, he walked towards me. "He's going to look at it, but he's not sure he'll have the parts. He's a little strange. The whole time I was there, I was talking telling him what the car was doing, and he didn't say a word. Just kept staring at me like he didn't speak English and wiping his hand on a greasy rag, but nothing was on his hands; his hands looked cleaner than the rag."

"I think we should go," I said.

"I hear you, but we can't. I don't know what's up with this guy, but I don't think the car can go any further."

We pulled the car up to the entrance of the garage, and I got out without taking my eyes off him. He came over to us after about an hour and said that he would have to order the part, but he couldn't get it till next week sometime.

"Next week!" I blurted out. "I'm not staying around here till next week."

My husband walked over to talk to the creepy man, then came back and said, "He thinks he can fix it well enough with what he's got till we get to a bigger town where there's a dealership, but it's going to cost us $300."

Again, I yelled, "Three hundred dollars!" to this possible serial killer. But blowing up was useless. He would have his $300 plus tax, and I would live to see Montana and the Canadian border.

Finally, we got to the Canadian border, pulling in slowly behind a line of four or five other vehicles. I remember a great sense of fear rushing quickly over me while looking at the border guards with their guns on their hips and flat, neutral expressions.

"Excuse me, can you pull over here? Thank you," the stoic guard said while surveying the car with x-ray eyes. "Where ya' headed?"

"Alaska," my husband answered with a cheery voice.

"Alaska, eh?" said the Canadian guard. He surveyed the car from the driver's window, while another guard circled the body of the vehicle with his hands on his holster.

My nervous, trained smile wilted quickly as I spoke out the window to the guard, who had walked around the car, "Is something wrong?"

Other cars passed the checkpoint while we waited. *Waited for what!* I thought. I became more and more irritated with the process. A process that wasn't explained and yet seemed somewhat familiar. My husband shot me a look that meant, *Don't start.* "They're just doing their job ... let them. Do you need my license or anything, officer?"

I was slowly going from fear and anxiety to anger. "Really, they just can't tell us what they want? What are they looking for?" I said, under my breath. "I don't see anyone else being stopped," I kept grumbling.

"Stop already," my husband growled.

"Could you please step out of the car?" The officer was now looking at us, looking at me straight in the face.

"Why, what did ..."

"Just step out of the car, please," he now demanded with a much more familiar demeanor. I can't count how many times I've been circled in a department store or my neighborhood grocery store by security. Their eyes would scan and crawl over me until I left. So many times, Black people had been stopped and asked where they were going, where they were coming from, and what they were doing "over here." It was feeling like that right now. While cars passed through the toll, I was ordered to sit on the curb, humiliated. I didn't know why. The fact that this happened a lot in America and was now happening to me in Canada chipped away at the hope that things might be different as we continued north.

The voices were loud and drifted into our window as the sound carried up the driveway and floated into our bedroom, "Oh, God ... what you do that fa'. Somebody help, she shot me ..."

I ran to the front of the house with my sisters in tow. "Mom, some-body's outside callin' for help," I spoke in my excited eight-year-old voice.

"Shut up … hush, I know it. I called the police. That woman shootin' cross the street … Oh my God." Mama had already extinguished the single dim Christmas light. The low wattage bulb made an excellent nightlight and kept the neighbors from seeing her movements in the house while saving on the electricity bill. We were plunged into blackness except for a small sliver of light that lasered in from the slightly parted curtains where my grand-mother peeked out. Soon the darkness was filled with red, blue, and white light, dancing about the room. We huddled in the back of the house, watch-ing my grandmother. A nervous excitement came over us from the lights and the crackling of the police radio outside. My heart pounded in my ears as we giggled with childish anticipation of what might happen next.

Suddenly, my grandmother turned on the chandelier light and opened the door to meet the red and blue lights of the police cars. She stood on the porch with our living room illuminated, showing the neighbors exactly her position. We ran through the bright light of the front room and into the dark of my grandmother's bedroom. Her room was in the front of the house, just off from the living room, and looked out to the street. We peered through a broken blind, and we saw her standing at the top of the porch stairs. Follow-ing her gaze, she looked just beyond the slope of our grass yard. Our eyes carried us to the sidewalk, then the curb where my dad occasionally parked when he came home. Right in his parking spot was where we saw what she was looking at.

The one-armed man from across the street lay partially on the street, partially on the grassy curb, dead and right in daddy's parking spot. He seemed as if he had been heading to our house. We ran back to our rooms. I felt sick and scared. Like death could happen to me in the next second and no one would stop it from occurring. The door came open and Momma came in, followed by other voices. I went to look. I wanted to tell her I was scared.

"What's your name? How do you spell that? Who else is in the house? How old? How old is the male child?" They were shooting one question af-ter another at her, hardly giving her a chance to answer. There were two of them, tall as the door and white—glaring white. I could hear Momma's tone change. She was getting annoyed, mad at the way they were speaking to her, and one of them started looking around the house.

"What you got to know that for? He's a child and my grandson. They all sleep … ya'll acting like I had something to do with it … anyway, I'm the one who called."

"I need you to just answer the questions or you can answer them someplace else, you understand?"

"I answered your questions, what else do you want me to say, I didn't kill the man. You don't need to be threatening me, I haven't done nothing wrong but call you. I'm not saying another word." I came out and walked slowly towards my grandmother. Her arms gestured for me and I ran into them. "What you doin' up, you ought to be sleep … school tomorrow."

My grandmother took me in her arms, which was only on rare occasions and I began to cry, "Mom, I'm scared."

"Of what?"

I looked up at the officers, my eyes only reaching their belted guns.

"I'm okay, Momma's fine," she glanced one of her looks at them without looking at their eyes and sent me back to bed—knowing I had served my purpose of diffusing the tension between her and the officers. It was rare for my grandmother to allow me to disrupt an adult interaction without me facing serious consequences. I did not fully understand then, but through many of my own experiences it would be made clear; big people can use their size to intimidate those of us that are small. Big people that possess authority have the power to do most anything they want.

We stepped out of our car and were instructed to step away from the vehicle. The officers opened up all of our car doors as well as the doors to the trailer and began rifling through everything.

"Those are my cooking supplies … they're messing up the way I organized it!"

"I can turn you around," he said definitively. "You don't have to enter Canada ... Now, may I continue?" I was silent, while my husband apologized for me.

"Sir, I need you to step inside and someone will instruct you further while we finish." We went inside where we were asked the same questions: "What is your purpose in Canada? How long are you intending to stay? Where are you from? Names? Address? Destination? And address of where you're going in Alaska?" The biggest question came next: "How much money are you traveling with?"

Seth thought he would need $800–$900 to go through the border, but we intended to have at least $1,000–$1,100 to be on the safe side. Canada had its share of Americans getting stuck in their country and needing assistance, and this was one way to ensure you had enough to be there and get out. Seth whipped out his wallet and counted out a little over $900. One of the officers that was checking the car looked in and nodded to the officer that was checking our IDs and cash, to indicate we were clear. I had gained a calmer composure while inside, away from the car, while the two officers were touching our things. When the attending officer said, "You need $1,200 to cross, you're 'bout $300 short, eh?," we almost soiled ourselves!

A different kind of fear came over me, the realization that we might have to go back to Kansas City. I stood there glazed over, not listening to what Seth was saying, catching a few words here and there: "Our car had problems ... Yeah, I understand $300! I know, what could we do? Can credit cards count? No, just camping! Straight through British Columbia to the ALCAN Highway ... Great, great! No, no, we're just trying to get to Alaska. Alaska or bust! Never mind, thanks. Come on, we can go! LaVern, let's go."

We got in the car and I said thank you to the officers. He looked straight ahead and waved us on with a "drive safe."

5

Chapter Five

After the challenges going through the border, we fueled up and treated ourselves to a quick meal at a stop. Seth opened a map he had purchased and announced that we could cut our trip down by following a truck route through Canada into Alaska. I wasn't altogether comfortable. "There's going to be a lot of big trucks," I warned.

"Don't worry about it," Seth, in his New York way, said emphatically. He continued his hustle, "It's fine! Look how beautiful this looks on the map, and the roads should be good. They have to be for trucks to be on them."

The road was fine enough at the start, but we started climbing the side of a mountain. The road began to narrow, and the trucks were not the dreaded sixteen-wheelers of my imagination. Oh No! Far worse. They were logging trucks!

"Turn around," I yelled, watching a fully loaded truck with twenty-foot logs weighing a few thousand pounds a load.

"Oh shoot. That was close," he stated, matter of fact.

"Just turn around."

"There's no place to. We have to just keep going."

That was pretty much the last conversation we had until we came off the mountain. The trucks just kept coming. It seemed like there was one every ten to fifteen minutes, and the road, I swear, was not much bigger than a single lane. Just when I thought it couldn't get any worse, we neared the top of the mountain. We were about a quarter of a mile before the descent when around the bend came the umpteenth logging truck, hugging the mountainside of the road, which meant we had to go to the opposite side, facing the cliff.

Now, I had said that the conversation had stopped, but the reason our talking had ceased was that I was paralyzed. I had been holding a visitor's guide which, by this point, I had twisted into a sweat-soaked clump of fibers. Before visually seeing the beast truck, Seth was acting as my scenic guide. He extended his entire arm across my chest while pointing to the view from over a thousand feet high. At that point, I managed to say, "I don't want to see it, put your hands on the wheel."

"Come on, it's beautiful, you're gonna miss it."

"Okay, okay, just put your hands on the wheel." I snapped a look out of the window as full panic gripped my body. My breath became shallow with every sip of air I took. Sweating profusely, my body was cold and clammy until the moment I saw the truck coming around and down, right at us.

I heard Seth talking out loud, trying to decide if he should go to the outside or the inside. I'm not sure if the shouting was coming from me or if it was in my head, but I heard a voice screaming, "Inside, inside," and Seth saying, "He's not getting over ... he'll crush us on the inside."

The road on my side disappeared. I was looking at the view with no visible road out of my window. It was beautiful, the view, for that split second. Some part of my mind and body separated, and I could appreciate what Seth had seen.

"Oh God! Oh God, there's no fuckin' guard rail ... please don't let me die!" Seth navigated the gravel curve until the beast passed, and with two hands on the wheel of the car, we rode in silence the entire descent of the mountain and made no more detours off the course set by *The Milepost*.

We pulled into Fairbanks after miles of dust, dirt, and gravel on the ALCAN Highway. The road had been a beautiful stretch of highway with tall spruces wrapping every turn. The sun had shown bright and made gilded patterns through the birch leaves across the road. It was like spring in the newfound joy of reaching Alaska. Finally, we were here. Even the trees seemed refreshed and grander in the last frontier. For all the elation I felt about the trees, I remembered plenty of times I'd thought, *If I see another tree, I'll kill myself.*

We headed straight for the University of Alaska in Fairbanks. Our trusted *Milepost* told us exactly where to find a place to stay. Home ended up being a campground a quarter of a mile from the university campus, and we managed to get the last space. The campground sat on a small corner lot. A patch of overgrown land, like a micro forest in the middle of town, surrounded by a busy road and houses. The first night we pulled in, we set up the tent and sleeping bags, and crashed. That morning I slept in, and Seth went up to campus to find out where to register and to start the process of getting a job teaching in the bush. When he got back, I hadn't left the tent. Deterred by insects the size of birds, along with not knowing the lay of the land, I was content with staying put. I watched families I could see from my tent through the sparse woods. They moved in and out of their homes, seemingly unbothered by the constant winged companions.

I made us lunch from our little cardboard box of food and cooler, happy to be out of the car and with nowhere to go. I was like a 1950s wife who was setting up housekeeping in a tent, and preparing food was my top job. I was a drill instructor about keeping our supplies in order. Every knife, spoon, and fork had to be exactly where I put it in the box because it made it easy for me to make us food while on the road. I could reach in and get a cutting board, knife, tomatoes, sandwich meat, lettuce, bread, etc. as if I were in my own kitchen. I took pride in being able to provide a freshly made sandwich, served with chips and a wedge of pickle on the side, New York deli-style. Seth was banned from touching my supplies. I knew if I let those soft dough fingers into my box, they would be shoved in a bag of chips, followed by the mindless eating of folded slices of white bread.

When I went to Seth's apartment for the first time, I thought I would gain insight into whether he was the right or wrong one for me. Waiting for a red banner to fly up, I watched for anything in his room that would tell me he's a murderer and to get the hell out! The truth was I hadn't a clue as to what to look for in him or myself. He had a roommate, and in the common area, they shared what seemed a typical male space—sparse with TV, sofa, and some exercise equipment—nothing special. Then, we went to his room. It was fairly neat except for a few mounds of clothes with an odd fermenting smell of food and socks that wafted through the air.

I asked at some point to use the restroom and he pointed to the en suite. I felt around a minute in pitch black for the light switch, only to find it didn't work. It was a bright sunny day, and the bedroom was bathed in sunlight. The transition from the bright bedroom to the bathroom, which caught no light, rendered me blind. I could barely see light reflecting off the white porcelain sink. I yelled out to him, "Hey, there's no light, I can't see." I finally groped around and found the toilet. Just as I'd finished, found the sink, and washed my hands, he came in and fumbled around to replace the lightbulb. And then, there was light.

I was mortified! I had just used a restroom with a toilet and sink that could have been a science experiment. I bolted from the bathroom and when offered something from the kitchen, I said a big fat, "No!"

In retrospect, God was preparing me for the process of discovering the many dark places hidden in myself and my relationship. These hidden ruins would prove to be a greater challenge than a dirty bathroom or kitchen. The muck inside would be far more insidious and require a deeper look to be unpacked.

We planned to go to the campus the next day to try and get a dorm room. The university offered cheap dorm space for teachers and visitors during the summer months. It was first come, first served. There seemed to be availability but for tonight we would be in a tent. We settled in for the night with a mass of dark-winged shadows at the tent door; the Alaskan mosquito. As the sun went down, the hum-and-hiss-song was nonstop. Those humming-winged night creatures waited with anticipation of a blood meal from anyone that dared to leave their tents. Paranoia? Maybe, but the raised smooth, hot bumps on my skin were proof enough that Seth's New York plasma was less desirable than the muddy Missouri water that coursed through my veins. Most nights I convinced Seth to play me a tune on the guitar I had bought him the birthday before we married. He would pluck and strum, and we'd sing together. He never made it through a bar without a mistake, but what patience there was in our young love.

When we woke up, I bolted to the camp bathroom, back to the tent, and got dressed. The plan was to get to the office early, score some free breakfast, and sign up for a dorm. This would cost us a little more than what we were paying at the campground, but in the dorms there were showers and a bed! We headed down the road away from the camp. It was a very busy street with both sides heavily wooded and a sidewalk only on our side. We hadn't walked more than a minute from the campground when I began to feel like I was being followed. The inner city had created a hypervigilance in me that seldom rested. I grew up in the trenches of our society and one of the first rules is to know who's on every side of you.

Out of the corner of my eye, I thought I saw something. I caught a glimpse of movement that mingled with the dark and light shades of the trees. I started walking faster to campus as my husband tried to keep up and continued to carry on a conversation with me. Then it happened, something hit the side of my neck with an almost piercing hum. I spun around and there behind me were six, seven … twenty, twenty-one black mosquitoes, bigger than anything I had ever seen. They were on me like a squadron of kamikazes, flying straight in at me! Some followed at a steady speed until they could strike. I began to swing my arms to keep them off, but it just seemed to stimulate them more and the numbers kept increasing. My husband didn't seem to be bothered by them as much. I believed his time spent on a remote tropical island in the Peace Corps acted as an inoculate. His scars from biting flies and mosquitoes are proof that he was no virgin, but I had untainted blood and I felt they knew it.

He yelled to me, "Just walk faster."

"I am."

"Did you put on the mosquito dope?"

"Yes," I said with impatience and waited for a more helpful response. I was risking my life and any future offspring with the level of DDT sprayed on my body, and these damned things couldn't care less. Finally, any desire to appear sexy, smart, or retain self-respect went out the window. I got flat out mad (as was my usual response to anything I was afraid of or had no control over). I was swinging at those mosquitoes like I was in a street fight, but they were winning. I could see my husband was amused, embarrassed, and a bit perplexed. I didn't care at that point. I had taken proper protection, and they were not respecting it. I was not giving up my blood without a fight. I finally realized that if I stepped off the curb into the street away from the trees, walked faster, and waved my arms like a windmill they were not so bad.

Moving into the dorms at the University of Alaska Fairbanks and out of the campground was finally my saving grace and defense against all things flying and crawling. Being married we had a dorm room to ourselves, while singles had to share. There was a small kitchen down on the lower level of our unit to share with other residents, as well as gym-like showers. After a month of traveling by car these accommodations felt like we just got put up at the Hilton and I could thumb my nose at the mosquitoes. So, take that you blood-sucking raptors!

6

Chapter Six

"Mom, we got mulberries."

In the backyard of our neighbor, a wild untamed jungle grew a prize of fat, black, shiny berries. Only by the sampling and surviving did we know delight and not death. The fingers, lips, and tongues of my siblings and I were stained purple. I carried a muddied cup of half-mashed mulberries into the house and offered them up to my grandmother.

"Mulberries! Where'd you get mulberries?"

"In the backyard," I said.

"Whose backyard?" she questioned.

"Next door at Tammy's"

"You bet stay out of there! You don't know what's in them bushes. Snakes or somethin' gonna get you, climbin' around out there."

"Uh-uh, Mom, there's no snakes out there. Here, I brought you some," I said holding out the cup.

My older sisters always stayed somewhere in the background when I approached my grandmother. They waited to see her response. Often I became my sisters' litmus test to determine whether a calm or storm hovered in my grandmother's atmosphere. They choose to wait at a safe distance for the results. I came to realize there was little difference between being used to test my grandmother's mood or the berries to see if they were poison. This time she was not the storm.

"Y'all go on and eat 'em. Mom don't want none. When I was a little girl, you couldn't get me out of Mama's and Daddy's fruit trees. We had 'ery fruit tree and ole berry bush you could think of. No, thank you! I dun' ate my share of mulberries. I sure miss them big trees: peaches and plums, blackberries big as my thumbnail, and mulberries cover'd 'em trees like crows roostin' in the evening ... Hey y'all bet not get that mess all over everything and I mean it, wash your hands."

I saw Vernice occasionally in the kitchen, sometimes when I looked in to see if it was in use or when she passed by as I was cooking. Vernice had skin like cream heavy on the vanilla extract, hair black as a raven's wings that hung to her waist, and dimples so deep water could pool in them. I had never seen a raven before moving to Alaska. Oh, we had plenty of crows where I grew up. But the ravens here were fat, juicy, black mulberries, clustered on a bush. A murder of ravens filled the trees every evening caw-caw-cawing outside our windows, darkening the sky.

"Are you almost done?" Vernice's voice startled me.

"Oh, aaa yeah ... you can bring your stuff in if you want, I was just cleaning up."

"Ya! People leave a mess, don't they?"

"You should've seen it when I first came in. I had to clean before I could mess it up."

Vernice smiled revealing her dimples, the kiss of God on both sides of her face.

"I'm Vernice Marvin," she said.

"I'm LaVern Schwartz. My husband is Seth if you see him."

"Ya, my husband is Rick ... Are you one of the tourists staying here?"

"No, my husband's a teacher and he's trying to get a teaching placement in the bush."

"Ya! We are teachers too. I just finished my teaching degree and my husband is workin' on his, but we look to teach in the bush too." She smiled. I stayed in the kitchen as she prepared a simple meal of rice and fish. We laughed about how poor we were, shared where we were from, and told stories about the men we'd married. But most of all, that meeting made Vernice my first and best friend in Alaska.

Vernice and I spent every day together that summer while we waited to go out to the bush. Her husband Rick studied in the library, while my husband went to training seminars and info classes for teachers looking to go to rural and remote areas of Alaska.

I couldn't help but worry a little about how much attention my husband would give to the practical needs of living in the bush. He was the kind of guy that would be laser-focused on the information he needed to teach, but the rest would fall to the wayside. I'd have to figure out the survival skills he didn't deem important and I didn't even begin to know what those might be. The craziness of it all was that I might have been better prepared had I been invited to the classes. I was left dependent on what he told me, hoping it was correct. "Ehh! I'm not worried about that right now, we'll figure it out later," was his favorite comeback. *Right!* I thought.

Vernice didn't attend many of these info seminars. She was focused solely on teaching in the remote village she had lived in most of her life. Vernice told me her mother was Eskimo and her father was blue-eyed and white like my husband, but both her parents had died fairly young. I later found out that her mother died from cancer and other alcohol-related health issues. I don't recall her saying how her father died. We were both married that same year, 1982, with the exception of a few months difference. We cooked most of our meals together.

We started cooking together one day, when we both showed up in the kitchen at the same time with our food boxes. She asked me what I was going to make. I looked and realized I had no idea, as I pushed around the contents and found there wasn't much there. She looked through her box and asked if I wanted to put what little we had together and share the meal.

Cooking was my wheelhouse, and as my grandmother would say "makin' somethin' out of nothin'" was what we knew how to do. The box contained mostly odds and ends. There was one can each of green beans, corn, pinto beans, tomato paste and a lonely can of pork and beans. I had some additional fresh items, including an onion. Onions are an ingredient I must have and are sometimes called Black folk's apples. There were also a couple of carrots and my last can of tuna fish. Vernice wrangled up a fresh apple she had in her room and I whipped up a tuna salad with onions, diced apples, shredded carrots, fast food packs of mayo, a little sugar, salt, pepper, and a touch of mustard.

That was our lunch along with some slightly stale potato chips. Meanwhile, I set to boil the chicken frame I'd tucked away in a brown bag with my name on it, stuck way in the back of the communal freezer. After lunch, we began to throw together a quick stew for dinner. Using canned vegetables, beans, the rest of the fresh carrots and half of the onion, Vernice chopped up the veggies using what she called an ulu. She handed me her ulu to use. It was a sharp, curved blade about four or five inches long with a shape that reminded me of the rockers on a rocking horse. It had a rounded bone handle you gripped with all four fingers and the whole thumb wrapped around the other side. Useless in my hand, I was like a baby trying to find their mouth with a spoon for the first time, a mess. Eventually, I learned to be pretty good with it.

From that point on, I made most of our meals. Vernice's contribution was showering me with praise and how much she loved my cooking while contributing whatever she had to make the meal. Though she claimed she wanted me to teach her how to cook my way, she mostly helped prep and wash dishes. One day, she shared the most precious gift of food, and it was the first and last time my palate would experience such an extraordinary taste, other than through memory. Her family had sent smoked fish from their village, and it was so unlike the canned fish I'd always eaten. It was especially precious because she had little of it left and it was a staple food for her and her people. They would spend the fishing season catching, smoking, drying, and canning all the fish they needed for the winter. It would be a while before she could go home to get more, or smoke fish herself. Despite this, she shared everything, as did I.

Most of our cooking time was spent talking about sex and love, husbands and old relationships, and mean racist people that made it hard for her to get her teaching certification. She shared with me something awful that I knew all too well. A teacher she was training under said that she would never be a good teacher or get certified because Natives were too stupid. I could feel the hurt she felt. It could only be matched by my own rage that burned from my own memories. My fist rolled into a knot as I listened to her, and said the only thing that came to my mouth, "If anyone ever says something like that to you again, let me know, I'd like to meet them."

I had developed a scab over the years from such nasty words. I understood how it kills everything in you, including your dreams. The thought of such evil beliefs ripping her dreams out of her hands when she had just begun to hold them was unthinkable. I was ready to fight for someone I hardly knew, because I wanted her to feel like I had her back and would stand up for her, which was more than I ever got.

We took lots of long walks, talking and giggling like high school kids. All the while forgetting about the time and our husbands, as they began to resemble our parents, sitting around waiting at home while we broke curfew. That was one of the best summers I have ever had. She made me feel like an ordinary young newlywed woman, anywhere in the world. My skin color didn't change anything. We had so many things in common even though we looked nothing alike and came from very different backgrounds.

One day, Vernice came to my room and asked me to take a walk with her. She told me the great news that she and her husband got the teaching placement she wanted in her home village. We were screaming and jumping up and down like cheerleaders and hugging each other until the reality set in that they would be leaving in a few days. We spent whatever limited time we had together, which were snatches of moments in between her preparing to leave. We encouraged one another and prayed that my husband and I would get a placement soon. Time was running out. Vernice hoped we would get a good village, one we would like, and that we'd stay in touch and get to talk often.

I didn't know what a good village was, and I was too scared to ask what a bad one could look like. I was just so happy to have found a friend and was hopeful that the village would be much like our friendship. The subject of how Black people were viewed negatively by some Alaskans had come up. The response I got was that most opinions came from what people saw on TV and heard from others. She admittedly said most people she knew didn't know any Black people personally. So, I figured I might be able to change their perception. Because once they had a chance to meet a real African American in the flesh versus some mythical creature seen and distorted on a box, it would change their view of us. After all, if Vernice and I became friends over a short summer, surely it would be easy to get people to like me, having a whole year to do it.

A strange sense of loneliness crept in and a pang of profound sadness was taking over. For once in my life, I had felt a sense of being important and special to someone, different from other relationships I'd had. Even though I had grown up with two sisters, we were never friends, because they never wanted to be close to me. That day on our walk, despite the sadness, my friend gave me a different gift. She gave me a secret to hold, something she said she had never shared with anyone. Vernice confided in me the hurt and betrayal she'd experienced when her husband had cheated on her. But this was not the secret. What she told me was not something she had ever shared with him or anyone. I realized secrets are strange little gifts that could be both beautiful and horrible, yet often a burden. I kept what she gave me stored deep in my heart, and that day for the first time in my life I knew what sisterhood was.

When I was nineteen, my fourth job was at Gillham House. This came after working at Gates and Sons Bar-B-Q Restaurant and Western Missouri Mental Hospital. Gillham House was a small facility for the mentally ill and disabled. It was run by a husband and wife team with two other young female employees in their late twenties and early thirties. I interviewed with the female owner. She was a prickly, uptight, demanding, but attractive person. Yet, for someone that owned a care-focused business, my impression of her was that she didn't seem to be a people person. Nevertheless, with my fragile stability, I needed the job. Through the grace of God, the interview went well, and I was hired.

This time I would be surrounded by women, shrouded in sisterhood. I could finally feel safe, safe from having managers feeling all over my body with their eyes and giving me stupid nicknames based on my sexualized body parts. At this job, I could feel less threatened by aggressive patients. Like when I was pinned to a wall by a six foot four 240-pound male mental patient. He groped me, while the male staff I worked with at Western Missouri Hospital took their time, enjoying the entertainment.

This new job felt like it was going to be different. So much better and safer for me, having so many women in charge. I did meet the male owner after I was hired, but I saw him only in passing, along with two of his sons that worked at night. I was told I was not to bother him and that I should report to the wife if I had any questions or concerns. However, if her husband instructed me to do something, I was to do it, since he was my boss as well. Doing what I was told was not hard, for I had been doing that my entire life. It seemed someone else always had control. All that mattered to me at this point was that I had a job and I kept it, or else I could find myself homeless, again.

One of the women I worked with was the resident social worker while the other was studying to be a nurse. The social worker had a solid build, short and sturdy. Her voice was slightly raspy, and she had an unwavering confidence that matched her stature. The nursing student was the opposite side of the coin. She was tall with long, corn-husk thick blonde hair. She seemed shy or maybe just nervous, all the while she pulled on her blonde mop, taking large swatches and draping it over her eyes. She used her blanket of hair when she talked to you. Her head would slightly bend, one dark orb concealed by the thick, blonde strands draped to one side. The exception was her mouth, the only thing you could focus on when she spoke to you.

There was a feeling of distancing right from the beginning, like I was a suspect before a crime was even committed. They watched my every move, correcting the smallest infraction. Even placing a staple instead of a paper clip might be treated as a federal offense. The first months remained mostly the same as my female boss barked demands at me with just enough polite disrespect that anyone watching, if they cared, would not have any grounds to complain. The other women were not much better, speaking to me only in regards to work-related issues, while they conversed socially with one another. It was clear I was the outsider and anything they didn't finish or didn't want to do was passed to me, job description be damned. If I wanted to keep my job, I figured I'd better do it. I was determined, however, to make them like me or at least accept me as an equal. So, I started by bringing in baked goods to share several times over a couple of months. I would kill them with kindness and work my ass off, doing whatever job that was thrown at me, even if it included taking on someone else's task. I knew I was up against perception. I'd been taught all my life you have to work ten times harder than anyone white just to get into the door.

"Make sure the doctors sign the paperwork. Pick up any new prescriptions and get them all back here in one piece." I almost shit my pants! I didn't even own a car and I had only been driving for a few years. Keys in hand, I was expected to drive the equivalent of a small bus, with disabled passengers. What was I going to do? If she only knew I had, at best, racked up a total of twenty or thirty hours of driving ever. People I knew, if they had a car, didn't just hand you their keys with a "Sure, no problem, use my car whenever you like!" It was by hook or by crook that I even learned to drive at sixteen and just barely got a license. I've found most white folks believe the world operates for everyone else as it does for them.

My boss, however, made it clear either I drive the van or I'd have no job. Terrified, I begged and pleaded with my boss not to send me. But (with my job on the line) I opted to drive and faked as much confidence as I could as I rolled that big monster van down the drive onto one of the busiest throughways in Midtown, Gillham Road. Hardly breathing. A van full of mentally-vulnerable people were depending on me not to freak them out, and I was depending on them not to freak me out.

We made it to the clinic and came back in one piece. It was so successful that I began volunteering myself. Driving, I learned, gave me a feeling of freedom I didn't realize I could have. It also made me less available for all the crap jobs and cold shoulders I got from the rest of the staff.

On one of our van outings, I stopped at the intersection of 31st and Gillham Road, a rush of emotions engulfed me. The radio was playing "Me and Mrs. Jones," one of my mother's favorite songs. It hit me for the first time *where* I was and *what* that corner meant. My father and I had stopped at the same light, the same intersection almost two years ago on my way to the Western Missouri Mental Hospital.

I was working the night shift around eleven p.m. The streets were empty and dark, except for the yellowish tinge from the dim streetlight. It felt like a desert with the hot air blowing back into the window.

A sound broke through the murky hot air. A fast car with a loud muffler and screaming music pulled up beside us. Two white men in their twenties pulled up next to us at the light. Abruptly, the music stopped, while the red light lagged on, holding us there for what felt like fifteen minutes. Suddenly their engine roared and snatched my attention. They were yelling at us out their window.

"Hey! Hey nigger, what you doing over here …" My head whipped around to my father. He always drove leaning on the door with his shoulder slumped down hugging the left side. He sat up straight now, never looking to either side, just straight ahead, waiting for that *damn* light to change.

"Hey old nigger, you hear me? I'm talking to you! What you looking at, nigger bitch? Hey you Black nigger bitch, I got something you want …" The light turned green, we pulled away and they tore off past us, laughing and yelling out their window with music playing. I rode the rest of the way in silent anger and rage at my father (and at myself for not saying anything). My thoughts jumped around in my mind to similar assaults that I'd stuffed away.

Peeing in a drug store parking lot at five. Why? Because we were Black.

I remember when my father tried to start a cleaning business, Zodiac Cleaning Services. I was no more than nine or ten when my dad, me, and my siblings took a job cleaning three apartments. There was a promise that if these apartments looked good the guy would hire dad for all of his "move outs." The apartments were disgusting but we finished them ten hours later, sparkling clean. He paid my father twenty dollars, out of the $200 agreed on. Because he knew there was nothing my father could do.

Sitting at that corner this time, did not just awaken past traumatic experiences. Instead, a completely different and deeper revelation came to me. That very intersection where I had felt humiliated and defiled in front of my father was the same intersection that had been instrumental in changing my life.

An ice cream shop called Velvet Freeze sat on the corner of 31st and Gillham Road. That ice cream shop was robbed back in the early '60s, and the man at the counter had been stabbed during the crime. Those involved were my mother's friends and this was the event that took my mother away from me. I was sitting at the crossroad of my life.

A horn sounded behind me and I pulled away.

The girls in the office and I finally became friends. We had bridged a gap of race, female rivalry, and class (so I believed). They even invited me on a holiday weekend to the beach in Manhattan, Kansas. We planned to go swimming (or not) and hang out with the local college students and party. The weekend was mostly a success.

My period started the week following the beach trip. I spent most of the morning ragged and frayed from pain. I was a gray string mop slung over the fence to dry. One after another, the staff asked me what was wrong, and I replied, "I'm not feeling well, it's my time of the month." The endless morning crawled relentlessly on, and so did the requirements for me to perform my job. I tramped around the building in an attempt to locate clients for various staff, for various reasons. My boss needed one of the residents to sign their check for rent and another client had not come down for morning meds. One of the residents had not been answering his family's phone calls, and they insisted I locate him so they could verify he was okay. There were conflicts to resolve between clients, arguing over someone stealing from the other one's room. There were spills to clean up or clients to be sent to shower for soiling themselves. There seemed to be one mess after another that needed my attention, and I soon found that I needed attention too.

About noon, I headed to the restroom, and I spent my lunchtime there alternating one end of myself on the toilet to the other. If enduring those symptoms was not enough, I was also delirious with pain. I don't know who came and knocked on the door first, but what followed was the female owner along with the other two female staff. Finally, the owner had the girls carry me out of the restroom. I hung over their arms as though I'd been dragged from a car wreck. They laid me on a cot in the small med room, usually used for ill clients or those that needed a little time out. One of the girls handed me over-the-counter pain tablets, while I lay on the little cot for an hour or so until the pain was manageable. I worked the desk a couple of hours before I was allowed to go home early. Heading to the bus stop, the pain pulsed and the warm sensation of blood poured from my body as I made my way home.

I returned to work that Monday morning after having the weekend (thank God) to recover. The awkwardness I had experienced when I first started hung over the office once again. I didn't see it coming, being called to the male boss's office. I walked into the dark leather cave of a room and sat before a massive desk facing a slightly balding, short broad man that illuminated the room with his whiteness. He sat back in his easy chair and said, "I have to let you go."

"Why! What did I do?" I protested.

He just stared at me for a while as I pleaded to know what I'd done and to be given another chance.

"I can't have late employees."

"But the bus broke down, and I was only twenty minutes late once, I was told it wasn't a problem."

He stared at me and said that behavior with you the other day won't be tolerated around the clients.

"But, I was sick! I couldn't help that. I stayed and worked. Your wife told me to go home early. I need this job. I'll work weekends. Pay me less. I'll do whatever you need."

He finally said, "I'll think about it. Come back at the end of your shift and we'll talk then."

I knocked and could just barely hear an audible voice say "come in" through the thick chamber door. The female owner had left early for a doctor's appointment, and the girls were heading out the door while the next shift, the male owner's two sons, were coming in. I entered smiling and hopeful after a good shift and no indication from my co-workers that they were aware of anything being wrong.

"I'm going to put you on a probation period and see how you do." I was smiling ear to ear. "But I don't want to hear that you've been late anymore, or complaining when you're told to do your job, and your job is whatever you're assigned to do. I have to leave, but I would like to stop by your house, so we can discuss this further and go over some new rules."

A cold chill washed over my body, but I couldn't say anything. "You live … by yourself or with someone?" He read off an address that was likely mine, but the numbness that had now moved down from my head to below my waist and could only allow a response of a nod.

"How about I stop by around seven p.m. this evening?" I just stared. "Do you have a problem with that, because we don't have to do the probation? I have enough to fire you today."

He came to my apartment without his wife. I can't say I didn't know, but I hoped she would be there. I had been prepared for this all my life. After all, my mother's first daughter was a street whore and ran her pimp husband's stable. My step-grandfather had every girl in our house, including me, at the tender age of three. I smiled an uncomfortable smile as he stepped across my threshold, and he would step across my threshold at least two or three more times. Other than the shame and humiliation of what I had to do, I was grateful that he was impotent.

Three weeks later, the female owner gave me a choice to be fired or quit, but it was highly suggested that I quit. So, I did what I was told, and as a result, I was not able to draw unemployment. My co-worker "friends" apologized for my getting "fired." They said the owners asked them what was wrong with me the day I got sick, and they told them they thought maybe I was using drugs. They didn't stay in touch and neither did I. Years later after many months of suffering severe pain and bleeding during my periods, it was determined that I had endometriosis.

Chapter Seven

I had become more than weary of our stay in Whittier and the dusty smell of books. Nights in the school library disoriented me. There was no other source of light except for an exit sign or our flashlight. It was the kind of dark that made your mind blank and your body absorb into its surroundings. I was thankful that Nyal provided a space for us to stay while we waited to leave, but this little cave we were in almost prevented us from leaving Whittier at all.

Jumping straight up from his sleeping bag, Seth shouted, "What time is it? I didn't hear the alarm go off."

We could hear a sound like a foghorn blowing in the distance.

"That's the ferry, we're going to miss the ferry, hurry up, run!" he screamed.

We got our clothes on, backpacks, and carry-on bags, making it out the door in what seemed like ten minutes. We could see the ferry as we ran over the hill about a hundred yards away. The captain blew the whistle again to signal the departure. My husband was ahead of me yelling, "Come on, they're leaving!"

I couldn't run anymore, the pack on my back and the bag in my hand felt like a 300-pound moose with two weeks of that damn hotel pie. My husband had slowed, waiting for me since the ferry was pulling away.

I could barely speak. It was more of an airless whisper, "Keep going and stop them, I'm comin' … wave at … them … God please … I can't run anymore, don't let them … leave."

My husband made it to the dock first, and as I got about ten yards away, I heard a voice on a loudspeaker, "Take your time." I made it down to the dock, and I sat there while the big boat pulled back in. I looked up and saw a man dressed in uniform, then watched the huge mouth of the ship open up to let us on. I mouthed *thank you,* too tired for sound to come out.

Once on board, a man in uniform told my husband, "In twenty-five years, I've been with this captain, he has never pulled back in for anyone, but he saw your wife and guess he felt sorry for her. You were lucky," he said with a smile and walked away. I thanked God … finally, it was time to say goodbye to Whittier.

During that first ferry trip out of Whittier, I sat inside, completely surrounded by glass while the passengers who were seated quietly had begun to flock to the front of the boat. A voice yelled to those of us still sitting inside, "Hey, there's a whale!"

My husband jumped up, and turned to me, "Come on, let's see?"

"No, I'm okay, go ahead."

It was as if my anchor had been taken away when my husband left me to see the whales. I felt like I was drifting out to sea when his arm detached. The glassed-in space of the ferry where we sat began floating around me like a puzzle in my mind. A puzzle I could not hold together. Several people asked me if I was going out to see the whales. They assured me that there was nothing to be afraid of. I guess they saw the fear in my face.

I was terrified. There was water that went to the ends of my vision. Bigger than any bathtub I'd been in, and there was no chain to pull out the stopper and let the water drain away. I could feel the eyes on me of those that had gone out to view the wildlife. They had returned to their seats, and now I became the spectacle, since I hadn't moved from my spot. The ferry rocked right, then left, and I gripped the seat with fingers and nails, attempting to keep myself from rolling like a marble in a child's game. Mustering all my courage and dignity, I finally got up, swaying side to side, unstable on my feet, as the big ferry bobbed in the ocean. I made my way to my husband. I shuffled quickly to the inner wall and slid along it until I reached the door to the deck. I just stood there looking out, willing myself not to be afraid and to see a once-in-a-lifetime scene.

My husband was not aware of my standing behind him in the doorway for at least ten minutes until the woman next to him beckoned me to come up. She broke through the few minutes of triumph I had accomplished then injected another dose of fear as she waved me closer to the edge. This woman was bent on drawing attention to me! *No one would notice or care,* I thought, *with the exception of Miss Flappy Hands.* I decided that before she started flapping and waving her hands again, I would try for the rail. I pushed off the wall and momentum took me the rest of the way. I made it, close enough to see the whales but standing just behind them. Frozen in place be damned, I made it! She was standing next to my husband, very white, likely from Wisconsin. They talked with excitement as they watched not just one whale, but a pod of humpback whales. They, like the whales, could have been more easily mistaken as family.

"No, no, I'm good, I can see fine from here."

I tried hard to get them to ignore me, but she had now alerted my husband. He grabbed my arm, pulling me between them, and I shut my eyes, protesting the whole way, "Oh God, oh God, no-no-no-no! I'm good, I can see."

The ocean water sprayed my face; I opened my eyes quickly, gasping for air as if I was drowning. The whale's tail, black like crude oil, rose in front of me as if it was waving, waving at me. For that moment I was not afraid, and I stood there waiting for the whale to come up again before fear returned.

The ferry took us to Cordova, the last leg of our trip to the village. We stayed one night and got an early start, waiting on the dock for our last transportation. The sound of the seagulls had finally quieted from their earlier barrage of screams, and I took some comfort in their silence. I indulged myself in the belief that the quiet was a sign that what I had been anxious about wouldn't materialize. After thirty minutes, there was still no sign of what I thought would be another ferry or boat of some sort.

"What time is it coming?" I asked Seth.

"Soon."

I didn't ask out of excitement and anticipation to be back on a ferry again, it was more out of preparing myself, as well as wanting to get it over with.

When I think back to when we were first thinking of going to Alaska, it seemed like an impossibility. We initially talked about going to Africa, to work with friends my husband knew in the Peace Corps who were starting a school. When those plans did not work out, my husband said, "How about Alaska?" and I simply replied "Yes" with no understanding of what that meant, how far away it was, and the challenges I might face. I didn't know at the time that this was the beginning of what would ultimately be my escape from Kansas City, a place that held me captive in so many ways. I would head north in hopes of finding freedom from everything that had chained me. I didn't know then that the strongest chains binding me were invisible to my eyes.

I grew up in a neighborhood of working-class poor. The area had transitioned from middle-class white Americans, to middle-class Blacks, to us—the just-hanging-on class, the on-paper poor with middle-class aspirations. The neighborhood of my early elementary years had streets lined with large oak trees, cut lawns, and flowerpots. During the mid to late 1970s, it had declined from poverty. An open display of drug abuse, violence, sexual assault, and incest seemed to be the landscape everywhere. Yet deep down, I knew some of these things were always there in some form. Carried from generation to generation like the one stain in the carpet you keep cleaning, and in a few months, it's visible again. I had left Kansas City and headed to a place that might as well have been on the other side of the world, Alaska, where most people I knew still thought people there lived in igloos.

The quiet of the gulls did not last and the dock above me was filled with them, diving in and around us. The sound masked everything else. In the distance, I could see a small plane, and as it came closer in focus, the sound overtook the squall of the seagulls. The plane, a bush plane, had now lined up with the dock and began its descent when I saw it.

"What is he doing … is he going to land?" I shouted to Seth. The plane kept coming nose down. It was heading right at us.

"What is he doing?" I backed up. "Seth, move, get off the dock!" I yelled while at the same time backing quickly off the dock. I couldn't believe my eyes. The plane hit the water. "Oh my God, it's floating."

It wasn't just floating; it was driving on the water, right up to the dock. Seth walked up to the pilot and started talking, then waved me over. I began to walk up to them, smiling, when I heard the pilot say, "How much stuff do you have?"

"What! I'm not getting in that thing." I turned and ran off the dock with Seth in pursuit.

"It's okay, come on! We have to go."

"No, you didn't tell me we were going on a plane. I'm not doing it … No!"

"We have to. It's the only way in."

"How come we can't take a boat? I want to take the boat, where the hell is the ferry?"

The pilot came closer. "Is that everything?" He had taken all the bags that were on the dock and loaded them on the plane. He reached out for the bag on my shoulder. I walked slowly down the dock towards the plane, shaking until my teeth chattered. The pilot reached out his hand to help me in.

"I'm not sitting up front."

The pilot said, "Come on up, you're going to love it, you can see everything better up here."

"She's never flown before," Seth blurted out.

I was so afraid my whole body shook, and sweat poured from my hands and ran down my leg. *Take pity on me and let me crawl in the back on the floor of the plane. No seat necessary,* were my thoughts, but no!

"So, you've never flown before, then you have to sit up front." He grabbed my hand and pulled me in. We were strapped and buckled, with my husband seated in the back. The engine roared in my ears. The water churned and cut away from the floats on the plane as we picked up speed. I wanted to scream, "Please let me out!" and cry, beg, or just flat out stop breathing. At the speed of thought, we lifted in the air. For a moment I saw nothing but blue sky. A feeling I had had many times as a child washed over me, the feeling of flying way above the trees, over my home, and far away from monsters. During these childhood flights, in sleep and sometimes while awake, I flew without a pilot or plane, exhilarated and without fear.

The clamoring of noise from the restaurant dining room and the order line of Gates and Sons Bar-B-Q drowned out the Muzak to a background hum. Liquefied animal fat on burnt wood swirled around my head like a good high. The burnt fat and smoke mingled in my mouth and under every layer of clothes on my body. This place gave me my first real job with an official paycheck with my name embedded in the fibers with black ink.

I had always worked in some capacity since I was six or seven years old. It was the way of Southern Midwesterners, that work ethic. The one exception was a hamburger joint, Smaks. I was fifteen, working the weekend night shift. My mother came to pick me up after work. Ten p.m. was supposed to be my off-hour but the manager wouldn't release me till eleven. I was the new girl and he had me cleaning out rancid gunk from grease traps and scraping muck off the floors. I dug out petrified fries and dried-up meat patties tucked in corners or pushed under heavy equipment. I scrubbed, swept, mopped, and hauled garbage while my mother watched me, impatiently, come and go from outside the glass-front restaurant. That night she ordered me to quit the next day.

Gates and Sons was a stepping-stone, or portal through which I had to pass, to get away from what I was trying to leave behind. Living with my mother was another such stepping-stone. Having run away from my grandmother and into my biological mother's home, I entered a different world.

From the moment I stepped foot in her doorway, my mother made it clear I would work if I was to live in her house. Right away after she made me quit Smaks Hamburger Shack, she used her connections to get me another job. She contacted the father of her first grandchild, the only child she actually had custody over and raised, unlike her own children. It was always curious to me that we were a family of women raising other women's children.

My nephew's father was a manager for one of the Gates restaurants and secured me a job. I was sixteen and found myself thrust into a world that operated on a scale I didn't understand, coming from the sheltered confines of my grandmother's home. I eventually found that there were more similarities between these two environments than I had initially thought. In my mother's world, I came close to beautiful, sophisticated Black people with power and money, as well as a life of hustle and game, violence and theater. But at a level of intensity that distorted what seemed normal to me. It was nevertheless an education that I suspected I needed.

I watched the Black aristocrats of my community come and go from Gates and Sons restaurant. They were served their smoky, gritty pork bones and poor man's beef "brisket" in their board meetings while dressed in tight, white, crisp buttoned-up shirts and eating off of real plates. The rest of us ate our slabs, short ends, long ends, mutton heavy on the sauce with fries and dill pickles on paper plates. The education of my newfound job required knowing how to treat Mrs. Gates and the Gates family if they were around, as well as avoiding being included in catfights between the girls on the line over the men working the pit, and sometimes over the attention of the male managers.

Most fights occurred late at night when the Gates family were not around and no management was in. The fights were always very calculated. They never happened during a shift, especially not during the aggressor's shift because they didn't want to be accused of fighting while on the clock.

One such fight happened between my line supervisor, Denise, and a girl that hadn't been hired but a couple of months before I started. Denise was about seven or eight years older than me, putting her around twenty-three or four. A big girl with over-relaxed hair that was broken off and uneven and stuck up all over her head. She had two kids and had been with the Gates company for about five years. She also had a thing for one of the night managers.

The night manager was married, short, dark, and a loudmouth. He liked to give all of the new girls nicknames like legs, bumpers, or in my case, "jugs," because of my large breasts that stood out even more because I was super thin. I hated being called that, but was pressured to laugh it off as if it was flattering. That is, if I wanted to keep my job.

So, Denise saw the new girl was flattered by the loudmouth manager and was flirting with him. Then, the new girl made the biggest mistake. She went to the manager and asked if she had to do some grunt job Denise told her to do. That night after shift, Denise caught her at the bus stop, which was on the corner and adjacent to the Gates parking lot. Witnesses were made up of a mixture of bystanders: pit guys, line girls, and a handful of locals from the projects. There were no introductions or build-up to the fight, just Denise beating that cute little girl ugly.

The clarity of these life lessons and the role I would be forced to play became clear to me during every fifteen-minute break. I sat in a chair next to the doorway of the dish room and line manager's office while an industrial fan blew warm, wet dishwater air. That hot summer night around eleven p.m. I was racing fast to my twelfth hour of understanding. The first thing I came to understand is that nothing is given without something in return. Not being beaten up by Denise meant avoiding a beatdown, but it also meant stealing from the cash register for her if you were assigned cashier. I refused to steal money for her and the only reason I didn't face a beatdown for that decision was that I also refused to snitch on her. Plus, they all knew a family member had helped get me the job there, and he had been in management for years.

I was slowly understanding my mother and the people she introduced into my life, along with their world and what it took to survive in it. Gratitude was not just showing politeness and sometimes kindness, which is how my grandmother taught me when we were expected to say "please" and "thank you." No, gratitude was engaging in the game that was being played. Then using whatever you saw the other players do, whether you knew the rules or not. I learned that there is always a game being played between people.

When my mother told me that my nephew's father who had gotten me my job at Gates was a nice guy and he'd always helped her out, I decoded the meaning. When she said, "He wants to take you out and show you a nice time," it really meant I was expected to go out with him and be eye candy. My mother highlighted his important attributes, like the fact that he had money and always had something going on to make money, that he took good care of his wife and kids as well as provided protection for her if she needed it or anything else. He was an old man to me in his late thirties (or maybe even forties) and married with kids. I didn't get how my mother thought we'd have anything in common when it came to hanging out and having fun, but I was excited about the possibility of him getting me into a club to dance. *That would be cool,* I thought.

So, we went out. I was dressed in a new outfit that my mom and her lover, who I called my aunt, bought for me. I was always expected to have makeup on, nails painted, and my long hair straightened and curled before going out my mother's front door, even if I was just sitting on the porch or running to the store. This was in stark contrast to how I grew up with my grandmother, which was to be unremarkable in every way unless it was to make her look good.

I don't remember where we went to eat. I just remember riding around and being flaunted in front of men at dance clubs and bars he took me to. Before he brought me back to my mother's house, he parked the car a few blocks away on a dark street and attacked me. He was a big man, over six feet, and weighed close to 300 pounds to my sixteen-year-old body of 116 pounds. He turned towards me from the front seat of his car.

"You had a good time ... you're a beautiful girl, you like all this ... ridin' round in a nice car? We can do this again. Why don't you come over here a little closer?"

"Yeah! It was nice but I need to get home. Mom said don't come in too late." I could feel my body shrink, drawing up to almost nothing with every adjustment he made in his seat. Then he flipped the steering wheel up and out of his way. He was close enough to me now that his voice was heavy and hot and it felt like a wet wool blanket had covered my face.

"It's OK. She knows you're with me, she trusts me, you're safe. Come here!" One large hand reached around the back of my neck and like pulling weeds, he snatched me to his face. His other massive and fat hand groped my blouse until he exposed my breast and kneaded it like silly putty before the force of his hand moved down to plow between my thighs. I now could see us and watched myself and him from a safe position above the roof of the car. My eldest sister Janice's voice began to run like ticker tape across my subconscious:

I was raped at fourteen. That's how I got pregnant. I was sleeping, when I felt someone on top of me. Scared for a minute until I saw it was my friend, but then he grabbed me and covered my mouth. I couldn't make sense of what was happening until I tried to get him off of me, and then I realized he was raping me. But he was my friend! It was your nephew's father that raped me and our mother treated him like he was her best friend or worse, her son ...

My mother's survivor story played out with horrifying similarity:

Rosey, my mother, and her men would come in every night on the weekend drunk. It wasn't the first time one of her men tried coming over to where I was sleepin', but I'd always fought 'em off or she'd come get them. This one night she was passed out drunk when he came in on top of me, and I fought him with everything I had, and my mother just lay there drunk while that dog raped me. I was just fourteen, and your eldest sister was the result of what they did!

...the thoughts of their voices evaporated, and I was there again with his hand in my underwear and his large face and lips covering my mouth and nose. For two or three seconds at a time I couldn't breathe from all the wet saliva and flesh covering my mouth and nose. I pushed as hard as I could, turning my head from side to side to catch my breath, and yelled *"Stop!"* but he didn't.

Something clicked in my head and I remembered something that happened once (getting away from the grip of my brother when I was eleven). He'd lure me into the basement pretending to want to play a game of ball on cold days when we couldn't go outside. There were these two red-painted iron support columns in the middle of the basement floor. We would use the columns as our goals. I would try and kick the ball past him scoring a point, and he would try to do the same past me and my pole.

That day he decided that we should see who was the best climber. We pulled ourselves up the pole by our arms and legs and saw who could hold themself the longest at the top. This was a game that worked far better when I was smaller than four feet. I was now reaching well over five

— 70 —

feet, trying to climb an eight-foot iron pole. But the joy of playing with my brother of sixteen, who now seldom had time for me, sent me over the moon.

The game he wanted to play originated with my step-grandfather, when I was only three or four. I remember being high up on his shoulders, giggling from him galloping me around in the backyard driveway like a horse, going in a circle while I bobbed up and down on his finger he had worked between my panties and the tender delicate folds between my legs. My brother might have been his apprentice, because during those early years he could always manipulate me into complying. My brother used promise of attention, treats, or threats. So, it was a surprise to me when I finally figured out I didn't like it.

I'd made it to the top of the bars and he ran underneath me and started pushing me up, saying I had to stay at the very top and hold on to win. His finger found a small hole in the crotch of my thread-bare pants and like a worm inching its way towards the center of an apple, he dug past the weak seams until the seams of my pants split, exposing me to his full hand. I swatted at his hand and tried to get down before my body betrayed me as it did as a child in the past. This feeling was different and new. The desire to resist any physical urges I might have experienced before was overtaken by a feeling of confusion, but mostly a sense that this was wrong. That feeling overwhelmed me. My stomach churned with a feeling of sickness, then panic, as he manipulated the flesh between my legs. Swinging my legs wildly, I got down off the pole with no resistance. Face to face with him, I saw a look I had never seen in his face, at least not towards me—rage. He grabbed my arm and wrenched me to himself then glanced towards the darker end of the basement where the light bulb had gone out. That was the place I knew I didn't want to go.

"Stop, you're hurting me. Mom is going to hear us!" I tried to speak to him in a calm and measured voice, then like some wild animal he started ripping at my torn pants. I pushed him off balance and ran to the top of the stairs' landing. He grabbed me again and was about to pull me back down the stairs when I told him I'd scream if he didn't let go and mom would hear us. He covered my mouth and gave me a look that said he didn't care. Followed by a deeper look that meant *go ahead, she won't believe you, she always believes me.*

I kicked the door as hard as I could. The door flew open and hit a small hutch just behind the door with whatnots that rattled, teetering on end with a threat to fall. My grandmother yelled out from her seat in the living room, "What in the world y'all doin'!"

I yelled back, "Nothing, just playing," and he let me go.

Here I was again. This time pinned against a car door and needing to escape once more.

Hey, it's late ...

Mom will be mad if I'm home late ...

I don't want to do this in the car ...

Let's get together again ...

Okay! I had a nice time, OK ...?

Slowly, he lightened his grip and sat back in his seat panting from excitement and obesity. To my surprise, he started the car and drove a few blocks to my mother's house, while I wiped my face and put myself back together. When we arrived, I calmly thanked him for taking me out, still afraid of what he might do or what my mother might do if she found out. Then he did something strange. He grabbed my hand to stop me from getting out, reached in his pocket, and took out a large roll of money. He peeled back several large bills and pulled out a $100 bill for me to take. I waved my hand at the money in refusal, but he grabbed my hand and squeezed it hard, pushing the money between my crushed fingers. I said nothing, took the money, and went inside. I never told my mother what happened but I never went out with him again. All of us, including him carried on when we saw each other like everything was normal because for us, this was normal.

At Gates, the line girls stood behind the counter waiting to serve the first customer that cracked the door. We all wore a red, white, and blue polyester top with a blue cap. It was a cool-looking uniform as uniforms go, but this day I made the mistake of coming to work straight from a summer park party. I changed out of a cotton summer halter dress in the restaurant's restroom only to discover that I forgot to bring a bra or a tee shirt to wear under my polyester worktop. I couldn't know what would come from such a small mistake. I wasn't concerned about exposure, because the uniform was heavy and opaque, but I soon found out it was scratchy.

I walked on the line and got into position to take orders as soon as a customer came through the door. I was forced to tug at the top and adjust the shirt after every movement because the material twisted and rubbed against my breasts. It was distracting pulling at the cloth while trying to work at the expected speed. Then came a rush of people and I was reaching up pulling the top, reaching down to grab something under the counter. Reach down, pull down, reach across the counter. *Ahh!,* feeling pain in every movement. Every movement of the man-made fibers across my nipples felt like fiberglass making razor cuts in me.

I walked off the line a few hours later for my break in tears and with sweat pouring off my chest, adding to the discomfort. My supervisor, Denise, walked up to me and asked what was going on. When I told her, she laughed and said "Com'ere, girl." She grabbed some Band-Aids, the big knee type, and told me to go to the restroom and put them over my nipples. She shared she'd done the same thing once. Denise saved me that day. I thought it funny how you never know who might end up rescuing you. I never thought it would be her.

After fixing myself up in the restroom, I finished my break in the combo dish room and line manager's office. I always took my break there because I felt uncomfortable outside. From where I'd sit, I could look down the line at the girls, listen to the pitmen, hear the customers, and experience the whole restaurant, especially the dynamics of the line. "Hi! May I help you?" rang out in unison, some of the girls pleasantly smiling and others barking their orders with disinterest to the men in the pit.

I watched the people ordering their food. White men in business suits with their equals in female form, lined up out the door for noon lunch orders. A greater mix of Black and white patrons came in during the evening hours. I listened to the voices of the men in the pit exchanging fresh jokes with one another, while puffs of smoke billowed out through the pit window. One of the girls stood at the pit window trying to get her order, which the men sometimes intentionally wouldn't send out as payback if the girl had complained about their flirtatious or crass behavior. In her case, none of the pit guys liked her. Maybe it was because she didn't put up with their shit. So, the pit guys got back at her, claiming she didn't call out the order loud enough for them to hear. The customer would be mad and take it out on her that they had to wait longer. That meant no tip for her, for sure. Sometimes it ended up in a shouting match between the pit guys and some of the girls.

I became aware of how great the sounds were while sitting on break and how vivid everything felt. I was disgusted by my smell of sweat and the smells of smoked meat and fat that penetrated everything, including my underwear and hair. In these moments, I was awakened to everything in this life. In a few months, I had perfected calling orders, retrieving and wrapping three to four different customer orders with speed, accuracy, and joyful competitiveness that helped make a monotonous job pass quickly. I escaped fistfights that continued to occur on occasion. I even avoided getting fired for the stealing that continued from the registers. I watched the poorest of us do whatever they had to do to survive, including fight over the scraps and bones of existence. And with clarity, I decided this was not going to be the rest of my life. As long as I could find some kind of choice, I'd just keep choosing until I got where I was meant to be.

Chapter Eight

We climbed the hill from the ocean's shore. The sun was high, and there was a bite to the air coming off the water during the last week of August. A baby-blue dome on top of a Russian Orthodox church was a beacon, guiding our direction. My mind floated over the village, over the ocean and Copper Mountain that towered above us. I drifted in and out of awareness. A documentary of an African village with children pouring out from everywhere, clamoring all over the Western outsiders, came to mind. My imagination echoed with the sound of faraway chants of these imaginary people greeting the outsiders. Present again, we were almost to the top of the hill and still not a soul to be seen. Dead silence met us as we rounded the first house, leaning and dilapidated, but pointing to the continued road.

"Where are the people?" I asked. "Did they know we were coming?"

"Yes, someone was supposed to meet us."

I really didn't know what to expect. TV and old-school textbooks were all I had to go on, and not seeing one soul made my anxiety intensify. We headed towards what looked to be the school. It was the largest building other than the obvious powder-blue domed church that evoked thoughts of gnomes and Oompa Loompas from *Charlie and the Chocolate Factory*. It felt magical. The contrast of the ocean, church, and dead silence made it all a bit unnerving. The whole time we saw no one, heard no one, not a child crying or a dog barking. I couldn't help thinking and feeling that though I saw no one, someone was watching me.

I was born into the Christian faith. My grandmother was a Baptist, so we were Baptist, sort of. Her grandfather, my great-grandfather, built a church in Conway, Arkansas, and it stood to serve the Primitive Baptist. I never knew what that meant, and the word primitive along with Baptist always frightened me a little. My grandmother worked several jobs after I started kindergarten and we began to go to whatever church my eldest sister could make our little feet travel to. There was the Catholic church down the street, Baptist several blocks away, and I think there was one nondenominational church.

They were nothing like the church that sat on the next block behind our house, which I could see and hear from our backyard. That church was a Pentecostal church. I would sit on my back steps and listen for hours to the bass that came from a hundred, maybe a thousand, stomping feet, a percussion of hands clapping, tambourines, and the harmony of voices singing and shouting. We never went there. My grandmother was not a woman to put up with making a scene. She thought loud, outward expressions were just putting on a show or making a fool of yourself. One Sunday, she caught me listening and moving to the beat.

"You like all that carryin' on? Why don't you get up and go on over there?" she said. "Betta get off my stairs jumpin' round like a little fool."

My husband was Jewish, and his mother had remarried to a white Anglo-Saxon and become a born-again Christian. A few days before we were married, Seth's mother and stepfather came to Kansas City along with his stepfather's brother and wife, for what I could only call an intervention. I had been out of the church, all of the churches, since my preteens. I was a very angry young woman in all areas of life, and damn well blamed God for most of it. When my husband's mother and stepfather came for the wedding, they came with the hope of saving Seth's soul by leading him to salvation. That did not happen, though they got me to release some anger and rededicate my life to Christ. They had to live with the hope that they had planted a seed in me that could help save my husband's soul.

We had made it to the entrance of the dock and in front of us, a little way down, was the school. Out of nowhere a man appeared. He walked onto the road from the direction of the dock and stood in front of us.

"Excuse me, we're looking for Mr. O'Brennan, the principal." My husband Seth broke through the sounds of nature.

"You're the new teacher, ah?"

"Yeah, we just …"

"O'Brennan in the school." He pointed and walked away.

"Thank you," we called after him.

The absence of human sound filled the environment again, leaving only the occasional cry of seagulls, ravens, and the lapping ocean against the rocks. We made it to the school and knocked. A blonde, fair-skinned woman with jaw-length hair came to a door at the side of the school. The entrance she stood in was attached to a small residence provided for the teaching principal. The woman that answered the door was O'Brennan's wife, Lisa. She was about my height of five feet and seven inches, with a California or maybe Idaho look. They were the only teaching team there until our arrival. We knew there were around sixty-five school-aged kids in the village, but my husband wasn't sure what percentage of the students he would work with. It could be tricky for him since he was hired to teach fifth and sixth grade, but also to deal with the special education needs, since he was a certified special ed teacher.

We'd heard from other teachers back in Fairbanks how overwhelming the workload could be for bush teachers. They spoke about teaching multiple grades, dealing with learning disabilities, and having little support when dealing with alcohol-related issues that affected educating and safety. They said trying to keep students and parents on board with coming to school consistently could feel like a full-time job all by itself. When asked why they are trying to go back out to the bush, some said they loved the challenge, the land, and the people. Others didn't really love it but loved how much money they could make, especially if they were nearing retirement. I was confident in Seth. He was a brilliant teacher, and the challenges they talked about, he'd already met in New York City, in the Peace Corps, and in Kansas City. I knew that if he had any struggle, it would be around his lack of disciplining the kids and himself. In spite of my confidence, I couldn't help but feel a sense that this challenge might take us to the limits of what we knew, and then some.

Lisa offered us tea while we sat waiting for her husband O'Brennan, the principal, to return. She said he was out visiting one of the villagers and would be back soon. We carried on the typical polite first-meeting conversation with an atmosphere that resembled our walk into the village, watched. Suddenly, the door opened abruptly, and O'Brennan entered the kitchen where we sat, still sipping on tea with long stretched-out silences in between. He was a short, fit man that seemed full of energy in every movement. He spoke with to-the-point punctuation and added overtones of sarcasm.

"I was at George Allen's. He fell last night and hit his head, or more likely got hit in the head, and he needs to go in for stitches." O'Brennan spoke as if we knew who he was talking about.

Seth asked, "What happened?"

"Who knows! The whole village was drunk last night, that's why no one's out, they're all sleeping it off. So! Where are you staying?" he said.

We looked at each other, bewildered by the question. "We thought you would have that information."

You could feel the discomfort in the air as Lisa got up and busied herself at the kitchen sink, then excused herself as she left the room.

"You didn't make arrangements before coming out?" He was standing again, posturing at the end of the table.

"We were told to see you."

"Well, you can't stay here. We don't have enough room, our place is barely big enough for us. Arrangements should have been made before you came out, but this is typical. The teacher you're replacing rented one of the local houses. You might be able to rent the same one, the Totemoff place. I can't promise. It didn't go well with the last teacher, but I'll give them a call in the morning. They live in Valdez, fisherman, and keep a house here too. Until then, you can sleep in the school, in one of the rooms." *Great!* I thought. *I'm back sleeping in a dusty classroom with a bunch of books.*

The conversation then shifted to their profession: testing, how many students there were, how many were in special education, and the level of support the school district would give the school. O'Brennan described some of the kids and their families while I sat quietly listening, like a third-world mail-order bride. O'Brennan eventually directed a few questions at me, like where I was from and what I did before coming to the village. Then he asked a thought-provoking question, one I didn't have an answer to. "What are you going to do to occupy yourself while your husband is teaching? There're very few jobs around here, and the villagers get the first choice of any that pop up."

I'm sure my mouth gaped for a few seconds as a quiver ran along my spine. I'd put off thinking about it because the feeling of being lost and alone with no guidance or purpose to ground me was terrifying. There was also the thought of so many people that were waiting for me to fail and prove I didn't belong in Seth's life. The question caught me off guard. For the first time, I really had to answer the question. I was out of time. I'd been asked before, by my family, but I saw their questions as more in the context of my responsibility as a supportive wife. When it came up in casual conversations with people staying in the Fairbanks dorms, it seemed rhetorical since everyone was trying to figure out what they were doing. I had mulled it over in my head, what role in this adventure I might have, but the thoughts of being useless and inadequate seem to keep clouding everything. I had focused on what I knew how to do and what Seth didn't do well, taking care of our needs. Plus, how could I have planned for something I couldn't even comprehend? It's like my husband telling me I'm taking you on a surprise vacation and to just throw a few things in a bag, but you don't know where you're going. I guess the answer to O'Brennan's question was, I didn't know. My husband said he wanted to go to Alaska, and I followed him. Seth and I never talked about what I would do in the real sense of the question. His answer to most things was, "We'll figure it out … I'm sure you'll be able to get a job doing something, at the school probably, or in the village."

I didn't answer O'Brennan when I heard him say he could introduce me to some of the village ladies. He said one of the women, Anna, was the health aid and very nice. O'Brennan also shared with us the dynamics of the village. For instance, there was one phone for the entire village, and you must stick to the time limit. He explained the kids had a lot of freedom and that the village was not a dry village. I listened as he told us numerous stories of alcoholic-related incidents. He spoke of many incidents including shootings, snowmobile crashes, murders, and rape. I sat quietly glazing over and thinking to myself, *I came 3,000 miles for what seems like the same mess I dealt with at home.* Yet, I knew this was not the same beast. My home and this place both had violence, and no matter where I was, I carried fear. My beast, however, was now 3,000 miles away. Another thought occurred; I had run to a place that could be far more difficult to escape, since a boat or a plane would be my only way out.

O'Brennan showed us where we would sleep and gave us one last piece of advice for the night: "Do not get high with anyone here, buy any drugs from anyone, or buy drugs for anyone if you don't want to get a reputation for being a partier."

He went on to tell us that the last teacher, who Seth was replacing, had a Grand Central Station going through his house and that's why he no longer taught in the village. I took comfort in knowing that Seth would never jeopardize his career and that he seemed content with not doing drugs anymore. He knew I had stopped using before we met and I was uncomfortable around them. It was the one thing I was sure would not be a problem; I had my husband's word.

When we were alone, I asked Seth what a dry village was. He told me that some Alaskan villages had voted to stop all alcohol and drugs coming into their village, because they have some sovereignty over their land and had the right to make those governing decisions. So, anyone caught bringing in alcohol could be arrested and banned from the village. However, this was not a dry village. *Yeah,* I thought, *but to know you have the right to govern yourself and protect your people from dangerous things coming into your community is mind-blowing.*

When I was around four or five years old, my Great-Uncle Dee came to live with us, one of my grandmother's many siblings. My Uncle Dee was something special to me, but my view of him would be muddied in a matter of a few years. During those early years, he was my playmate. We often would sit on the front porch rocking back and forth on a white rusting glider that my grandmother dressed in blue and green floral vinyl lawn cushions. Like most of the material things my grandmother owned, she took exceptional care of them, which was the way of Depression-era survivors and striving poor Blacks. So, every fall she ritualistically covered and stored those plastic cushions. In the seasons we sat outside, we were never allowed to play or tussle on them. On rainy days, she sent us kids out to tuck them safely behind the glider to be protected from the elements. My Uncle Dee was different; he didn't follow many rules, including my grandmother's most of the time. He would sit on the glider for hours smoking his rolled cigarettes and killing flies.

"Uncle Dee!! You kill all those flies?" I'd say to him with wide eyes.

"Yes, ma'am," he'd say, still gliding. Whoop, he'd hit another fly, not missing his stride, and sweep it over to the corner with the fly swatter.

"Want me to get the broom and sweep them up?"

"No, ma'am, that's for my soup," he said.

"Soup? Oh nooo, that's not for soup."

He would look at me with a straight face. "Moptop," he said, (that's what he called me because of my long hair that stood all over my head at combing time) "don't you know them flies make the best fly soup you ever had? You better leave my flies over there if you want me to give you some."

I looked hard into my uncle's gray eyes and believed every word. "Can I help you make the soup Uncle Dee?"

He handed me the swatter and sat back. "Alright, you gotta start killin' some flies if we gonna make a big pot of soup." He'd smile and that's how those days went.

Other days I would see him coming down the street towards home, and I'd call out to my sisters and brother, "Uncle Dee's comin'." They would run to the porch, look down the street, and watch him bump from one side of the sidewalk to the other, like hitting imaginary walls.

With a swoop, they'd grab me by the arm, snatch me in the house and lock the door. My sister grumbled, "Uncle Dee's drunk. Mom said 'Don't let him in if he's drunk'." No matter how much I protested, my sister would say, "Be quiet and don't let him know we're here, or else Mom's gonna be mad." He hollered and cursed over an hour before sitting on the glider, falling over, and going to sleep. We never made a sound.

Uncle Dee was my hero. Not just because he was in the army during World War II and received medals for barely surviving that special hell called war. He was my hero, because he unwittingly found himself in a different war and chose to take up arms and fight. This conflict was called The Piss War.

It started when my grandmother woke up at six a.m. and started ranting. It was an all-day siege of cursing, threats, shoving, and fist knuckling in the back or head of one child or the other. The list of things she was angry about went from not being able to find an article of her clothing that went through the laundry to "I'm sick of this damn filthy house and not one soul lift a hand ta clean unless I make-'em." Or, "I work like a dog ta keep a roof over our heads and I can't even sit down and have a cup of coffee without a mess starin' at me." Then, "There's four of you runnin' around here always lookin' hungry and tearin' up and makin' a mess. I'm sick and tired of it. These GD good-for-nothin' men can't even cut the damn grass. Guess that's for me ta-do, too. Get your behinds up and get something done! I'm not callin' you all but once too."

We poured out of bed on a Saturday morning and gathered up dirty clothes to wash, cleaning supplies to clean the bathroom, and polish to start dusting the living room and my grandmother's room before vacuuming. Two o'clock rolled around and we were still going strong without stopping for breakfast or lunch. That's when the teeth-gnashing started for not working fast enough. Then the name-calling led to the knuckle-grinding of heads. And everything would escalate because of a perceived look.

"You tryin' ta roll your eyes at me?" Then as fast as her short stout legs could carry her wide hips, she headed for her beating stick. The sound of a voice rang out from the top of the stairs where a tiny attic room housed my great-uncle. His voice trumpeted deep, slightly, gurgly and rough when he spoke. Years of him chain-smoking rolled cigarettes and drinking too much gin likely had ruined the deep velvet tone you could sometimes hear.

"Purnie, leave them kids alone. I'm sick of listening to all that damn noise!" Uncle Dee's voice sang like Gabriel. His voice reached her as she passed his doorway on her way for the beating stick. I had started crying and stopped when I heard his voice. My grandmother backed up to the attic door and snatched it open wide, and yelled up the stairs.

"What you say to me, man?"

"I said leave them children alone. They ain't doin' nothin', and I'm sick of listenin' to you hollerin' at them over nothin'. You been yellin' all day. Be quiet and go somewhere and sit down and let-'em do what they got to do." We didn't move a muscle with the exception of our mouths falling wide open and staring at each other.

"Who the hell you talkin' to sittin' up in my house? This ain't none of your damn business what I say in my house and how I discipline these damn kids … you want-ta take a side and don't know if your ass is up or down. Now, I suggest you lay your drunk behind down and mind ya business before you get on my bad side too."

Uncle Dee was a thick, brawny man that had grown up on a farm doing hard labor most of his life just like my grandmother and the rest of their siblings. He stood up from the small bed tucked out of view to one side of the attic and faced her straight on. He had the high ground and the advantage. He looked down at her from the top of the stairs, readying himself.

"It is my business. I've been listenin' ta you yap all mornin' over nothin', you need to shut up now, I done told you, and just let-'em get whatever it is done." My uncle steadied himself on his one good leg. The bad leg had been injured in the war when the weight of a horse fell on it and crushed the bone. He refused to let them amputate, so they pinned and plated it up the best they could.

"You talk ta-me like that after everythin' I've done for you? Nobody wouldn' even give you a glass of water, let 'lone a place ta lay your head down. You come here drunk and stinkin', filthy and dirty, but I'm the one that took you in and you gonna stand in my …"

"I told you to shut up now else I'm gonna throw this piss jug at ya-head." I could see Uncle Dee standing there with the glass half-gallon milk jug almost full of amber piss sloshing back and forth, raised and aimed.

"Alllll right, you S-O-B, you want ta treat me like that after ever …" My grandmother's small feet pounded the ground loudly with the weight of her legs. We giggled and shook with fear, not knowing if she was coming back with her stick to beat us, just to spite him, but nothing prepared us for her next move. She returned with my step-grandfather's hunting rifle. She pumped it once and leveled the gun up at the top of the stairs.

"Okay, negro, you want ta throw a piss jug down on me you go right ahead, and I'm gonna blow your ass right out of there and straight to hell."

Well, Uncle Dee retreated. Though the war ended in what might look like defeat, we were liberated from my grandmother's tyranny that day because of him. She spent the rest of the day seething and talking out loud to herself towards the attic door. Her angry words and comments had shifted from us and were now centered on Uncle Dee and the other males attached to this house. Like a magnet to metal, she soon gravitated to the yard, where the sound of the lawnmower roared from my father's arrival to cut the grass. Within seconds, the sound of the mower cut off with my grandmother's presence outside.

I had few intimate interactions with either O'Brennan or Lisa after our initial meeting. I saw them on occasion in passing or when I was at the school, but that didn't produce a great deal of socializing between us. The O'Brennans had established themselves well enough in the village, having been there about two or three years prior to our arrival This gave them time to struggle through whatever cultural or social differences they might have had.

The fact is being white gave them an advantage. After all, this was a white system of education that was being provided to the village in order to further the Inuits' understanding of their place in their world. The O'Brennans, my husband, and others like them became the overseers of their educational system that intended to inculcate everyone into it. The school was placed in a position of power like the church and its pulpit in front of parishioners. Even the O'Brennans' residence was located away from the rest of the houses in the village. The only building positioned higher and further away from the people's everyday life was the church.

None of this I can say was consciously done on the part of the O'Brennans. Since the school had been there long before the O'Brennans came to the village, they, like my husband and I, were following a system already established. Their whiteness, in spite of whatever conflict indigenous people might still have with the original colonizers, had been softened through marriage and the reshaping of Native lands ever since Russian and other Europeans invaded in the eighteenth century. Unlike my people that were marked by slavery and sifted out from the human race because of the darkness of their skin, the Alaskan villages screamed a different story. As a Black person, my relationship with most white people was tenuous at best, and I was used to being kept at a polite and sometimes not-so-polite distance. Now, I would see what my relationship could be with the indigenous people. I'd chosen to see hope in our shared history of suffering for our otherness and looked to find a bridge between all three cultures.

We got moved into the Totemoff's place, a red-painted wood-framed house that sat at the end of the main road. Going straight along this dirt road would bring you to where the church and school sat. The only crossroad ran downhill to the shore and uphill to where the new housing was being built. Our house, near the intersection, was surrounded by the old housing. There were no other roads because there was no place else to go.

We had one phone and that was in the phone shack for everyone to use. The phone shack was on the main dirt road at the intersection. You paid for a calling card and when you needed to make a call, you punched in a gazillion numbers, assuming the one phone was not occupied, in order to do the tedious process. There were no stores, cars, or restaurants. Just seventy-five houses, and half of that number was made up of the new houses. There was one school, one church, thousands of trees, several valleys and mountain ranges, and one massive ocean. My God, it was the most beautiful place I had ever been.

Our house had one bedroom, which had very high windows that ran across the top of the wall, the sunniest room in the house. There was a storage closet I used as a pantry, a living room that flowed into the kitchen, and the kitchen had a backdoor that faced the other older houses on the main road. Our house was directly across from Anna and her husband Haze, whom O'Brennan had said he would introduce me to.

That introduction came a few days later during the open house and potluck at the school. The community always attended the open house to see what new plans or changes there might be in the new school year. For the teaching staff, it was a time to encourage parents and students to participate in making it a successful school year. Subtle suggestions from posters speaking to the importance of sleep, parents' help with homework, and being on time were artfully taped everywhere. Then there was meeting the new teacher and his wife. Everyone brought a dish to share, making the potluck feel like a real social event. I had heard the word *potlatch* used in passing and thought it was the same thing as a potluck. I made the social faux pas of calling what we were attending a potlatch and was quickly educated it was not.

The potlatch was a ceremonial feast that celebrated marriage or death, and gifts would be given to the guests according to their importance. If it was a potlatch between groups that were rivals, then a lot of showing off of wealth and competition took place, and the host might even break things of value to prove his prosperity. This was not that different from Black people I knew that came together for funerals, graduations, and the infamous card parties where the fried chicken, mac and cheese, collard greens, potato salad, cobblers, and sweet potato pie flowed like water. As far as its similarity to the potlatch, we competed about everything from who cooked the best fried chicken, had the flyest outfit, had the best dance moves, or had the best-behaved kids. Where we differed from the potlatch, we were not about to break a doggone thing of ours to prove nothin'. Deep down we all knew none of us, in the big scheme of things, had shit.

All I could bring to the potluck was a sacrificial bag of chips from the pantry, which was a big deal because you couldn't just run out and buy a bag. It would be a month or longer before we could get more

Lay's potato chips. In our new home I had yet to figure out how to light the cookstove. This was important beyond cooking because it was also our source of heat, and the cold was here, especially at night.

My grandmother, being a farm girl, imparted many skills and knowledge to me from her farm life. Things as a child I didn't want to know and I never thought I'd use, but I was wrong. The stove was not unfamiliar. I had been told every story of my grandmother's life on the farm from bringing the cows out to the pasture to the proverbial walking ten miles to school in the snow with cardboard in her shoes. At some point she shared about the many stoves she'd cooked on, and being a great cook in her own right; this stove was like one she'd mentioned. I just didn't know how to prime the oil to come into the firebox. My husband Seth was not the handyman type, in spite of his attempts to try. So, solving the stove issue was up to me, and a request went out to O'Brennan. A few days later he came by, and we got heat.

On the day of the potluck, I arrived about an hour before everyone else. Seth had spent the whole evening the night before preparing, and he was up and out early to work on his classroom. When I got to the school, he was still frantically doing a few last-minute things, and I was put to work. I helped hang several affirmation posters and tidied his room. I stood around while people came in, walking past me as I spoke, occasionally nodding or saying hi, but no one made any real attempt to have a conversation–until I was introduced to Anna Allen, a connection that would change my time in the village. She kept me company for what seemed like an hour but was likely only twenty minutes. We set a time to meet the following day. A few of the other women finally decided I was safe enough to approach. They made light conversation with Anna and me over the potluck food.

"You eat fish, ah."

"Yes, I love fish."

"I make this one, fish good, ah. You teach?"

"No, just my husband," I'd say.

I didn't altogether know how to view what was happening, whether it was because they were a shy culture, they didn't like outsiders, or they didn't like Blacks. I had plenty of experiences of walking in a place, be it a store or a school, and knowing I was not welcomed. I had it in my mind that the Native people could not possibly be racist against Blacks; they were Native. We shared a common truth of oppression. Plus, I, like most of the Black folks I knew, had Native American blood that coursed through our veins, even if in my case, it was just one-sixteenth. Anna turned to talk with someone else and with barely a pause between their actions, the other woman walked away as well.

I remembered looking at old pictures of my grandmother's father and mother, who I knew up until I was thirteen. The picture of my great-grandfather was of a stern man with coal-black straight hair. My grand-mother told me her father had both English and Native blood. I was so happy at the time. I thought someone had handed me the keys to the kingdom until she said, "I don't know why you so happy, they treat them just as bad as Black folk." Something sunk in me again. I thought nobody could be treated as badly as people treat you for being Black.

O'Brennan told me at some point that most of the people had never met or interacted with a Black person except for what they saw on TV. That helped, but I had to later come to the reality that they were just people. They could be kind, mean, and discriminatory like the rest of us. I felt some kind of responsibility to give them a different view of Blacks, other than what TV offered in their portrayal of Black Americans.

The school was all abuzz with people laughing and talking. They were not quite like my friend Vernice that I'd left in Fairbanks. Her face was round like the moon, happy to see me with her deep crater dimples on the sides of her face even when she didn't smile. Their faces seemed different to me, all different shades of light summer brown with slimmer faces, but the same raven hair. There were a few of them, maybe a little more than half, whose skin was fair with only a tinge of pigment and hair that went from dark to a light brown. Maybe this was the Russian influence on the people.

I stood off to the side and watched them. They filled the room like a field of spring flowers, some wearing a *kuspuk* printed in delicate colors and patterns. The kuspuk reminded me of a dress my grandmother made for me as a child. It was a simple tunic pullover with short sleeves and little pastel flowers. The kuspuks were worn mostly by the older women. These traditional garments were pullovers with a hood, long sleeves, one large front pocket, and a gentle ruffle on the bottom. The women made me think of Russian nesting dolls as they turned and moved in the small school space.

Towards the end of the potluck, I saw a tall, dark-haired man walk into the school. The energy shifted the way bees behave when the queen was present. I remember him addressing O'Brennan with a punctuated tone and asking an unrelated question as if he was there for a conference or meeting. O'Brennan answered him with a smile and his short and to-the-point manner, "It's open house, Meddy, we can talk about that sometime this week." With his usual high energy, O'Brennan moved away quickly, busying himself. After everyone was gone except the teaching staff and me, O'Brennan let us know that the man I saw was Meddy, and he was the village council president and an asshole. He said that everyone was afraid of him and he pretty much did what he wanted. That was the first time I saw Meddy, but it wouldn't be my last.

Chapter Nine

My days were long and quiet without Seth, and I missed our days together coming up to Alaska. Our trip to Alaska took us nearly a month. Driving his yellow Volkswagen Rabbit, we pulled a used trailer that resembled something meant to carry a dog team. The roof of the car was stacked with our belongings, two feet high, as we chugged along the highway. Seth mapped out a route that would include sightseeing as we traveled. I always felt this was his way of making up for a lousy honeymoon, which consisted of a campground with a holey, borrowed tent that leaked from the rain that poured the whole time.

Seth plotted a route that went through some of the most beautiful parts of the country I had ever seen. We were in Big Sky country, Wyoming and Montana. I fell in love. At some point on a whim, he decided to make a slight detour and take us through Yellowstone Park. He was spontaneous like that. For instance, when we were dating, in the dead of winter with a few feet of snow, he said, "Let's drive to the Ozarks and rent a cabin."

The thought of going there with Seth brought back bad memories of the first time I was in the Ozarks with a previous boyfriend. He too was a white guy I dated for a minute, and he decided it would be fun for me to see the fall colors in the spectacular Ozarks. It did not go well. We stopped to eat at a country restaurant. It was Baptist Sunday and the place was packed with elderly blue-haired white couples and white families of four and six, plus a white waitressing staff to boot. It was wall-to-wall white folks, and I was about to be the speck of pepper.

You could hear the clamor and clatter of dishes, eating, and talking before you opened the door. We walked in and like in an old Sidney Poitier movie, everything stopped and their eyes all looked at me, then him. We ordered to go, and I waited in the car. Going to the Ozarks with Seth turned out very different from that first time. It was winter, and everyone was inside, somewhere protected from the bitter cold Missouri temperatures. We spent the entire weekend huddled together in the warm little cabin. On our first day out, we shot cans in the woods with a borrowed .22 rifle that belonged to the cabin owner's son. That weekend, unlike my first visit to the Ozarks, produced a moment of peace, joy, and the promise of marriage after dating for ten months.

Yellowstone Park was incredibly beautiful, but as incredible as it was, this ended up not being one of his best whims. Yellowstone Park is 7,733 feet above sea level and we were in a fully loaded Volkswagen Rabbit, climbing. That is when I learned that my husband also had no mechanical skills. The car would go two feet and shut off, go another two feet and shut off, all 7,733 feet. A few people stopped to offer assistance to no avail, other than a possible diagnosis of something called an airlock. At that moment, of course, Seth suddenly recalled hearing that there was an issue with the vapor lock in that specific vehicle.

Seth had a great sense of humor in a way that was different from mine. He could be self-deprecating without loathing himself. He was sarcastic, which was a form of humor I wasn't used to. People I grew up with saw sarcasm as a white thing and as someone disrespecting them, and they were obliged to respond to sarcasm with an ass beating. He had an almost childlike habit of making statements or asking the most inappropriate questions to people. We were out once and this very eccentric old white woman had her hair up in what looked like a sculpture made of dirt and paste. It had the appearance of not being combed out in at least twenty years. He said, right in earshot of her, "Whooo! Did you pay someone to do that?" I remember when it was popular for women to wear loose bohemian lounge-type dresses. I loved them because they were so comfortable and colorful, but he made it his duty to tell any and every woman he saw that they looked like his grandmother in a *schmatta*. Though these kinds of outbursts were uncomfortable and not always funny, his ability to laugh at himself and his ridiculous behavior became one of the greatest gifts he gave me.

My humor was more direct and survival-based. If I got a beating from my parents, I'd laugh about it with my siblings. That's what we did, laugh together, turning our whoopings into something humorous to ease the pain. There were endless jokes about how you looked dodging and dancing from Mom's stick, belt, or some other flying object. We made fun of one another a lot and played "the dozens" (like "your mama so fat" jokes) with friends. My easily bruised emotions about my mama made me short-tempered and didn't allow for playing the dozens very often. When I would inevitably get mad, my grandmother was always there to dole out her unsolicited advice, "Don't dish it out if you can't take it."

One of the ongoing jokes between Seth and me, by his omission, was that he wasn't the guy to have physical fights for someone's honor. Even safety was debatable. He would share in social settings that if he and I were walking down a dark alley and thugs were about to jump us, he would push me in front to handle it. I didn't believe this to be true, especially after he stood up when my supervisor at the boarding home made derogatory remarks about Black people. Even if he was too cowardly to fight physically, I was good with that. It was knowing that he would stand up for my people and my honor that held the greatest value.

Seth was one of the smartest people I knew. When I met him, he was enrolled in a calculus course and seemed to have a general knowledge about everything academic. His falling in love with me I didn't quite understand, nor his belief in my intelligence. The constant encouragement was confusing, especially when I couldn't handle simple adult tasks like filling out an application, calling a bill collector on the phone, or organizing my thoughts and words to ask for information. These things seemed to paralyze me.

At times I felt more like a project. I knew he'd gone into the Peace Corps in a desire to reject and prove he was different from his father. I couldn't help but think I might be a continuation of this pathology. If so, then it would leave me as less than a formidable partner. Yet I had to consider my own internal battle of self-doubt and whether I could quench the negative voices to believe that I was worthy of being loved. The idea of the latter, for now, was so much more desirable to me. I could not ignore that I still had so few marketable skills. I did, however, have strong opinions and I guess that's part of what made us work—he was opinionated too. We liked each other and talked about everything, fought about it all as well. We made love a lot, partly because we could, and because it made me feel secure and it made him feel connected in an otherwise physical world he was disconnected from. We bore one another's secrets, and we became each other's friend. Surely that was enough.

The honeymoon seemed over; every day Seth was leaving earlier. During those first weeks in the village, I would get up and we would have breakfast together, but then he began to just have time for coffee. I started sleeping later in the mornings, having little to do. He would say, "Why don't you get with some of the women in the village. What about Anna, you like her?" The other woman in the village would hardly speak to me, and Anna and I got together one day for tea before she had to leave the village for almost two weeks for some training as a health aid. The days not only got longer now when Seth went to school, but the evenings as well.

Seth was always at school preparing. He was not just a regular teacher, he was also their special education teacher, and there were so many more demands on him in a village with alcohol-related learning problems. When we met, he had been dealing with the same or worse challenges teaching in the same inner-city schools I had attended. Alcohol, drugs, neglect, and abuse were just a few of the problems his students faced in Kansas City. The apathy of the adults on all levels that were supposed to care about these children was the biggest crime.

The weekend would finally come, and he was almost all mine and always up for an adventure. I had learned that Alaska had wild berries, and I bought several books on wild gathering when we were still waiting for a placement. Our first real weekend had us up early and out to hunt for what Alaska had to offer us. Most days were rainy and cloudy, or cloudy and rainy, but we put on our rain gear and headed out. Over a hill or down along the shore, it didn't matter. On our first weekend out, we found berries. I was crazy excited. There were raspberries and a beautiful almost peach color berry that looked like a raspberry; I later found out it was a salmonberry. We picked enough to eat right there; wet, cold face and hands, but satisfied, we returned home four or five hours later.

That Monday seemed to come quickly, and I was on my own again, but this time I was ready and excited for my long day. I had purpose and motivation which would take me back to where we found berries, but this time I had a pail to catch them in. Most people seem to have something innate, that draws them to nature in some way, no matter what environment they grew up in. I believe I have always been the hunter-gatherer type despite living amongst a deluge of grocery stores as the primary means to feed oneself. My ancestry of farmers and woodsmen and women ran in my blood.

We were completely surrounded by houses with lawns and property lines, but a mulberry bush in the wild brambles of a neighbor's yard was a call from nature to whoever dared. I loved gathering from underneath the window of our house. A weed we called pickleweed grew there. It was sour like my favorite food, pickles, but came with a warning to not eat too much else you'd get a stomachache. I spent hours by myself gathering shiny flecks of stones from the sand. I imagined they were rubies and other precious gems. I ate my pickleweed and fingered through small mounds of sand in my dusty palms hoping to find enough treasure to make us rich, so my grandmother wouldn't have to work so hard and be sad.

One Mother's Day weekend I expanded my hunting range to a house that cornered our property in the backyard. It was on a corner lot that faced the next block over, but their yard touched our property. Sunday was to be Mother's Day, and I wanted to do something extra nice for my grandmother. I was about six, and my grandmother had not yet fenced in the backyard. The house directly behind us had a high cement slab that covered most of the yard. It sat higher than our yard and made it hard to climb up and over to their side. Plants grew in a three-feet strip of grass along the sides of the concrete and in every patch of soil that was not cement.

There were two elder sisters that lived there, and it was established long before I was six not to go in their yard. Next door to them and behind our neighbor's garage was a small little yard. I thought of it as an enchanted wild field with magical creatures. No one ever went in the yard, and it was grown up in Easter-green grass and wildflowers that drew butterflies and birds of all colors. It was waiting for me. I got up early and walked down our drive, to the corner of our block, and up the long side street to the grassy, unused driveway that was between me and the magic field. I hesitated. I had never been this far by myself. My heart was pounding with fear as I now stood at the grass edge. Fear of being far away from Mom's sight washed over me, yet excitement nudged me forward to see so many beautiful wildflowers I had never seen before. I stepped in on tippy-toes, trying hard not to step on flowers or fairies, as the sunlight danced and patches of light turned the shaded emerald grasses a spring green. My soft but holey sneakers were now on point like a ballerina. I danced, not crushing a leaf or ant mound. I picked, taking great care not to damage the purple, white, and yellow flowers I found. Only taking one each, I moved gently out of the yard the same way I went in. Running all the way home and straight to my room, my grandmother yelled out, "Where are you going in such a hurry? And stop slamming doors."

I yelled back, "Yes, ma'am! I have to go to the bathroom." I stopped in the bathroom, flushed the toilet, and washed my hands, so it wouldn't be a lie. I took out my meager art supplies: scraps of construction paper from other projects, scissors, and white paste that was going hard, so I added water to it. I glued the fresh flowers to a piece of my sister's white medium-ruled writing paper. I cut and fashioned the best pieces of my construction paper into a mosaic of shapes and colors to paste around the flowers. I glued the paper with the flowers to half of the construction paper, then folded the other half of the construction paper over to form a card. I then pressed the card with my sister's Webster's dictionary just like I saw on TV, ladies pressing flowers.

The next day was Mother's Day. I took the book off my pressed flower card and opened it to write my message and to show my eldest sister my gift. To my horror, the flowers had molded in places where I put the paste and stuck and tore in other spots. Whenever I was upset or punished, I liked to go in the closet. I would climb over our clothes folded in plain brown boxes, serving as an organizing unit. Over my grandmother's purse that was hidden from my step-grandfather, I would curl up in the corner, lost amongst the colorful fabric of clothes and cry quietly. That was where my sister found me and told me that mom (my grandmother) wanted me. She had heard me crying and asked my sister what was wrong with me. My sister gave her the card, and she called me to come out of my room. "What you cryin' for, did you make this for me?"

"Yes, ma'am."

"Look at those pretty flowers."

"Yes mama, I was gonna write you a poem on the white paper."

"You better get ta writin', so I can hear it."

My smile was as wide as all outdoors, as my grandmother would say. Then she said, "You been pickin' my flowers?" She answered her own question. "You better stay out of my flowers, else I'm not gonna have no more."

I skipped off to write the poem and got the bright idea that I would go and pick some more, but this time make a bouquet. It was not unusual for me to be left alone for hours. My siblings had little time for me, and my grandmother was too tired or too busy to notice. If I wanted to hang around my grandmother, that would mean doing something work-related, and most of the time I couldn't avoid work anyway. So, I skipped off unnoticed and headed back to my enchanted forest to pick more flow-ers. This time I heard the voice of a giant. From a window of the gray pebble stone house, a coarse female's voice came: "Get out of my yard and go home." I looked up, saw no one, and plucked a violet. "I said get out my yard, I'ma tell your mother too."

That was all I needed to hear and ran home. I had escaped, no one was behind me. So I went into my room, tied blue yarn in a bow around the bouquet. On the dresser was a small jelly jar with safety pins and rubber bands. I emptied it out and filled it with water and the flowers. I slipped into the dining room, crawling on the floor between the dining table and buffet, to carefully place the flowers on the table next to my grandmother's chair. Now, I waited for her to find them. As in most things in life, timing is everything, and this proved to be the foreshadowing of a life of bad timing. She saw the flowers and I smiled, awaiting her happiness, but instead, her voice rang out in a harsh tone, "LaVern! I told you ta stay outta my flowers. You bet not go back out there …" The doorbell rang. Mom went and opened the door. I could hear the coarse voice of the giant and my grandmother calling my name, and they both sounded the same.

Wet, everything in the village was wet; it had been raining for days. I put on my rain gear: an army-green hooded jacket, matching rain pants that made a swishing sound when I walked, and brown and tan water boots that came to the knee. By no means was this an inner-city fashion statement, but I loved it. It gave me a feeling of confidence that I could gear up with the right equipment to protect myself from the elements. I headed out along the muddy road. It felt like pottery clay slip mixed with chunks of rocks under my feet. I saw no one as I headed to the end of the road and onto the mossy carpet of the tundra. My feet stepped, laboring as I sunk deep in the mossy tundra. Water would pool around each step of my foot, squeezing the rain-saturated carpet of plant life. Someone told me that the moss could be used to dress a wound or absorb a woman's monthly. I reached down and felt the soft fibrous plant and wondered if it would be comfortable between my legs, soft and fuzzy, or dry and rough like the old torn towels my sisters and I had to use when there was no money for proper sanitary napkins. I continued, and the rain fell softly and cold on my face. My heart was beating fast, and sweat trickled down my arm from my pits. *Was I going in the right direction? Would I remember how to get back?*

Copper Mountain loomed black and ominous in front of me. I turned left and walked into a valley out of view of the village and the ocean. Soon the sound of my warm breath panting, the swish of my rubber pants, and the sudden call of a raven brought me to stop and catch my breath. I was told that when going into the woods to remember to make noise, clap, or hit sticks together because of bears, but I didn't. Instead, I was like an animal foraging in the woods. I tried to go unnoticed, but was still alert, so I looked around carefully. I saw and heard nothing dangerous. Listening to the quiet, I became fully aware of myself and decided I should sing a song just in case. "Sometimes I feel like a motherless child, sometimes I feel like a motherless ..." The only songs I could ever remember were spirituals when I was scared or nervous. A cry from the sky came again. A raven, the same raven? I didn't know. "So, Mister Raven, are you my guide for the day? Let me know if you see any bears, let me know if you see any berries." Kaaa kaaa, he answered. I walked a couple of steps forward towards the raven, and there in front of me, I saw the most beautiful patch of raspberries. "Oh my God! Thank you." The raven flew away.

I picked and sang when I remembered to for hours. I followed the patch farther and farther from the village, unaware of time or distance. The patch sloped down off a hill, and there I found the prized salmonberries. My two-quart bucket was more than half full with raspberries, and at least a pint or more were salmonberries. My face felt wet and icy hot, my hands felt the same, but stained and sticky with berry juice. I raised my head up from the bushes, smelling the air, it was fresh and clean. I looked to the right and then the left, wondering which direction I had come from. It was well into the afternoon, the sun was sitting low in the sky, and evening was fast approaching. I started walking towards the mountain. I used it as my North Star. Since I'd walked with it at my back getting to this spot, I would go towards it to return. I could feel the fatigue in every step, sinking deep in the bog. My muscles burned, and the weight of the berries added to the overworked tendons. I could feel a tightening in my chest with every labored movement I made to get home quickly. I counted each step I made, something I did in my head to order my thoughts and calm myself.

The light was fading quickly, and I couldn't stop focusing on the big things around me because everything seemed bigger now. The mountain I needed as a guide loomed black and heavy on top of me as I struggled to get back, safe. *You'll make it back. Don't worry, sixty, sixty-one, sixty-two ... he'll look for you ... seventy-six, seventy-seven ... look at all these berries you got, you did good! Just keep going. I came in here with a purpose ... Yeah! I feel good, I'm excited. I can't wait to show him ... getting back is another thing ... come on you can do it, don't give up now!* I tripped and a handful of berries rolled out. I started over counting in my head until I saw the faint smoke from the stacks of houses in the distance. My breathing slowed and my mind focused as I walked and sang out loud, not with a clear voice, but breathy and just enough to keep any animals, especially bears, away. When I saw the village and church dome, a smile came on my face, and there was no sound from me left.

I stepped on the village road. I found new energy and waved at a face looking out their window. I spoke to a couple of ladies on their way to the phone shack. "Hi, how are you? I've been out berry picking, did pretty good, have a good evening," I said as they passed nodding, or maybe they smiled, I couldn't tell. I reached my door, I was safe, and I had two buckets of berries for my efforts. I stood there a moment with my back against the closed door. The room was gloomy, and how I'd left it with some laundry in a basket and a mug of cold tea on the small table. Now, I had to move from this spot, start a fire, and make dinner before Seth got home.

The next day kept me home due to more rain, and I would be making jam. The house was gray from the dark clouds and rain as I brushed my teeth and got dressed at eight a.m. Damp and cold, I moved through the house to set the stove ablaze, make tea, and look out at the empty streets, eight thirty-five a.m. *Tink, tink, tink,* the rain fell softly on the tin roof like music. I sat at a flip-up wooden table and ate eggs, toast, and tea with thoughts of home and my grandmother.

"Vern, time ta get up, can't sleep the whole mornin' away," my grandmother called to me on Saturday morning, eight a.m. I had been awake hours earlier, listening. I could hear her soft feet walk through the house to the bathroom next to our rooms. She would speak to herself conversationally as though someone sat on a stool beside her, "No, I said you ain't gonna do it. Yes, I told him that and he bet' not ... I said I mean it ... I mean it." The sound of rushing urine followed by minutes of it trickling from her body. She was quiet for a while, then she prayed "Lord is my Shepherd I shall not want ... Lord what in the world am I to do?"

Water rushed from the tap, the door creaked, and then silence as I drifted off at five fifty a.m. I aroused once again to the smell of coffee and eggs floating over my bed. Bacon, my grandmother's final assault on your senses, came before she called my name. I loved my grandmother's eggs. When I entered the kitchen, she would be sitting with a cup of coffee and a small plate of scrambled eggs.

"That smells good, Mom."

"You want some, go on make you an egg, the skillet's still hot, bacon already done."

"Oh, Mom, I can't make 'em like you do," I'd say as we played our little game.

"I can't even eat an egg without somebody wantin' it, here girl, take these and eat 'em."

I smiled, and she laughed. I think I was the only one Mom let do that. She had a way of making eggs that were not like ones most people made; theirs rolled around on your plate. The old iron skillet would be hot, but not to the point of smoking. A pat of butter, then she would drop the egg in like making a fried egg and begin to let the whites cook a little before she broke the yoke. She would make sure the cooked whites were minced up in the egg yolk well to give it texture, add salt and pepper, and that was the best-scrambled eggs I ever ate.

Chapter Ten

The rain was pounding the metal roof. I could hear the water rushing from the downspout to the trenches along the street. We'd been here almost a month, and my life had changed so much from my small little apartment in Kansas City. Seth was up early and out by six thirty a.m. every morning. It was dark, and I could hear him moving around the room, then in the bathroom. I would usually doze drowsily in and out to the sounds until the front door closed. *I'll get up soon in a couple of hours,* I'd think to myself, *and have a cup of tea.* This morning I coughed and he stopped moving, I lay there and said nothing. I'd leave lunch out for him since he no longer came home to eat with me. He would work past dinner time and when he did return, we spent our evenings talking about the events of the day, his job.

I felt like I couldn't breathe sometimes, wondering what I was doing here or if I was capable of handling this. My mind felt like it would implode trying to answer this for myself. I needed air. I ran to the porch and gulped the sea-filled breeze until I could bear going back in again. Sometimes at night, I'd lay in the dark for hours staring into the black emptiness. My mind would flash on arguments with Seth or the family I left behind, while I desperately tried to shut it all out and sleep.

Flipping like frames in a slide projector, the images in my mind were nonstop. A game came to mind that I played as a child while lying awake at night. I would extend one arm straight above me and point my finger towards the ceiling in the dark. Despite the darkness of the room, I'd close my eyes. I would try to keep my arm straight while pointing at some imagined spot, but it never worked. My arm would always end up swaying and moving in a circle. Around and around, it went until I was too tired to hold up my arm. I would fall asleep, just before dawn.

Seth was given the task of testing all the students in the school. He would comb through record after record checking to see what tests had already been performed. This was in addition to his regular teaching assignment. Then there was the responsibility of establishing a relationship with students, parents, and the other two teachers. I realized all of it must have felt daunting at times to him. In the evenings, I'd watch him reading intently and writing notes for hours. He was completely absorbed in those moments. I no longer existed. Nothing existed. The dinner on the table I'd spent two hours making. All the laundry washed and folded. The pants he asked me to repair and iron. Even me walking past him almost naked didn't break his attention. He shared on occasion, grumbling his annoyance over a disorganized record system or other teaching modalities not in place. Mostly he stayed lost in his thoughts, rubbing the light reddish-brown mustache into a tangled wiry mess. Sometimes anxiety caused him to reach into his pants to twist his pubic hairs until he was relaxed and could focus again.

Isolation and loneliness can be a slow suffocation. It requires routine to survive. I ordered my everyday steps and created a schedule for chores, creative projects, and learning new skills. My grandmother became a valuable resource during this time. When I was a kid, she'd shared stories of growing up gathering wild plants, canning foods for winter, and how Black folks survived the Great Depression. All of this knowledge was an advantage to me now. Growing up under her was training in Great Depression survival skills. She inoculated us with those skills as if we were being prepared for the next near apocalypse. I called her as often as I could, depending on if I could afford minutes and there was an opening at the phone shack. My grandmother and I got closer during this time. She was up in age, in her late sixties. Her hard life of physical labor and limited resources made her body's age somewhere around that of seventy-year-old. She was the worn, cracked vessel that held our family history and knowledge, and I was the young clay pot ready to be filled. I began to see our love-hate relationship of the past shift with every phone call and letter.

We found common ground in our love for cooking, wildlife, and nature. I began to live for each call. Letters did not allow for the same connection. They were mostly pleasant little notes between two people that struggled with the mechanics of writing. I was careful never to share details of my struggles with Seth. I feared our newfound relationship would return to judgment of me. I had been receiving enough judgment from Seth's family and friends and had so few allies. Seth's two best friends since elementary became his contact with the outside world via phone and letter. Seth's relationship with these two men, I'd soon learn, was as complicated as my relationship was with my family. There was one exception; I wanted to get away from my family, but his family and friends seemed to be involved in everything we did.

I met his friends for the first time when they flew into Kansas City for our wedding. I was so nervous and excited to meet the people that had been in his life since he was a kid. They pulled up in a rental car in front of my grandmother's house. Seth and I met them coming up the driveway. Reuben was tall with dark hair and olive skin. He was Jewish and had an actor-like swagger and charm. It turned out he was an aspiring actor. Robert or Rob was short, blond, attractive, and of mixed-German descent. He had a more grounded energy compared to Reuben. Although he was a teacher like Seth, his personality type fit with teaching at a boarding school or college-prep school. Seth introduced us. I, being the more touchy-feely type, went to give them a hug that ended up awkward, with a half hug and handshake thing.

Seth had shared painful childhood memories of growing up in a non–Jewish community and being bullied almost every day for being a Jew. Both Seth and I grew up in a dysfunctional family with cultural oppression. This may have been why we were drawn together. Reuben and Rob were the childhood bullies from some of the stories Seth had told me but somehow they had stayed friends. Now that they had grown up, I assumed their relationships must have matured and evolved into a true friendship.

That night we went out for dinner and drinks. I sat through most of the dinner having very little to say at first with very little directed to include me. Instead, I listened to them bark laughter like hounds as they caught up and told stories of their childhood adventures. Other than answering my questions of the when, what, and where nature, I noticed I received very little direct eye contact, especially from Reuben.

We headed to a bar for drinks. The liquor flowed, and after two or three drinks, their tongues, lips, and every locked door flew open. The stories they'd told earlier were funny and silly kid stories that didn't always show Seth in the best of light, but everyone laughed with him, not at him. Now the stories shifted. Reuben and Rob seemed to take on size as they got louder and more aggressive. Even Seth, who laughed joyfully at dinner with just a glass of wine, was now adding to their characterization of him, but in an obnoxious and buffoonish manner to their every insult. The flowing of alcohol allowed them to jump the curve, and we had to ride it all the way down the hill. They roared about him being called a fat Jew boy. They laughed about how he followed them everywhere, how they hit him, made fun of him, or got him to do stupid things, but he just kept hanging around.

They turned to me, somewhat restrained and calculated, ready to extract what they wanted to know. I was not drunk, at least not enough that I wasn't aware of what was happening. They went in, asking me about my neighborhood and how dangerous it was. Were there drugs or people killed? They expressed shock over the poverty of the area. Would they be safe if they stayed there? Eventually, they got to it, "Seth didn't grow up like you, and he's a good guy. Have you really thought about if you're right for each other?"

There it was, like the clinking of the ice in their glass of single malt liquor. Were we really right for each other? The real question, was I right for him? The man they treated like their pet boy. Reuben, the " actor," and Rob, in a supporting role, turned away from me without wanting an answer, as if I was the waitress he'd asked to remove his dish. Reuben shifted his body away from me and began a story about his acting career and working in Canada.

I was now completely sober from anger. Not for myself so much but because of how they treated Seth. I didn't understand what was going on. I kept thinking, *These people are his friends. Why didn't he defend himself? Should I do something?* I'd never been unsure about how to deal with bullies if it was about protecting someone else. Yet I was confused. I thought maybe they were trying to make me lose my composure and behave in a way they felt was stereotypical for a Black woman. I willed myself to stay calm and to not give them the satisfaction of, *"See, this is what happens with those people."*

I straightened up, took a deep breath, and said, "Look at the time. We have to be up early in the morning. I'm really tired and need some sleep." I paused and started gathering my things. I decided to add to my exit, "I thought that the two of you needed a place to sleep, so we made up beds for you." I didn't wait for an answer and went in again. "But, if you prefer to stay at a hotel, I completely understand." They hung over their drinks, then quickly looked up as I stood there in silence. Seth followed suit. He agreed we needed some sleep and would see them back at my grandmother's place. I added, "Oh! By the way, if you're staying with us, please be in no later than twelve, so you don't disturb my grandmother or the neighbors. It's a pretty quiet block."

I woke from my restless night to rain and sneezing. I straightened out the covers on our empty bed, making it neat for the day. My nose drained and dripped to the outside sound of raindrops. I caught it with wades of tissue while leaning over to tuck each pillow in tightly with the bedspread. *A cup of tea*, I thought, *might be the cure for the tickle in my throat.* Getting sick always came on so quickly for me. I smiled at how others could play in a cesspool of muck and germs before getting sick, but I just had to breathe.

The debate warred on in my mind as did the sickness in my body. *I should have wore a hat in the cold. I shouldn't have stayed out so long picking berries in the rain.* My grandmother would certainly have enjoyed admonishing me with, "I told you so."

This did not feel like a place where I could be sick. I wasn't even sure we had aspirin, let alone cold medicine. I was afraid of getting sick, even the basic kind of sickness that everyone gets from time to time. A stuffy nose or not being able to breathe panicked me as much as my fear of mice terrified me. I could deal with pain, being punched or cut. I even thought being shot or hit by a car was something I could cope with, but throwing up or not being able to breathe was psychologically debilitating.

On the floor by Seth's side of the bed was an opened letter. Clearly read, it lay unfolded on top of the envelope. I saw the letter was from Reuben. I sat down on the edge of the bed and began skimming through the first half. I thought I knew what it would say:

Hi Seth,

How is it out there in the bush? Did you land in a beautiful place? How big is the village? What are the other teachers you work with like? And the kids, do you have a large class to teach, what's the pay? The district, do they have money? So, you're not spending half your pay on supplies this time. How's the weather?

It read mostly the way I thought until it didn't:

So, how's married life? I got your letter the other day, that's a lot of debt. What are you going to do? It probably wasn't a good idea to get married yet until you had money put away and could afford it. You should have been putting money away for a house or some kind of investment. I have to ask: do you really love this girl? She is not your type. Have you thought that maybe it's because you spent too much time in the Peace Corps around too many of those Brown people? It's possible you became too used to that life, but that's not your life. I'm not saying she's not a nice girl, but she doesn't know anything. She's ignorant, uneducated, and not like us. So, are you going to be stuck with taking care of her for the rest of your life? She can't even contribute. That place, her grandmother's house we stayed at, was scary. You didn't grow up like that. Listen, your dad is disowning you because of this. Everybody is concerned about your choice. You made a mistake, but it's not too late to get out of this. Your dad is upset, but he'll still help you. She is using you as a ticket out of the ghetto and I get it, but you have to think about your own life, future, and career. Don't throw it all away because of a misstep. Hey, send some pictures, the wildlife must be amazing ...

The truth, something I believed in my whole life, lay across my chest in a letter with the weight of a slab of granite. When I met Seth, I was working at Rockhill Manor Boarding Home. He came in, looking for a friend of his, my co-worker. He had recently returned from the Peace Corps. I was standing on the wide formal stairs of this once grand old building on my way to check on a client when Seth walked in. I stood there for a moment on the stairs (like a parody of Scarlett O'Hara in *Gone with the Wind.*) Seth looked up at me, I turned, and we locked eyes. At that moment, our destiny was put into motion.

Seth became a bright light of truth for me during that time. He shared with me after we had been dating that the staff I worked with, all older white men, were talking about me and other Black people disparagingly. These were people I naively thought of as friends, because we had been to one another's homes, laughed with one another at staff parties and picnics, and encouraged one another when illness or tragedy struck. They thought I was good enough to try and sleep with (although I refused), but they did not think I was good enough to be a friend. The truth was they saw me as nothing, less than nothing, and Seth defended me, standing up to them all.

Slowly, it all began to drain the life out of us, the letters and calls. He never said anything, not anything that mattered. Everything seemed to be harder, even making love. We were different and came from different worlds. Now the discovery of our difference was accelerated and exploited by others with their judgment and expectations.

We'd had our own plans in the beginning. Head to the wilds of Alaska where we would be safe to explore and live a simple life. Alaska was that kind of place. The kind of place that people run to, to be something different from the rest of the lower forty-eight, to have the freedom to choose their way. Whoever we had planned to be, the dreams we were beginning to form, were changing with every letter and phone call.

I saw him shift away from me and become obsessed with his career and whatever message his friends and family shared. I retreated into that lonely place I had always known. I kept order in the space given to me: cleaning, cooking, and washing clothes. I was doing what I was trained to do: keeping a house, expressing myself creatively with my hands, and having sex.

It was an early morning on the weekend. The sun came in, and we woke slowly. I touched him and coiled around his body, and he responded with a kiss. I usually initiated sex between us and he would always respond in the third person penis, "You want the little guy?" It was silly and playful, and I didn't mind in the beginning because we were creating something new, us. He lay on top of me, kissing and working his way down. The further down he went, the further removed I became. I didn't mind oral sex, but it could not replace the feeling of a man inside of me. It was a feeling that made me want to consume and hide inside someone else, and I needed that feeling more than ever. I reached down and tugged at his arms to come up and couple with me. He entered, and I could not go to that place that gave me safety, though sweat poured from our bodies and the bed was mangled. He fell to one side, exhausted, and I stared at the sun coming through the window.

"Did you … you know?" he asked, slightly breathy.

"Cum," I said bluntly.

"Yes. Did you?"

"No, but it was still good."

I'm not sure how we got on the subject of past relationships, but I'm sure his pride and insecurity prompted the in-depth pillow talk. The exploration of past relationships surfaced on both sides, and my being Black, the question of size came into the conversation. He knew my first true love was a six foot two Black Marine that had a package to match. Though Seth was only five foot eleven, he was slightly bigger than average, and there is something to the saying, "It's all in how you work it."

But the question of size and whether it was satisfying led us to the most unusual experiment and that's the only word to describe what happened next, toilet paper. Yes, I had the idea of wrapping his penis in toilet paper to thicken the shaft. He had a substantial length, and the condom would hold the toilet paper in place giving him added thickness. I took charge and straddled my enhanced stud, but after only a few strokes I fell to one side in defeat.

"What's wrong? I was getting there."

"It doesn't feel right," I said; maybe the disappointment came in my tone or in my face that shows everything.

"Come on, let's try again," he said, trying to urge me on. I turned towards him, ignored what I felt, and looked down at his penis bandaged in stark white toilet paper as if it was broken. He kissed me again, and down, down, down he went, and I succumbed to his world.

The tasks ahead of us to leave Kansas City and head to Alaska included getting married and finding any extra money to do so. It was Saturday morning, and we were hauling bedroom furniture, kitchenware, and clothes onto the porch and yard for a moving sale when the phone rang.

"It was my dad, he just flew into the KC airport," Seth said.

I was too excited to read his face. "Is he coming here? Does he want us to pick him up? Oh my God, look at this place …"

"No, he wants me to come to the airport; he wants to see me first."

"Oh, okay, that makes sense, he hasn't seen you in a while. Go ahead, I'll have the sale anyway, but see if he wants to have lunch or dinner, I can make something," I said, distracted by the job in front of me. I spent the whole day selling the antiques I had collected and refinished over the years. It was late in the afternoon when Seth finally returned. The sale was over, and I had dragged in what was left.

"What happened? Where's your dad?"

"He is flying back to New York."

"Oh," I said in true disappointment, "How come you didn't bring him to the house? I would have made lunch for us."

"He wanted to talk to me alone ... we ate in the airport lounge."

"So, what did he say?"

"Ah, he's a jerk."

"What! What did he say, Seth? Was it about us getting married? What!" That's when I didn't need to read Seth's face. He dropped the bomb.

"Maybe, we should wait to get married ... I don't ... I don't know what to do?"

"What the hell are you talking about? What did he say?"

"He said he doesn't support this marriage, he's not coming to the wedding if I marry you, and he will disinherit me."

"Why, why would he say that, he hasn't even met me yet?"

Then the words came from his pink lips, "Because you're Black. He said that you sleep with girls like you, you don't bring them home. 'Fucking a nigger is fine, but you don't marry them.' I'm sorry LaVern. I don't know what to do."

"You asshole, I've been here selling everything I own for us, and you stand there and say you don't know what to do? I will kill you, asshole ... we are getting married. How can you just do that? I gave you a chance to walk away and we just be friends, and now I have given up everything to be with you ..." I sat weeping. He reached for me and held me while apologizing. We moved forward with our plans despite that day, but evil in the form of many people would continue to plague our marriage.

Chapter Eleven

In a heavy pot, I poured the berries I had sugared down the night before. Sugary juice splattered out and jumped across the red-hot iron surface of my homestead stove. I'd watched my grandmother and great-grandmother do this hundreds of times, and now it was my ritual. You had to be patient using this method because it used no commercial pectin to set the jam quickly. You must stand and stir slowly, trying not to break the boil, but at the same time not letting the jam stick. The steam rose, sweating my face, and sending the sweet and sour perfume of the berries to fill my nostrils.

When I was a kid, my grandmother would get bushels of seconds (slightly bruised and over-ripened fruit), such as pears, peaches, and apples from the local fruit stand at the City Market. Or, sometimes from the men that drove slowly through our neighborhood, calling out their cargo that filled their vehicles to barely drivable capacity. My grandmother favored the latter, nomads that had traveled from Arkansas to Kansas City. From her birth soil to my stonewalled crabgrass lawn with one tree, they brought the smell of rich fertile earth macerated with early morning dew.

They brought the juice of ripened fruit of all kinds and the guarantee of satisfaction. My grandmother would hold counsel with the nomads briefly on things I knew nothing of, but I was there to bite the flesh of the fruit and give my approval in silence. We would take our bounty to the back porch with newspaper to cover the rough dirty lumber flooring. There we peeled and cut the fruit to ready it for pies and jam. My knife skills began on that porch, cutting bushels of fruit at the age of six or seven with a paring knife and juice running along my arm and mouth.

My mason jars were now ready, clinking from the boiling water. Sterilized, drained, and hot, they waited to be filled. I began to ladle in the syrupy hot fruit and counted almost twelve jars capped and sealed afterward. The jars presented as rubies, shimmering on the small dinette table. Bread! Bread was what was called for now, and the house was soon filled with the warm smell of bread and wild raspberry jam. It was peaceful, but much too quiet with no one in the house to share my accomplishments. I smirked to myself, pridefully, thinking about the village women and what they would make of my efforts.

"*Screa, Screa, Screa,*" I heard a sound come to me while I sat on the couch. Sitting quietly, I listened, turning towards the kitchen and closet area along the same hall. The wind blew, and I could hear metal brushed by debris and tree limbs sweeping across the side of the house. The damper on the smokestack to the stove squeaked with a proper gust of wind. "*Screa, Screa, Screa ...*" There it was again. The noise was coming from somewhere inside the house. Somewhere in the area of the stove. My ear was now fine-tuned to hear it. My heart began to race wildly, and I could feel the vein in my neck pulse and pump blood rapidly. I laughed at the thought of myself afraid of a noise coming from an old house. I took deep breaths, trying to calm myself down.

Really, what's wrong with you? Nothing's probably even there ... It's a mouse. I know it is, oh man. Come on, LaVern. Shake it off. Quiet again, I began to relax a little and think that maybe my imagination was getting away from me. I hadn't seen any signs of a mouse before now. The scratching began again. "*Screa, Screa, Screa!*"

Breathing deeply didn't work, nor did the self-talk. I could feel my breath becoming shallow and a tightness squeezed my chest. *Maybe I'm having a heart attack.* The sound seemed louder. I couldn't hear the wind blowing the trees or the damper singing in the chimney pipe, only the sound of something from across where I sat high on the back of the sofa, holding my legs.

Memories had a way of tearing through my life like worn sheets, splitting in the middle. I watched the thin threads shred and cotton lashes like dust float in the air, gliding down, down into …

"*Screa, Screa, Screa.*" I heard the noise coming from the wall between my bed and my sisters.

"Are you awake, you hear that?" I spoke to the dark, and her voice returned in a similar whisper.

"Yeah, what is that?"

"I think it's a mouse. Turn on the light," I said from under the bed covers.

"The light switch is at the end of your bed. You turn it on." The muffled sound of her voice returned, and we giggled nervously. The scratching sound continued. Followed by a mighty snap of metal hitting metal and wood popped like fireworks, and we jumped, releasing a squeal, startling ourselves even more. Darkness and silence engulfed the room for a moment until we heard what sounded like the trap being moved. We knew that a trap my step-grandfather had set on the orders of my grandmother had achieved its goal and caught a mouse.

Well, partially caught. From the sound of the trap, it was still alive. I begged my sister to get up and turn the light on. She refused, fearing this mouse might get out of the trap and climb on her. My sister had good reason to be afraid. She had experienced a mouse running across her face when she and my older sister shared a bed and I slept on a little cot next to them. Now I was eight and she was ten, and we were still just as scared. Finally, it was decided that I would go and tell my grandmother we caught a mouse and turn on the light at the same time. When I finally moved, I moved like lightning. Covers thrown, light on, door open, "Mom, there's a mouse in the trap." I was rubbing my eyes from the light spots and could only see her in blotches.

Her voice cleared everything, including my sight. "Why are you telling me? Go, get rid of it!"

I returned to the room defeated. For a while, we hid in our beds trying to come up with a plan of how to get it out of our room and not touch it. We laughed and teased each other nervously until the half-dead creature moved and we dove under covers. In the bat of an eyelid, everything changed when my grandmother came into the room. The sound of words began to narrow immediately.

I could barely hear her voice yelling as her arms moved wildly. I could see us all. My sister in her bed. I was sitting up in mine, and my grandmother was standing between us and in front of the dead mouse. That image of us began to spiral into a dark tunnel where only at the end of it was I able to see light focused on the three of us and the mouse. I saw my sister shaking and her face frozen in horror. My grandmother's hand had me by the back of my neck, and she was pushing my head down towards the floor. Her right hand had entangled her fingers in my hair. She was controlling me, where my face went. I closed my eyes tight.

I was screaming. I could see my mouth was open, screaming, but I could only hear my thoughts. *Don't open your eyes, don't open your eyes.* I opened my eyes. There was the dead mouse. My lips and nose were so close I could smell its foul death and feel the slight warmth and fur of its body. *Freeze one, two, three seconds.* My eyes scanned this thing, its tail, the scratching little feet, until I saw its coal-black beads for eyes. I fought to get away and my grandmother's voice brought me back to the corner of my bed, knotted up in covers:

"Pick it up! Pick the damn thing up, and throw it away! "

Knock, knock, knock, came at the front door. Startled, I jumped back into my seat on the sofa, straightening myself. The knock came again, and I walked to the door with measured steps and opened it. The men had brought the gift of seal to the village. My visitor, a neighbor, invited me to come down to the beach if I wanted meat. I thought maybe I'd made a better impression than could be measured at the school's potluck. This was their way of letting me know I was a part of village life, and that made me feel hopeful. When I reached the shore, I found two seals laying beached, and one of the seals already splayed open. Two of the women were squatting over the seals like surgeons in a great outdoor operating room; they sliced the flesh away from the animal with precision. Standing up and stepping back, hands bloody, they asked, "You like seal meat?"

The question came and the women laughed under their breath. "You know how to cut? You have knife?" They laughed again and spoke a word or two in Aleut to each other. "Here, you can use my *ulu*," one of the women said. They all flew back away from me like a murder of ravens; they watched. I bent down and began to slice through the black and maroon flesh of the seal. The meat opened like a ripe watermelon, and the thick layer of fat was like its rind. I cut the meat as I'd seen the women cut it and with the discipline and quick assimilation that my grandmother expected. They couldn't know that I had been in training my whole life for a moment like this. I didn't know either. I survived by imitating those around me and doing what they expected. I would silence their laughter that intended to humiliate this *Cheechako* (newcomer) by calling up the hard lessons of my life. I took the meat home and for all of the self-respect I gained on the beach, my background did not prepare me for cooking seal meat.

I had been raised to eat wild game like squirrel, rabbit, raccoon, and fish from lakes, but this, I thought, was not going to taste like chicken. The seal meat looked like liver, and so I decided to cook it as such. I seasoned the seal with homemade seasoning salt and black pepper; lightly flouring the meat before frying. Boiled peeled potatoes were cooked down to make a creamy potato sauce with lots of butter, salt, and pepper. This seemed the perfect side to go alongside the crispy fried seal meat and sweet green peas I'd prepared. The table was set with food that looked Southern and comforting. I sliced into the meat with a knife and fork and found that the color was still deep artery blood red, unlike liver that turns brown when cooked. I placed a small slice in my mouth, while my brain was prepared for what it believed was liver. When I tasted the meat, its flavor confused me. I couldn't find it anywhere in my brain or taste sensors. The meat was sweet, deep sea–like and earthy at the same time. The rich flavor differed from other meat I'd had. It was so unfamiliar I couldn't imagine that there was any way to prepare this meat that would help me relate to it. Yet, the truth be told I had eaten worse things in my life, and if ever I was starving and there lay a seal I would eat it, but not tonight.

Returning to my jams, I wrapped a couple of jars and tucked them down in a bag, then headed out to make my deliveries. A jar of my jam went to O'Brennan's wife, and in turn, she gave me a quick lesson on how to make yogurt and the recipe. I headed down the road happy and anticipating trying my hand at making yogurt next. I was feeling quite accomplished. I was halfway to Anna's to deliver the jam when I ran into O'Brennan on his way home. We started to chat, and I became aware that this was not going to be a quick, pleasant little conversation. Well, at least not without some advice, and the kind that always seemed to restrict me in some way.

"So, I hear you've been berry picking?"

"Yeah, I just came from your house and dropped off a jar of jam. I was heading to Anna to drop off a jar there. How did you know?"

"Well, people have been saying it's a bad season for berries, that's why nobody's picking," he said.

"Oh, really! I found plenty. I wonder why they're saying that?" I mused.

"Too much work, especially if the bushes aren't practically dropping berries into their buckets. They're used to getting buckets in a matter of minutes. The women don't like you picking, especially when they've already said it's a bad year," he cautioned.

"Really! Why don't they talk to me and tell me these things! So, does that mean I can't pick berries, because they don't want to go out and get any?"

"No, you can, but you won't make many friends doing it."

When I got to Anna's, I asked her about going out to pick berries and if it was okay. I treaded very carefully, not wanting to offend her or to seem as if I was trying to get her to take my side. After all these were her people, and I was an outsider. She looked at me and asked why. I searched to find the right words that didn't sound accusing or entitled.

"I was told when I first got here that it was alright to go out and pick berries and I ... just don't want to do something I'm not allowed to and upset people." Anna was quiet, holding the jar. She thanked me and placed it on the kitchen table.

"You find 'lot of berries, eh, me too. I put 'lot in my freezer, good for when I make sweets when it's cold, eh. I make 'lot of jam too! Two years not 'lot of berries on bushes, so we don't pick 'lot those years... that way they go back into the land and return strong ... Young people don't like picking, too much work. The old people still like to pick. Sometimes the young ones pick berries for their grandma. You make lots?" She turned in my direction and asked without looking directly at me.

"I have about two cases!"

"You give some to Tommy Kenikoff, Leanna's grandfather. He's an elder, and he likes jam 'lots."

I gave Tommy Kenikoff, one of the oldest elders, two jars of jam along with jam to two other elders. Anna had a way with truth that made me realize that there were always more sides to reality. The implied message that I shouldn't have gone out and gathered berries was clear. Likely because I was an outsider, and they felt the need to protect what was theirs. Yet, for me, it was one more thing that made me feel outside of things.

Anna and I were now visiting regularly. She was teaching me how to crochet new stitches. I had learned to knit and crochet simple stitches in the fourth grade from a young, bright, wide-eyed, white optimist that was subbing for our permanent teacher for a few months. I watched all the little Black girls in my class fly and circle like crows, crowding around to touch her long blonde hair. When she allowed the first of them to play with her stringy strands, it became an open invitation to all of them to draw their brown fingers through it like a comb. I sat and watched her crochet in the middle of class. While the art of our braiding took place on her head, I, in turn, learned the basics of knitting and crocheting over those two months.

Anna taught me how to salt fish when the village's fishermen came in with their boats. They brought silver salmon and tanner crabs to share with their family and the whole village. The silver salmon flopped around, glinting in the sun, but the prize was the king salmon and that was for the elders. Fresh live crab was ours by the fifty-gallon trash bag full, and we took two. But my first harvest of salmon did not come off a village boat. We headed out to reap the bounty of Alaska for ourselves, from a cove just over a hill.

My husband came home excited one Friday. One of the men in the village had told him that the salmon run was winding down, but there was still fish to be had. We could literally reach our hands out and they would jump in our arms, but we'd better hurry because they would be gone in another week. I was so impressed with the abundance this land had to offer and the resourcefulness of the land's people. I had so much to learn and was hungry to do so. It gave me a sense of self-reliance and self-respect I had lacked and longed for.

That weekend, Seth and I headed out with two twenty-five-gallon plastic buckets and the instructions he'd received from the villager. He was told there was no need for a fishing rod, we just had to reach in and grab them. I had a hard time believing that catching fish would be this easy. They were making this place sound like a utopia, as if the fish would jump in our bucket with a smile on their faces. Yet I'd already bought into this being the nearest thing to my version of utopia. The isolation seemed less isolating to me here. There were fewer than two hundred people with no stores or malls, which I didn't seem to miss, at least not yet, and definitely not today. Today I was walking in a backyard that went on forever. I could pick berries and catch fish, but fish that you didn't have to do anything for except lift out of the water. We had walked about a mile or a mile and a half, which was the equivalent of two miles on wet tundra, and there it was, a pool of water filled with fish that seemed to be meandering about. I assumed that their lackluster appearance was due to their journey upstream and our advantage was that we would get them before they gained energy.

"Oh my God! Seth, I can't believe it. Look at how much fish there is! I thought they were lying." I had never seen salmon before coming to Alaska.

Instead, Midwestern men caught catfish, trout, and buffalo, or I ate canned tuna and fish sticks from the frozen food department. The first salmon I ate that didn't come from a can came from my friend Vernice. She had shared smoked salmon from her village, and we ate it during one of our shared meals with rice. She also gave me some dried salmon that was like sweet fish jerky. The mild flavor was nothing like the smoked meats I grew up with. We had the flavors of hickory, cherry, and apple wood; this fish was smoked in cotton-wood or alder wood which gave it a mild delicate flavor. My mouth watered with the desire to taste those flavors again, because I had never eaten a piece of fish better than the fish I ate with Vernice.

Seth leaned in over the water and readied his hands to grab a big fish that cruised by in front of him. I was so excited, I could hardly contain myself. Seth had told me so many stories of his Peace Corps adventures, and I imagined him as in pictures I had seen, bare-skinned, handsome with only a loincloth and fishing spear, but now he had his bare hands. He grabbed the fish and flipped it onto the tundra moss. One, two, then fifteen filled our buckets, and happy with what we accomplished, we headed home. At the time we gave little thought to how easy this all was or for that matter how hard it would be to walk back with thirty to forty pounds of fish and water.

The walk home was long and arduous. We wondered why no one else was getting fish or if they had already. We questioned our intelligence to take so many fish, since they would be almost impossible to carry. We mused over how I would prepare the fish, and soon we did not talk at all except for the occasional consideration to leave a bucket behind. The trip was an hour from the village and two and a half hours back. We finally made it, exhausted and relieved. After resting a bit, we began the work of preparing the fish for the freezer and cooking for that night's dinner. We worked intensely, gutting and cleaning all the fish, while the first fish I cleaned was seasoned and already cooking in the oven. This fish we'd caught seemed very different from fish I'd cleaned in the past. First of all, it smelled different, not like what I thought freshly caught fish should. I was expecting a clean sea-like smell with a hint of fishiness, but this fish gave off a murky smell and parts of the flesh were soft and mushy. Seth thought maybe it would be okay once it was cooked.

The table was set. I'd made rice and peas with herbs. The salmon took center-table dressed in caramelized onions, lemon slices, and seasoned with salt and pepper and a drizzle of olive oil. I served each plate. Seth lifted his fork to take the first bite, and I followed in seconds, "Aaaah, it's putrid." Seth spat it out on the plate. I ran to the trash gagging and spitting. "You think it's all like this?" We looked at each other and the fish while still wiping our tongues and dousing our mouths with gulps of water. I decided we would not take the chance, it would all be dumped tomorrow, and we had to accept the joke was on us. We later found out that we had been a part of local Native humor. They enjoyed occasionally making sport of an outsider's lack of skills and/or knowledge. We fell for it, all two twenty-five-gallon buckets worth. All of our work ended up back in the ocean from whence it came.

We found out more about salmon runs. The fish will run back up stream, jumping and fighting against the currents, battered against the rocks. Those that survive the currents and have not been eaten by bears or other animals, were the few lucky fish that will spawn and soon after, die. That is why it was so easy for us to pluck them out of the water with little fight, they were on their last fin, almost dead.

On rare occasions, Seth came home and ate lunch. Today had been one of those rarities, but he headed out quickly after. I looked out over the flip-up dinette table and through the window at Anna's house, while I mindlessly wiped up crumbs and hoped for a visit. It was a crisp day, and the sun bathed the front room with light through the picture window. The sound of a knock on the front door came so slightly I dismissed it at first. I heard it again, two quick light raps to the door. I moved towards the door, anticipating Anna. After all, she was the only one that ever visited in the middle of the day, except for Seth, who had already left for work.

The local preteens and their young siblings liked visiting throughout the village regularly. Late-night visits of nine p.m. or ten p.m. were no exception. Shortly after we first moved in, we were finishing dinner and cleaning up when the front door opened, and four preteens walked in.

"What the hell?" I forgot myself and blurted out, "Excuse me! Can we help you?"

"Come visit, ah," one of the girls said.

"Sorry, but you have to visit tomorrow. It's nine thirty at night. Do your parents know where you are?"

"Yeah, they're out too," one of the boys said. They laughed, all walked out, and closed the door. As always, the next day O'Brennan was our go-to person to explain what was unexplainable to me. He told us that this was customary for people to walk in without knocking because everyone was related. Most of the kids had no set time to come home or go to bed, particularly if their parents were out partying. It's considered rude to lock your door or turn someone away that's come to visit. Every part of me railed against this. I simply could not be in a house that just anybody could walk in, whenever they wanted, especially at night.

"Hell no," I said and thought to myself, *my ass was just going to have to be rude.* From that night on my door was locked by nightfall.

I had reached the door to open it and called out to my would-be guest. "Anna? Why would you come all the way around to the front door?" I swung the door open, smiling, then gasped as the air in my lungs did not exhale. I stood there, staring, startled by the thick, muscular man that stood at my door, glaring at me with no expression on his face and no words uttered from his mouth. I didn't know this man standing in the doorway. I'd seen him before coming in and out of one of the houses down by us, but I saw plenty of people here that didn't introduce themselves or had nothing to say to me. A lot of the Native men reminded me of family. He in particular reminded me of a few of my great-uncles, my grandmother's brothers. They had that light brown skin with red or yellow tones underneath, broad and thick with fleshy muscles, and serious, empty eyes from too much drink.

"Oh … can I help you?" I stammered. He said nothing at first, then muttered something about Seth. "Oh, you're looking for my husband? He already left and went back to school."

He said nothing, and I stood there confused, not knowing what to do. I began to think he was expecting something else. Maybe I was supposed to offer tea, which seemed to be the custom when visiting here.

"Would you like to come in and have a cup of tea?" I asked. He came in without a word, and he sat on the black leather couch while I put on the kettle and grabbed two cups. The silence made me nervous, the same way it made me feel as a child. Silence, the intentional kind, meant something was about to happen, and I would try and prolong the storm coming by filling the air with talking or doing. I could feel his eyes on me as I busied myself in the kitchen, waiting for the water to boil. I stared at the pot and thought of one of my grandmother's sayings, *a watched pot never boils.*

I thought of something to say.

"You're Mark Allen's nephew, right?"

He muttered the answer under his breath; the teapot whistled and made me jump.

"Were you supposed to meet my husband here, because I'm not sure when he'll be back? What kind of tea would you like?" I continued to fill the time.

He stood up and seemed to grow wider and bigger, standing now between me and the front door. However, I had the back door and I was only a couple of steps from it with a cup of hot boiling water in my hand. He opened the door, and I heard him say my husband's name again.

I replied, "I will tell Seth you came by looking for him or you could go by the school!" The room grayed as the sky clouded over.

There is nothing like the sounds you remember as a child of the area from which you came. Missouri, or misery as it was sometimes called, was hot in the climax of summer accompanied by a wet, sticky, heavy humidity that took your breath. For poor people at night, it was a glimpse of hell. My two sisters and I slept in our ten-foot by ten-foot sweatbox without air condition-ing or a fan for years. Windows were always up as high as they could go or as much as the paint-layered window seals would allow. Curtains pulled back for the moon revealed twisted nightgowns and underwear of three little girls. One night the wind was enough for us to catch a breeze and the cricket songs didn't labor. We slept much easier, drifting off to the rhythm of nature's night music, pausing only to the fear of threat. The pauses pricked our conscience, disrupt-ing our slumber with the breaks in the sounds of its lullaby.

The sound of someone in the driveway focused my listening, as my brain in its dreamy state tried to sort the noise: feet, loose gravel, crickets, a creaking fence. I could hear the sound through the weight of sleep. The thought *my father's coming in* was my brain's answer. A breeze floated me away. *The sound of crushed rock under foot? Outside our window?* It stopped and started again. *Coming closer, or is it moving away?* I was now listening. I didn't move, still as a cricket, and the sound didn't move either. Being still was a part of my training, to freeze like a rabbit with no sound. The sound changed, not gravel or footsteps, but something on the window screen. Nails digging across it, catching on every tiny square while running quickly across the screen's surface. My heart pounded, about to burst. I halted my breath for long periods, waiting to react, and praying it would go away if no one moved. Maybe my big sisters would hear it and make it leave. Finally, the sound of feet moved away, giving relief.

"Pum ... .screeechscratttch." Something pounced onto the screen, ripping at it.

"Aaaahhh ... Ahhh!" My sisters sat up in bed, screaming. I sat up and saw the grotesque head with a twisted face, black, empty holes for eyes that stared at me. My grandmother flung the door open, and the light from the lamp next to her chair blinded me as I cried uncontrollably.

"What's wrong with yaw?" We pointed to the window, she looked out to the laughter of my Uncle Dee, her younger brother, pulling off a rubber mask. She yelled at him. "Dee, cut that mess out, and leave these girls alone." She turned on us, saying, "Stop all that screamin'. I said shut up now and go on ta sleep, just your Uncle being silly."

My Uncle Dee was my playmate sometimes and a mean drunk other times. I was in my late twenties when I heard the full story, around the bits and pieces of rumors, about what happened to my eldest sister, my mother's first child. My grandmother had always said that my mother was telling lies to stir up trouble and my father mumbled anxiously and would not confirm or deny anything.

There was a picture of my sister in a white dress with a ruffled petticoat beneath it. She had on lace ankle socks and black patent leather shoes. She's sitting on the floor at the feet of my grandmother, a sphinx with deep plum skin like that of our mother's. She sat there without a smile on her face in contrast to my grandmother whose skin was like ivory, her hair turned in curls and falling long down her back, and a lovely smile pressed her lips. On the photo's border was a date, 1959. She was nine years old, and I was born some months later. That first year of my birth also was the last year my sister and I lived together under the same roof. She was sent to live with our maternal grandmother, while my other two sisters, brother, and I stayed with my paternal grandmother. That was the year my paternal grandmother's brother, my Great-Uncle Dee, brutally raped my sister and hospitalized her, after ripping her vagina clean to her rectum.

A shadow casts itself over my heart whenever I think of Uncle Dee. The next thought that comes to mind is the first dog we ever had. His name was King, a beautiful German shepherd. My grandmother, known to prophesize, but most of the time was just her giving her unsolicited opinion, said King was a trained police dog, he was so well-behaved. He became my brother's dog, since my brother was the one that spotted him in the back of our house. King had been sleeping behind the haunted leaning garage that cried creaky noises in the wind. Coaxing King with food, he eventually came to him.

King was a mysterious dog right from the start. He was well mannered and trained beyond the tricks of beg and sit. He was clean and well-groomed for a stray dog. He wasn't boney and starved like most of the strays in the neighborhood. My grandmother was suspicious to the point she'd behaved as if the dog was planted for us to find him. I later began to think that might be true, just not by some government agency. Maybe, he was a spirit sent to help us, I thought, to help my brother and whatever was tormenting him and making him change into what he was becoming, mean! For a long while King did just that, made my brother better.

My grandmother agreed to let him keep the dog. From that moment on, my brother and King were inseparable. My grandmother had to even be wary of the dog if she tried to discipline him, because King would stand between my brother and her like a man, unflinching. A year or so came and went until the night that there was no moon. Everything was black, the kind of black that enveloped life.

My great-uncle came to stay with us periodically. That is, when he'd used up all of his military pension or wore out his welcome elsewhere. With only a half-empty bottle of gin left to fuel him, he would head to our house. It was always the same: a week's worth of a clean bed and body, shaved face, combed head, and a full belly; Uncle Dee would become restless. The night he grew tired of cleanliness was a "haunt's night"; that's what Mom called it. Haunt's night was a night of no moon and all things corrupt and even evil came out. Both men and haunts could do their mischief under cover of blackness. So, off Uncle Dee headed to the liquor store to commiserate with his demons and the like. His pockets filled with his allowance, which my grandmother, his eldest sister, had doled out to him from his pension money.

Uncle Dee, hell-bent on getting his way, shamed my brother into letting King accompany him to purchase his slow death in a bottle. My brother gave in to Uncle Dee's persistent tongue-lashing. My brother watched his dog, King, disappear into the dark with only the sound of Uncle Dee calling the obedient King to serve as his companion and witness. If only he had waited and brought his bottle home, got drunk and ranted and raved here, in his room. But he didn't and death's playmates found them.

On the way back to our house from the liquor store, they had to cross the busy thruway. The same thruway he'd crossed sober earlier, but now he had to cross drunk off of a fifth of gin with a spare pint in his pocket. Uncle Dee's persistent tongue-lashing that my brother heard earlier was nothing compared to what King likely had to endure when he was forced to cross the busy thruway that spared no man nor animal on haunt's night. King was gone just like that, in the same way he came, quickly. Uncle Dee continued to come to the house for years to come. Hatred grew, or at best a deep resentment by most of us children, because of King's death and the many things that were to follow.

O'Brennan was my grim reaper of bad news. Seth had put to rest the mystery of the uninvited villager that came to my door. Seth told me that he ran into the wide silent man coming off the docks on his way to the school. The man mentioned that he had some old fishing gear and offered the equipment to him. I was glad to hear the explanation. It helped to make sense of what seemed to be strange behavior on the part of my male visitor.

O'Brennan shed a different light on the man's visit. A firm loud knock made me jump and hit a dish against the side of the sink. We had just finished dinner and begun cleaning up when Seth went to open the door. There stood O'Brennan in a light-colored rain jacket. In spite of the dark sky behind him, he seemed to disappear into the muted light within. I greeted him from the kitchen with a smile when I heard his voice.

"Hey, O'Brennan, what ahhh … you doing here, something wrong at the school?" my husband said, surprised to see him there.

"Hey O'Brennan, come in, you like some tea or coffee?" I said, repeating that stupid mantra that now fell so easily from my mouth.

"No, I'm not staying. I need to speak with the two of you a minute."

"Oh, okay, you want to have a seat?" I asked. It was a grim reaper time when he declined to sit.

"The news is going around the village that the new teachers are partiers."

I'm sure the look on my face matched the words that fell from my mouth. "What the hell does that mean?"

He looked at Seth, and so did I. O'Brennan was, much like myself, to the point. "It's going around the village that the new teachers are looking to score some pot."

"What! Who said that?" I blurted.

"One of the Allens said he shared a joint with Seth, and he was asked who to buy from."

Silence.

Silence for an uncomfortable minute with Seth neither confirming nor denying.

"Listen, it's not my business if you get high on your off time, but I would suggest you keep it to yourself and not ask people in the village to get drugs for you. The teacher living here before you had people knocking at his door all night every night and got beat up a couple of times when he tried to stop the traffic of people looking for drugs. The owners finally kicked him out and refused to rent to him or teachers anymore. So, I would suggest you not smoke or drink with the locals," O'Brennan said in a corrective tone.

"Ahhhh really, I don't know? Um … who said, who said it again? … I didn't smoke, I mean … I think I asked him for a cigarette maybe."

"It's not my problem, just thought I'd warn you. See you in the morning, Seth," he said as the door closed behind him. I'd learned that discussing issues with my husband, when he was to blame, required the appearance of being in agreement with him. That is, if I wanted the truth, my hardcore, straightforward approach would never glean the answers I sought, so I played good cop, bad cop all rolled into one.

"So, you copped a joint and didn't tell me?"

"Get outta here! You don't smoke? … I got half a joint left. I didn't think you'd do it with me. I can get more. He just gave me a joint to sample," Seth said, spilling his guts.

"Have you lost your damn mind? What are you doing? You could lose your job over this."

"Ah, come on, it's just a little pot."

"Did you not hear what O'Brennan said happened to the other teacher?" I said, glaring at him.

"I want to smoke a little pot. What's the big deal? Nobody's gonna know. I'm in my own house."

"How old are you? Grow up. You could lose your career. And what do you mean nobody's going to know, clearly everybody does. You drag me way the hell out here to do this! Now I know why that man came here, sitting there, staring at me, he probably thought I wanted to get high and party with him … you jerk. How could you put me in that situation?"

"I'm sorry, I didn't know he was going to come here. I'll tell him not to come to my house anymore."

"What do you mean not to come to your house? You tell him you're not interested at all! I don't want people thinking that's what we do." I could see it in his face. He was only half-listening to me.

"Come on, how about I just do a little bit? I'll go down to the beach and smoke." He pinched his fingers together to indicate the amount he intended to use and spoke in a cutesy voice to try and persuade me.

"If you get high here, or buy anything from anyone, I'm leaving and going home, I mean it." He looked at me, unsure. I went back into the kitchen and finished my evening chores. I felt bad about giving him such a harsh ultimatum.

We lay in bed next to one another. Perfectly on our sides of the bed. Quiet in the darkness. I broke the silence. "Please don't buy drugs here and get high, promise me."

Silence.

"Ok, I promise, go to sleep."

Chapter Twelve

Winter could be smelled in the air, and snow would come over the mountain sooner than later. Seth announced we were invited on a boat trip to see the Columbia Glacier. O'Brennan and his wife owned a boat and wanted to get it in the water one last time before winter set in for the long haul. As usual, these plans were all made behind closed school doors without my input.

The decision-making power seemed to have come to Seth by default. In any case, the default was based on Seth having experience from the Peace Corps and living on an island with indigenous Pacific Islander people. This made him the best decision-maker, so he seemed to believe. If I was going to have a voice in anything I would have to yell to be heard. I didn't always feel that way. When we were back in Kansas City, Seth was different, and we enjoyed curling up and planning our next moves, together. That was only months ago, but it felt like a lifetime had passed. Yet, I wondered if this personality trait was always there beneath the surface, waiting to erupt. Or was it possible something else had called this behavior forth and made him forget that I was here too?

Saturday (nine a.m.) it was a cold and partly cloudy day, with temperatures in the low fifties. We headed for the beach dressed in full rain gear with layers underneath. I reminded myself over and over again as I slunk to the beach, that I had taken a boat before. How hard could it be the second time? I visualized a boat not quite the size of the ferry, but large like the fishing trollers that came into the village. It would be a large boat, one set up high, away from the water with a small cabin I could go inside. *After all, I thought, what else would you put on an ocean for God's sake?*

There O'Brennan and Lisa were, sitting in a skiff bobbing up and down. The boat looked like some great bird clacking its beak in laughter at me, as the ocean waves jostled this boat around in self-pleasure. I tried to protest quietly to Seth, but everything was changing between us. He was growing in-different to my fears and no longer took to comforting me. I had denied him his means of self-soothing, by asking, no, demanding, he not get high or drink in the village, and now he began to deny me.

"Ah come on, you'll be fine … Get in, he's already here with the boat, what! You're not going to go now? Come on, get in, and just hold on, you'll be fine." Seth pushed and insisted to the point of annoyance. I did get in. To my horror, there was nothing to hold on to. Black self-pride flew in the wind as we sped across the water and waves. The boat skipped across like a stone, and I slid my butt from the plank seat to the lowest position of the craft, terrified of my fate. The sprays of the salty sea bit my brown skin as the wind reshaped my facial contours. I was clay in the potter's hand. I could do nothing except press my hands to the sides of the boat while my butt became one with the hull, and the water smacked the boat with a force that felt as if it was smacking my behind directly each time it hit the water's surface.

I was seven or eight when my grandmother and step-grandfather took us to our first traveling carnival. It was dark by the time we were able to go. I remember how black the sky looked and how it held the lights of the carnival in one spot of the sky. The air carried the smells of buttery popcorn, syrupy cola, spun sugar, hotdogs with mustard, and gas-fueled generators. My heart raced at the herd of happy people moving in a rush past us. Men carried children on their shoulders, and mothers hushed and wiped the tears of crying little faces with promises of going home soon. Laughter and talking, going and coming, while lights and sound were everywhere in a way I had never experienced before. I wanted to skip and laugh, scream and run just like the rest of them, but mostly I wanted a hand that would hold mine tightly. My grandmother had bought a string of tickets for rides, and as we approached each of these extraordinary metal contraptions we would be asked, "You want ta try this one?"

My siblings would answer, "No, ma'am."

This went on at each ride as I stared into the joyful faces of others. Slowly the laughing voices of others faded until I could hear them no more. I could no longer hear the music of the merry-go-round, the screams of joy from people spinning in the saucer and cup or children laughing and running from one ride to the other. My attention was refocused, keenly to a more important sound, vibration, and image. My step-grandfather, soft brown sticky lips, whispered close in my grandmother's ear.

"These kids of 'yarn don't want to do nothing, why you lettin' them waste a bunch money?" His lips smacked up and down in her ear. "What you gonna do hon! I don't want to be out here all night … don't want your legs hurtin' you, baby d'all." She'd half roll her eyes at him, but at the same time, a smile would come across her face. Another moment of childhood blotted out with the familiar voice of my grandmother. In these moments, my grandmother always grew from five foot four to six foot four, blocking out everything, and he, my step-grandfather, was the black shadow behind her. We were standing in front of the Ferris wheel.

"You want ta ride this?" she asked me.

"I think so," I said, smiling, then looked to my sisters for approval.

"Y'all want ta ride this one?" her tone sharpened.

My sister, a year and a half older, said, "No, ma'am, I don't."

"What the H-E-L-L do you want to ride? I bring your butts out here to waste my money. How come you don't wanna ride?"

"I'm scared, I don't want to," my sister's voice trembled.

"Scared of what? Get yo' little behind on that ride, worried me to death to come out here and you haven't rode one doggone thing." She reached for my crying sister and shoved her in the line. As her cries of protest got louder, my grandmother's anger got bigger. I looked up at the big wheel, spinning in the black sky, while hearing the screams of fear from my sister and slaps of skin on skin as we walked away from the Ferris wheel, never to ride.

O'Brennan slowed the boat as we approached the glacier, and he maneuvered through the floating ice. I was relieved. We were no longer plowing through waves, but had slowed to a speed where I felt safer. My sense of safety was short-lived after finding out O'Brennan was doing something far more dangerous. Lisa seemed unconcerned by her husband's plan. Floating glacier ice could go down under several feet to several hundred feet in the water. I could see the white-blue ice underneath the water like a giant stalactite vanishing in the brilliant ocean.

"Hey, keep your head in. Tell me if we're too close to the ice. We get trapped in between the floating ice, it could crush us like a can," O'Brennan admonished.

Great, I thought. "There's one on the right," I yelled.

"That's starboard," he said.

Whatever, I thought. "Hey, you're getting close to another one over here," I said.

We continued slowly, the engine sputtering along, like going through a minefield, until O'Brennan saw a moraine and asked if we wanted to get out and look around. "Yes," I said before anyone answered, desperate to have my feet on solid ground. There in front of us, what felt like only a hundred feet away stood a blue wall of glacier ice. Seth got out of the boat and ran up the dirty black hill of the moraine to see the glacier better. A small strip of the ocean was the only thing between him and the glacier, and yet it seemed to tower massively above, as if he was standing beneath it.

"Come on up," Seth called out to me, while O'Brennan stayed near the boat. I climbed the hill despite my fear of heights and gigantic things. I stood before the ocean and the massive blue ice with my husband by my side. Standing up higher on the hill of ice and dirt to face the massive glacier was like standing before a giant that could crush you at will. I could feel my legs wobble, I held my breath to still my nerves, and I felt my nervous tics jump around my face and eyes. All of a sudden, we saw a large chunk of ice begin to break away from the wall, sliding towards the ocean.

There was no sound, my eyes narrowed, and darkness formed in my peripheral vision. I viewed the glacier through a tunnel that my vision formed until the air from my lungs exhaled hissing like a gas leak, stabilizing all my bodily functions. In seconds, but with the feeling of minutes, my ears heard the roar of the ice reach us in an infinite exhale. The huge calving ice dipped down under the ocean, then came back up and shot towards the sky, as if it had been thrust up by another great giant under the sea. The bottom of the ice was black, like the rocky, silty soil we stood on. The black silty eye winked at us, while we stared back at it in awe, hearts racing. Down again into the water, it fell, in its choreographed dance. A wall of water swelled to what felt like ten feet, pulling the water from the small icy shore we stood on to itself. I froze in place, afraid and mesmerized to the point that I didn't see or hear my husband run screaming down the hill, running towards the boat for his life.

I followed, yelling, "Wait! What are you doing? Don't leave me," all the while looking behind to see if the wave was upon me. Seth made it to the boat first and I was halfway there when the wave hit the shore of the moraine. The wind and water lightly sprayed my face as it came to rest like a lap dog, splashing mildly on the shore. The O'Brennans smiled with a hidden chuckle tucked underneath. They knew that the distance between us and the glacier was greater than we could perceive. The mass of ice, though it was large and created what seemed to be a huge swell, was absorbed by the distance it had to travel.

We glided through the fragmented ice field quicker this time with me yelling "Starboard" and "Portside." The wind blew a mixture of salty seawater, and a light rain now fell. My face was cold yet blood rose to the vessels in my cheeks as I kneeled with my torso upright this time and faced the elements. On the way back to the village, I asked questions, pointed to landmarks, and asked their names. Sometimes I could feel the fear lurking just behind me when O'Brennan took a sharp turn or accelerated the engine, but something had changed with that glacier ice falling into the sea. Dipping down under the water in baptism. The ice came up different and so was I from this experience, at least the beginning of different.

Seth pointed and asked about a piece of land that stuck out into the sea like the stump of a severed leg. There were white crosses announcing a burial site.

"What's that?" Seth asked.

"It's called the point, an old Native burial site." O'Brennan, with Lisa by his side, pulled in slowly towards the shore as his voice lowered to almost normal. "It's also Meddy's favorite place."

"Why?" I asked.

"The villagers love to get puppies until they grow up and you see them running around getting into people's garbage or stealing game hunters brought in. So, they call Meddy!"

"For what?" I pressed.

O'Brennan brought the boat to a stop, and he and Seth jumped out and pulled it in. Lisa and I jumped out into the frigid water, which I could feel through my rubber waders and wool socks.

"They call him to get rid of their nuisance. So, he takes the dogs out to the point and shoots them. As soon as one of the kids wants a puppy for their birthday they get one, the dog grows up, and Meddy's waiting. They have a different view of pet ownership."

I was anticipating our morning flight into Anchorage with both excitement and trepidation. I was not disappointed on either account. We were going into the city to shop and see the family we'd befriended when we first went to Anchorage, before heading to the village. Then off to a dreaded dentist appointment before we returned.

The plane we had ordered was waiting on the small village runway, and the sky was gray and overcast. The small single-engine plane started up and sputtered loudly with the roar of a lawnmower, idling at the end of the snowy runway. I sat in the back of the plane this time where I could feel some small if false sense of security, while Seth perched boldly upfront.

As I climbed up in the plane, I discovered there were no seats in the back other than the two upfront for one passenger and the pilot.

There was nothing to keep me off the cold metal shell of the plane except the bags and a small wool blanket stuffed in the corner and offered up by the pilot. The worst thought I had was the realization that the thickness of the plane's hull that separated me from thousands of feet of air was probably one or two inches. The plane screamed louder and shifted side to side on takeoff, and I was transported to the back of my brother's go-kart when I was a kid. The force of my sister's hands, pressed on my back, pushed us down the hill for a faster takeoff, and my brother pulled left, then right on the ropes to keep us on the sidewalk.

Seth and I were again in flight as the plane took off just before the runway ran out. It lifted, and then banked right, dropping and rising on the air's crosscurrents. I quietly gripped, held my breath, and focused on each fall and rise of the plane while waiting for it to level off. We flew in front of Copper Mountain so close that I could feel its shadow and see the cracks and breaks in the mountain's face. I could see the village and the blue dome of the church inch out of view.

My stomach dropped when the plane rolled. I held my breath, gripped the bag next to me and then tried to sort my thoughts quickly. Scrambling to hold a positive thought while an overwhelming fear of dying pressed every synapse until the plane leveled off. A flash came to me. *Is this what it is like to have your life flash before you?* The exception was that this flight of death was longer than a flash, as I continued listening to the engine bang on. I was freezing, and it became a real possibility I could die from exposure. It was ten to fifteen degrees colder because we were thousands of feet in the air, in a metal can, and if there was any heat in this thing, it was not coming back to me. I snatched the blanket, wrapping myself, as thoughts of its questionable background invaded my mind. My mind started to drift again to anything that might help me not think about the frigid air.

Time seemed to slow and what felt like hours was probably minutes. The pilot spoke, breaking into my thoughts and yelling over the noise of the aircraft. "If the weather holds up, we'll be there in an hour and fifteen minutes, fifteen minutes early!" An hour might as well have been twenty hours, adding to the ten hours that it had already felt like. But I was grateful for a measurement of time. It made me feel there was something reliable, and a limit to this agony. We dropped a few feet, the engine went silent, and it suddenly roared again and snatched us upwards.

Mountains! More beautiful damn mountains and how much longer can I take it? I battled dark thoughts, from the "what if" tormentor:

What if the pilot found out moments before taking off that his wife left him for another man, and Seth looks just like him! Overwhelmed with grief and anger he plans to crash the plane!

What if the pilot has failed to refuel the plane before we took off? Thinking it's only a one-and-a-half-hour flight, not anticipating bad weather, so the storm takes us off course, and we're doomed! Doomed!

But a much darker thought seeped into my "what if" scenarios. A thought that never seemed to leave me; instead it urged and compelled me to jump out of the plane. I was trapped in the back with all the bags, feeling like luggage, away from the door's handle (thank God), tormented by "what if." The roaring of the engine was an endless sound that gave me no peace, but should have been a source of comfort. Yet, that moment of silence when the engine cut off seemed so sweet to my wrecked nerves. Seth was yelling now to speak above the roaring engine to the pilot while taking a quick glance back at me. I could see the worry in his pale face.

"So, I bet you've seen some really bad weather before?" Seth's voice nervously searched, waiting for the pilot's response.

"Yup! Pretty bad," the answer returned vacant, and the plane rocked side to side in the way a five-year-old zooms a toy aircraft before sailing it into a wall.

"So-ooooa ..." the plane dipped and rocked hard again left and right. I could hear Seth suck in air along with my stomach bottoming out before he spoke again. "Woo! So ... how would you rate this? Pretty rough conditions!"

The sky had mostly engulfed us in darkness, and there was nothing but black clouds, rain, wind, and lightning on the horizon. Seth continued with a measure of fear in his voice. "I mean on a scale of one to ten. How bad?"

"Oh, I'd say not too bad," he said, matter of fact. Then continued, "Probably a three."

"A three!" I screamed from the baggage area and startled both of them. "This is not a three," I announced (seconds away from clawing my way out).

"Yeah! This is nothing, been through ten times worse, it's just a little rain."

Seth's tone took on a calmer, relaxed, and chatty sound like he was believing this fool. "I bet you've seen some crazy times."

"Yep, I've seen a time or two. I'd figure I wasn't gettin' home to supper."

"Yeah! What happened?"

"Engine problems, bad weather. We fly bush planes in Alaska like they drive taxis in New York, you're bound to see something," he said reflectively. "You're from New York, right?" he asked Seth.

"Yeah, how'd you know?"

The pilot shrugged and just smiled, "I got a story for ya! About a crazy bush pilot and his wife … one hell of a pilot, but crazy! Him and his wife both flew. She was a Native gal, they always flew together. They could raise some hell, excuse my language. They fought all the time. I heard once they were flying out of Cordova. Been drinking and he said something, pissed her off, she hit him so hard, knocked him cold for a few minutes."

I listened to him spin his story as the clouds billowed black in front of us and we drew nearer to its center. I counted in my head and lip-synced, *One … Two … Three … Four …* Seth's voice was like background music. I could hear him urging the pilot to tell the epitaph.

"Really! Get out of here, that's unbelievable, they musta died?"

"Nope, sure didn't. He came to pretty quick, and she took hold of the controls … That's nothin', I heard they were flying down around Talkeetna, and they started arguing, and he got sick of hearing her or didn't want to get cold conked again, so he flew over this mountain peak; It was coated with a fresh coat of snow. He turned their plane and banking it right, heading for the mountain. He told her if she didn't shut up he was gonna push her out of the plane. She started screaming and trying to hit him, he reached over, opened her door, tipped the plane to one side, and out she went."

I stopped counting and was paralyzed with horror and fear, while Seth was completely and fearfully enthralled. "These people are fuckin' nuts, you gotta be kidding! He murdered his wife?"

It felt as if the very spirit of these people were playing out their revenge on us that very moment. The rain began to hit the plane sideways, and we rocked and knocked against walls of water and wind. I could see Seth grip the seat with everything he had, and the pilot intensely took control of the wheel to steady the small aircraft. The storm threw us about for what felt like an hour. Just as I felt I was going to go completely mad and have a nervous breakdown, we came around our last peak of the mountains. In front of us in the distance, there was light and a clear sky. The rain wet the windshield with tear droplets, and the wipers easily pushed them away.

"That was a five," the pilot announced in that same steady, matter-of-fact voice. "And she didn't die. The snow that fell earlier on the mountain was like she fell into a feather bed … It takes a hell of a pilot to do that and not kill her or crash the plane on the side of the mountain."

"Bet that ended that relationship," Seth announced, not asking.

"No, they were in love with each other and kept flying together. It stopped a lot of the fighting, I heard, at least while flying." The plane still roared in my ears and dipped occasionally, but we flew, almost gliding in the air with the wings of an eagle towards the light. The plane landed, and I was pulled out, stiff, muscles rigid, and every part of me quivering as I tried to stand, but Seth held me up as we walked away.

We would take the cab straight to pick up our car, do some shopping, pick up ordered supplies, and enjoy some 'R and R.' We finished our shopping and ordered pizza for the Grimes family and ourselves, and then arrived around seven p.m. at their trailer. Darkness had long rolled in when we entered the dim-lit home. We ate pizza while sitting on a blanket-covered sofa with cats, kids, and dogs climbing about the furniture while the adults discussed the state of Alaskan affairs.

I had never gone any further than the front room of their trailer when we first visited. So, I held no judgment when I saw it was a bit under kept. After all, they had four kids and the front room would likely be the most overused area. But *nothing*, and I do mean nothing, prepared me for the back bedroom and bathroom. I was raised to be clean and respectful, and I couldn't decide which should take precedence in this situation. The bathroom had layers of hair, soap scum, and body dirt in every corner. The toilet was a monument to the very thing it was created for, i.e. urine and fecal matter, and it was distributed to lots of places with the help of the animals and toddler. When they offered us their bedroom I seized the opportunity to rescue us. I told them we did not want to put them out and we had planned to stay in a hotel.

They however insisted and said they had already arranged everything. Her husband and son were leaving for a hunting trip, and she usually slept on the couch and watched TV when he was away. *Damn, now what?* If I pushed the issue it would be obvious how uncomfortable I was, and I didn't want to offend them. Seth didn't say a word and wasn't freaking out. *What in the hell is wrong with him?* I was losing it! So, I did what any polite, good Southern–raised Black child would do—I cleaned what I had to use, starting with the toilet. I refused to shower, lay on a blanket I had brought with me, and slept in my clothes with a hat and gloves on to protect myself. I was mortified while my husband snored away the night. The next day we were out before the house erupted in sound. We stepped out into a gray dreary day. It had just begun to rain and the thought of my dreaded dental appointment clouded my mind.

My siblings and I sat at our 1950s green mosaic Formica chrome table, each in our precise seats. The table was next to the stove in the crammed kitchen. The grownups took their food in the dining room on the formal table draped in an old Irish crocheted tablecloth. My step-grandfather was always served first, a plate of food with rice and baked chicken smothered in gravy and a smidgen of green beans with fatback.

My grandmother seldom ate right away after cooking and would sit in her chair next to the dining room table. She'd yell into the kitchen at one of us. "Fix Allen a plate and bring it in here before yaw start eating." If you were the unlucky female child to serve Mr. Allen, my step-grandfather, you had to choose how to hold his plate. Underneath meant burning the entire surface of your hand, but trying to hold the plate on the edge scorched your thumbs. Either way, you were sure to be burned, because he liked his food hot, boiling hot along with a plate that had to be completely covered by food.

The joke perpetuated by my grandmother was that he needed sideboards on his plate. We children failed to see the humor. So, he ate and received the lion's share every night, and almost every night that pain-delivered food was puked in the toilet before he started dessert. He'd look at us with that golden tooth and laugh. He'd laugh because he was a pig that didn't want us to have more of anything than him, and he knew we knew that.

"Yeah, baby, this looks good," he'd say, then count his pieces of chicken. "Baby, you know I like thighs, how many you fix?"

"I made a whole chicken. You know how many thighs on a chicken, what they give you?" she'd ask.

"Look like a half of breast and one thigh."

"Y'all know this man likes the thighs, bring that other thigh in here to him right now. I'm tired! Y'all gonna make me mad."

One night, I picked up my portion of the chicken, a wing. When I bit my tooth gave way, bending back into my mouth, bleeding but attached still to a chunk of pink gum. I hollered in pain. My eldest sister said, "Be quiet, you don't want them to come pull it out." She looked in my mouth and moved the tooth back in place. She told me the tooth was loose but not ready to come out. I was horrified, but excited that the tooth fairy would leave me a dime (maybe a quarter). But then I remembered the first tooth I lost around six years old. My step-grandfather wanted to pull it with pliers, but was convinced to use the string-and-door method (with the option of pliers) if it didn't come out. I endured the door slamming several times before it was over. This time it was different. I kept quiet until it was loose enough. In the middle of the day, while eating a peanut butter sandwich, out came the tooth stuck in the bread and peanut butter.

Chapter 13

I'm not sure when I conceived the idea or if it had always been a given, but at some point, between breakfast, coffee, and tooth extraction, I decided to look in the classified ads for a dog. Thumbing through the free section of the want ads, and there he was, the dog that would become my best friend.

"LaVern Schwartz," the dental assistant called out my name. Dental care hadn't happened until the age of twenty-one, just a short time before meeting Seth. When I did go, I had only one cavity to fill and my teeth cleaned, which to me was remarkable considering the level of decayed teeth in my family. Now it was my turn to have teeth problems. I had two impacted wisdom teeth with inflamed gums, and that made it difficult for me to eat. On top of that, the dentist recommended that I take out all four, or I'd be coming back. However, I had also discovered that I didn't numb easily. I explained to the dentist my brief but painful history of being able to feel what's being done despite several injections of novocaine in the past.

"Open wide," he said without the slightest indication he understood my concerns, and the torture of injections began. Five injections later and the partial extraction which left half of my tooth embedded in my gum. I gurgled cries of protest, with tears streaming down my cheeks, enduring each fiery hornet injection. I still had to face three more molar extractions plus the partial extraction. The dentist seemed exhausted and exasperated when he walked away to retrieve my husband from the waiting room. He explained to Seth that he was sending me over to an oral surgeon. He couldn't pull my wisdom teeth; they were too embedded and would have to be cut out. He didn't want to put me through any further pain. That was considerate of him. All of this teeth business reminded me of the elementary school hygiene program and the little red chewable they gave you, so you could see where the plaque was. I learned early on to be a great brusher from that program and from the bad teeth that were in my family. My father and grandmother both had missing and bad teeth. My father suffered from gum disease, which went from yellow to variations of greens and black over his nubby teeth and gums. I was so afraid of getting it that I spent hours obsessed with brushing.

When we arrived at the surgeon, I was happy to know that I would be knocked out. When it was done and I woke up, I felt like a truck had hit me, but nothing prepared me for the aftermath of the numbing medicine and gas wearing off. We arrived back at the Grimes' a few hours later, so I could rest instead of the last-minute running around we had planned to do before heading back to the village. By the time we reached the Grimes home, the medicine had completely worn off, and I was spitting and swallowing blood. I lay on the sofa, clutching a blanket that had been dragged from one end of that trailer to the other while catching every meal its owner had eaten. I couldn't care less at this point about cleanliness or filth; between the nausea, pain, and throwing up, I would have cuddled a homeless man. I had a stomach filled with blood, no food, and codeine pain pills. My final humiliating act was destined to come; running into the bathroom and hanging over the toilet that thankfully I had cleaned the day before. I was barely in my right mind while racked with pain and nausea. I had enough of my brain function to squat, so my knees were not on the soiled carpet and held myself while throwing up in that pit from hell. It always amazes me how in times of sickness you don't care if you're butt ugly and kissing the back end of a garbage truck … Well, I almost didn't care. I was in no shape to leave and we stayed another night, I on their sofa, Seth in a chair, and the Grimes family piled up in their beds, sound asleep.

For the working poor, as was my family, prosperity was revealed by what we were finally able to buy. Some bought clothes and new cars, but we bought an extra-large box freezer and filled it with food. The Wonder Bread's day-old shop with lots of bread and sweet treats was a prized staple. Our freezer was packed with Honey Buns, Twinkies, and Suzy Q's. There was meat of all sorts and cuts that I had never heard of along with summer vegetables bought by the bushel that were processed, packaged, and frozen by us. Prosperity also translated into my grandmother purchasing the house next to us. My earliest playmate besides my sisters was the little girl that lived in that house next door to us, the house my grandmother would eventually buy. Her name was Tammy and her little brother was Qualows. Tammy was a year or two younger than me, about four or five, and her brother three. We were relegated to her front porch or the broken pavement of the driveway that separated our backyards.

At nighttime, I watched them from the bed of my dark room. My eyes followed their mother as she chased her screaming three-year-old from the dining room to the bedroom, then out of view. I watched them like a movie, staring through their wide-open windows, naked children and arguing adults. How different they were with kids crying and playing while their mother encouraged in quiet tones, unlike the strict order that dictated our house. The house they lived in was a large two-story stone building. It had the most beautiful rose bush that graced the stairs to a large stone porch from our shared driveway.

It wasn't until I was six that I truly experienced the difference between my life and theirs. My grandmother's job as a domestic now required that she leave earlier. Before seven a.m. she would catch three buses in order to serve coffee to her mistress's husband before work. Not breakfast, but coffee. My grandmother must have made some damn good coffee.

All of this meant that I, at the age of six, had to head to kindergarten by myself from an empty house, even on my first day of school. I went from seeing my siblings go off to school while I ate oatmeal and my grandmother sipped on coffee to having to walk six long blocks across a busy fairway. The plan was that my grandmother would send me to Tammy's house a couple of hours before school. Tammy and I would often play on her front porch. My grandmother made it perfectly clear that I was not to go in their house or get dirty.

One exceptionally cold fall day the sky was gray and the rain fell lightly when my grandmother left me on their porch. I didn't want to go to Tammy's house. I didn't want my grandmother to leave for work. And I *didn't* want to walk across that busy street that no one stopped or slowed down on, not even for a little six-year-old trying to cross. That day Tammy had the sniffles and wasn't allowed outside in the damp and cold. Tammy's mother came to the door and asked me if I wanted to come in.

"No, ma'am," I said, "I'm fine." I went to the back of my house and swung on the metal pipe rails to our basement stairs. Tammy's mother called me back to the porch and said that my grandmother wouldn't like me being in the backyard. The sky began to darken like it only could in the Midwest and the lightning and thunder came along with sheeting rain. I was afraid and tears began to form, quietly.

Tammy's mother told me to come inside, and without hesitation I stepped inside the door. A man, Tammy's uncle, was to my right burning paper in a small fireplace. He looked at me and spoke quietly. There was only one light on in the house and it glowed an orange-brown from the kitchen directly in front of me. The living room was to my left with a lopsided sofa covered with dirty blankets, sheets, and clothes.

I took one small step when Tammy's mother spoke and said, "Come on in." But my feet smacked with stickiness between the sole of my shoes and the floor. There was no other furniture in the room except a broken wooden chair, torn shades, and dingy curtains. The room reeked with used diapers, greasy food, and a sweet-salty dirt smell, along with crumbs all over the wood floor. Tammy was sent to greet and encourage me to come into the kitchen.

Her mother spoke from beyond the dim orange glow. "You want something to eat? I don't think you should go ta school today. I think your grandmother wouldn't want you out in this. Tammy, tell your little friend ta come on in here." The smell of smoke stung my nose and filled the house while the thunder cracked outside the door. Tammy stood in front of me. The faint, gray light from a window lit her as she ate a white bread sandwich with nothing between it. Her cocoa-color hands made the bread almost luminescent in the dim room. Her small boney arms were bare, along with her chest, legs, and feet, with only underwear as her wardrobe. I stood there as she looked at me and offered some of her bread. Then I watched a brown roach crawl across her matted hair like some strange companion. I ran out the door, saying it was time for me to be at school. Her mother called behind me to stop, but I didn't. The rain sheeted and the thunder crashed above me, but I kept running.

My grandmother was determined to push out Tammy's family. She would constantly complain, "I can't stand that filthy house next door. They're the reason we can't get rid of the roaches in our house, no matter how much Raid we spray." She made my dad get one of those big canister sprayers you saw on the commercial, *'Hey Orkin Man.'* She would have my dad mix the chemical with water in the can and he would pump and pump to build pressure till *Sssssssssss,* out it came. He sprayed the whole perimeter of the house and around the windows and doors. I can still remember the smell and taste of that milky white poison I inhaled. My grandmother was obsessed. She complained to their landlord every chance she got, but I didn't want them to leave. Tammy was my only playmate.

"Can you come over?" Tammy asked, standing on the top cement stair of her porch, off the driveway. The stairs came out to our shared driveway and faced the rock wall of my porch.

I sat on the top of my wall, catching my breath after climbing and jumping off several times, "I can't ..." I huffed out each word, "come ... over there ... on your porch. My mom won't let me," I said.

"How come?" she asked.

I didn't know how to answer her. How to say, "The truth is your house is filthy and my grandmother is trying to buy it right from under you"?

"I don't know, I have to stay on the porch or in the backyard," I said. She sat on her top stair, wiping the hair of a half-bald naked doll. "Hey, you want to go play in the sand. I'll get some things, and we can play beach."

She ran to the back and I went into the house and found an old pie pan and sneaked a plastic cottage cheese container filled with water outside. Mom was in her chair, and I had to pass her slowly like nothing special was happening.

"Where are you going?"

"To the bathroom then outside in the back," She had been nodding, her head slightly slumped back, but still knew I was there even though I was walking quiet and closed the door soft.

"You get on in there and use it and then stop going in and out the house, lettin' in bugs and makin' noise."

"Yes, ma'am."

"Next time you come in here, you stay in."

When I thought about it technically, the sand was kinda in the fork between our driveway and our two backyards. And I'm sure my grandmother technically meant for me to be in my backyard, but I thought if I got caught I could just play stupid. We filled the pan with sand and water and made a beach for her doll.

"Where's your brother?" Tammy asked.

"I don't know, with his friends I guess."

"I don't like him, he's a mean boy."

"What he do to you?"

"My momma said I can't play with him anymore," she said, looking down as she bathed the doll in sandy water.

"My grandmother said, y'all gotta move because you have roaches and rodents." She got up and pulled her doll to herself and started down the drive. I called after her, "I'm sorry, got them too." I don't know why I said that. Maybe it was because of what she was saying about my brother, even if it was true. I knew it was wrong, soon as I said it, just like I knew it was right, what she said about my brother, well partly true.

At the age of nine, not long before my grandmother succeeded in purchasing their home, Tammy's mom asked my grandmother if I could go to the movies. It was Tammy's birthday and she wanted to treat her and a friend to celebrate the day. For me, it was my first movie in a real movie theater.

Before that we'd always gone to drive-ins in the back of my daddy's junk and garbage truck. We'd bleach, scrub, and hose out the truck on those rare occasions. But this was going to the real theater: Uptown Theater. We took a bus there, Tammy, her mother, and I. We walked across the street from the bus stop right up to the ticket window. I stood under the huge white and gold marquee. Lit up in big black letters it said, *The Ten Commandments*. We walked into the large auditorium with rows of wooden seats and red velvet cushions. Straight in front of us was a stage with huge red velvet drapes that went so far up I couldn't see where they stopped. She bought us popcorn and I held it close as we walked down the aisle past a sea of seats. We sat in our seats. Everything was quiet at first, then right before my eyes, the red drapes opened. *Wow, without anybody pullin' on 'em!* I thought.

The roar of the music started, and I sat through the whole movie with my mouth opening mechanically to receive the popcorn I shoved in without a thought. White patrons had long since left the area and abandoned the beautiful but aged theater. I didn't even know *The Ten Commandments* was fourteen years old by the time we got to see it. But what did I know, it was the most magnificent experience I had ever had, from start to finish.

We walked into a palace and then into a world and time more real than me. I couldn't believe her mother could afford this when we couldn't (or at least my grandmother didn't), not even for a birthday. A poor woman gave a poor and lonely girl the gift of her first movie. That simple act of kindness had consequences. Although the last of the Ten Commandments (Thou shalt not covet thy neighbor's house) was broken by my grandmother, the act of kindness opened me to the ideas in the New Testament, the new universal law, where *Love* is the greatest commandment of them all. I've strived for the latter ever since.

The next morning at the Grimes', I woke in much better shape than the day before and my mind was clearer except for a nagging pain and swollen jaws. We had a bush plane to catch around noon and it was seven thirty a.m. The ad for the dog came to mind. "I want to call about the dog."

"Really! We have to be out of here at noon," Seth demanded.

"Why can't you just call and see if she still has him?"

"I don't know, a dog? I don't want to take care of a dog. If we want to go somewhere what do we do with it?"

"I didn't ask you to take care of it. It's *my* dog and I'll take care of it myself. You're never around anyway." He sighed and continued looking through the newspaper until he found the ad again and reluctantly called.

"You still have the dog?" Seth spoke into the phone.

"Ask if we can come now," I whispered.

"Ok, and where are you?"

"Can we come now?"

"Ok, thanks, we'll see you in a few … We can see him at nine a.m. She'll meet us at her apartment."

"Yay! Thank you, I can't wait. Let's get ready to go," I said, as the pain intensified into a throb and my head swam. Seth had his work, family, and friends he talked to on a regular basis and I would have my dog.

Many times, I found myself missing a place I couldn't wait to leave. Familiar things like my dad randomly popping up at my apartment to tell me about his old broken-down truck and how he needed to get it fixed, so he could get hustling and make some money. I'd make food to feed us then slip him a few dollars to put gas in his old piece of a car he was driving. He always protested just enough to maintain some dignity. "Ah baby you ain't got ta do that," he'd say, rubbing the bills between his thumb and finger.

I'd say, "It's okay, Daddy, I'm glad you came to see me, plus that car can't run on air, can it?"

We'd laugh. He'd say, "Sho can't, Daddy 'preciate it, how'd you know I was about out anyway?"

"I don't know. An angel whispered to me."

He'd smile, clear his throat, and say, "Yeah, humm, thank ya',

Lord and angels." I guess I missed that familiar kind of loneliness more than this new loneliness.

We got to the woman's apartment, she opened the door, and we were greeted by her and Rocky. *That* was the dog's name, Rocky. It was love at first sight but I hated the name.

He was a big black shepherd with white markings on his chest and said to be mixed with Lab and wolf. After several licks, wags, and learning his history, we were on our way. It was on the train to Whittier that I changed his name to Rawsh, making him fully mine. Before we made our way through the tunnel into Whittier and caught our bush plane to the village, we were bonded. He became the first dog I completely gave my heart to.

I was dressed and out early to take Rawsh for his first walk on the beach. I kept him on a leash through the village until we reached the water, then I released him. We walked a quarter of a mile playing fetch as I ran into the water, allowing the waves to crash against my boots. Rawsh, however, refused to enter the frigid ocean water. Instead, he played tag with the tide, running out when it swelled then letting the wave chase him in.

I began to train him right away by calling him to me when he got only a few feet away. "Sit, stay," I would tell him. He sat on the wet sand until he heard his name. The sand clung beneath him, hanging from his black hair as he ran to me. We practiced over and over again, and I rewarded him with rubs, hugs, and more driftwood to fetch until we reached a part of the beach that was not easily passable. The rocky black cliff poured into the water demanding we climb if we were to pass. Rawsh leaped onto the black rock that lay vertical in irregular sheets. Pieces easily broke and crumbled underfoot and they lay washed along the cliff and beach. I followed Rawsh, while I became a different kind of four-legged creature, stepping clumsily in my rubber boots and pawing about with my hands, clinging to the black mass.

I notice blood on some of the jagged rocks in front of me. Raising my head from my lowly position, I saw Rawsh was limping. He was cutting up the pads of his feet on this haggard black monster. I removed my gloves and stroked the surface. The edges were sharp as a razor in places and had I fallen I would have sliced myself open. What was wrong with me following this dog out here crawling around on all fours? He was still very much a puppy at one-and-a-half years old. I backed down off the rocks, calling him to pause his movement forward. He struggled to turn himself around on the treacherous rocks. His momentum pushed him forward in the direction his nose was pointed and his hurt foot encouraged the urgency. He stopped, hesitating on the black monster, in contemplation of whether to come to the sound of my voice or follow his instinct. I called him playfully, then in a firm voice. He jostled from side to side before slowly coming towards me and leaping off onto the smooth dark sand. I hugged and praised my dog. Tears came to my eyes when I looked and saw a deep gash in his paw. He limped home leaving a small trail of blood and my tears for my stupidity.

If I could imagine God's face, Alaska would be His reflection. Alaska's imminent beauty, power, and majesty could play you like fool's gold, or worst, cost you your life. Winter had come with plenty of cold frigid air off the ocean, but nothing said winter to me like the first snowfall. It was late evening and the sun had long gone in. I looked out and saw the first flakes gliding down like parachutes. Each flake was huge and fluttered with the flirtation of fake white eyelashes. Seth was not home yet, so I threw on my boots, coat, gloves, and hat. I grabbed Rawsh and headed down to the beach.

It was a strange experience—my mind could not wrap itself around the idea of the ocean, a beach of snow, or my seeing such a beautiful thing. There were no lights except for the white of the snow reflecting off the black expanse of ocean. I stood at the ocean's edge with a dim hue of light refracting off sky and water, leaving just enough light to navigate. The water lapped and smacked at the beach edge as Rawsh and I played, childlike, close to it. Each flake melted on the water and sand, but lightly coated the rocks milky. I caught the gentle ones with my face and lashes, standing still for a moment. Unafraid, yet my heart raced from the reality of my simple existence compared to the largeness of an ocean I could barely see, knowing it could swallow us up. There is no other peace like when you are one with reality and in the midst of experiencing it as a miracle.

Chapter Fourteen

Rawsh was beginning to be well trained, at least in the sense that he came when I called and stayed when I told him. He had, however, one major flaw, rubbing in dead fish carcasses. The first experience I had with this was during one of our long beach walks. After that point, I avoided the beach with him, allowing only the occasional sniff at the bottom of the hill from our house along the rocks and beached ruins. I was somewhat afraid of the ocean, and I wasn't sure if Rawsh's curiosity and his youth would land him in the water with the sea claiming him for itself. I spent weeks when I first got Rawsh walking him on a leash along the road from my house to the school, practicing sitting and staying, staying and sitting. When we reached the bog behind the school and away from the village, he received his reward, to be let off his leash. As soon as Rawsh was off his leash, he would leap and jump over the bog and brush in a dance of pure joy. His body was graceful, leaping like spurts of black oil shooting up from the ground. He would stop suddenly as if to ask "are you okay?" "Good boy, I'm okay. Go on, go," I'd tell him. He'd run with his nose down chasing a scent until I'd call him when freedom might be claiming master.

Finally, I was confident of my command over Rawsh, so we headed to the beach. He was well ahead of me when I saw him lay on his back, rubbing and rolling on the sand. I assumed he was scratching himself on the coarse black sand until I reached his itching post. There lay the remains of rotting fish, and he was covered with bits and pieces of the smelly fish, all tangled in his hair. I soon learned this foul behavior was the one uncivilized thing I could not train out of my dog, and he in turn looked at me in disgust for my barbaric use of shampoo. I scouted ahead on our future walks to resolve the issue of dead fish rolling, but Rawsh and I would be in a game of wills over this issue. It was never so tested as when the school decided to go on a camping trip before the cold weather really set in. It was the beginning of October, and the trip invite was extended to Rawsh and me to accompany them.

We headed to Copper Mountain with junior high- and high school-aged students. Our group was made up of eight students, four adults, and one dog. We spent the day checking out the forest as we searched our campground. Every student was given a chore. Some gathered firewood. Most of the boys were tasked with O'Brennan and Seth to erect the tents and hang our food in a tree, but mostly they ran around screaming and being silly kids that had a day off from regular classes. A fire was roaring and the light from the sky was falling in the darkening woods. Some of the students went off in various directions to explore before the dark consumed everything. Rawsh became the students' escort into the woods, and the kids loved calling him to do everything from accompanying them to their woodsy outhouse to making him pull oversized logs. We eventually settled in around the warmth of the fire, and ghost stories changed the blaze in front of us to an eerie theater.

"Scary Mary, she was called, the young bride of Klondike Ike. They said he left her to wait for him while he made his fortune in gold." My husband began in a soft slow voice as the wood in the fire crackled and popped between each word. "They said weeks went by, then months, until a year had passed. The young bride no longer talked with townspeople of her beloved husband, and soon she took to longer periods alone in her room. The townspeople occasionally caught a glimpse of her pale face looking out the window of her hotel room while passing by on the street."

"Oooooow!" Melvin, one of the older boys, yelled and grabbed the arm of the teen girl next to him.

"Stop, you stu-pid," Leanna said, her voice trembling a little.

"Tell some more, Mr. Schwartz," Sandra, Leanna's sidekick, urged, so my husband started again.

"So, after a while, no one saw her at all and not a sound from her room was heard. Then early one morning the hotel owner knocked feverishly at the door to no reply, so he broke it down. There he found the gruesome sight of the young woman that waited for a husband that never returned. She laid in the bed dressed in her white wedding gown, dead!"

Some ooooed and ahhhhed while others sat quietly before my husband spoke again. "From that day on, many claimed to have seen the pale young woman staring out that same hotel window in a white wedding dress, looking for her young husband that promised to return for her, but never did."

Everyone sat in silence for a moment with only the sound of the fire crackling when Melvin spoke. "I saw a ghost," he said, looking straight into the fire. He was the handsome one, the smartest one, the one most likely to succeed, measured by someone else's culture. "That old house on the corner by you, Mr. Schwartz, that's my auntie's old house. She died there in the fire. We were out walkin' round one night, and I saw her. She was standing in the road by the burn' down house. She walked up to it and started whisperin' somethin' to me, but I got out of there and ran home. Told my mom and dad, and they asked me, 'You been drinkin?' and I told 'em no! Well, little." The teens giggled. "My dad said I shouldn't run, you should've stayed and found out what she want, might be somethin' you need to know."

"Yeah, you should've stayed," Leanna, the pretty, long-haired girl replied. "My grandpa said you have to grab them and push 'em down round the neck back in the ground." She stared into the fire. There was silence for a moment before they all burst out laughing and teasing.

Melvin said, "Yeah, why don't you go push her back in the ground then."

"Shut up, it's for real, my grandpa say so, show some respect." All the other teens turned on Melvin, now the "disrespectful" youth.

A loud sound came from behind us, crashing through the leaves, straight at us like a rush of wind. Rawsh came barreling through the brush, while every teen and adult jumped or fell off the logs they sat on. An overwhelming stench hit us like the bowels of hell, making our ghost tales a weak account. Seth grabbed Rawsh by the collar before he jumped in the lap of anyone, and discovered to our horror that Rawsh had rolled in human excrement that someone had failed to properly clean up based on wilderness edict. Rawsh was tied outside our tent for the night and cleaned the best that our supplies would allow. The next day, we headed home down the mountain, through the tundra, with everyone now ostracizing him the entire way. On our trek home, Lewis, one of the quieter boys, mentioned Meddy.

"Hey, Meddy's getting a dog … what kind of dog is yours?" Lewis asked me.

"I was told that he's a shepherd with some Lab and wolf in his family line."

"Yea, Meddy said your dog is nothing compared to how big his dog is, his dog can eat your dog for lunch."

"Okay, I didn't know there was a competition." Lewis, with his thick, black-rimmed glasses and academic look, reached down and ruffled the neck of Rawsh without thinking. "You're a good boy, Rawsh, we love you …"

And the other kids erupted in jeers, "Eeewwww, you got poop!" They took off running towards their houses, tormenting each other playfully, while O'Brennan and my husband went to the school with the camping equipment. Rawsh and I reached home. I tied him up while I went in to get cleaning supplies, then headed to the beach to perform the ritual of bathing in the frigid ocean water to remove most of the foulness he'd gotten himself into. Shivering from the cold, we headed quickly up the hill to the house and into a tub of warm water and shampoo that made him huggable once again.

That next week, late afternoon, I headed towards the phone shack, housed in the post office. The back of our house faced the phone shack. The front of the house faced the ocean. Neither entrance brought me any closer to the people here. We were centrally located, saw people in passing often, and were on the perfect visiting path. However, the O'Brennans being located farther down the road at the school seemed to allow as much or as little visitation as they wanted. They had the option of visitors or to turn off their lights and not answer the door, basking in their privacy. We were in the thick of things living in the center of town plus having to balance being newlyweds as a racially integrated couple and outsiders in an indigenous village. Most of the village didn't have or want interactions with me, particularly the women, except for an occasional hello. Yet I often felt watched like the day we first arrived. The men were a bit friendlier, sometimes stopping for a quick passing conversation like, "How you like living in Village … House good, eh?"

I seldom saw Meddy except walking in the distance or riding his four-wheeler. He lived up on the hill in one of the newer houses and was the president of the tribal council. Other than those distant sightings and Anna's annoyed reactions to things he did or didn't do, to me he was mostly a ghost that moved things and sent messages through others about dos and don'ts that affected our lives.

At the phone shack I ran into Meddy. He was walking, headed in the same general direction I was going. Except he was holding a leash and what could only be described as a horse on the end of it. Now I had grown up with dogs my entire life, and the biggest dog I had ever seen was a Great Dane, but this was a moose.

"Wow! Big dog. What is that?" I asked, trying to keep my distance and appear unafraid.

"Wolfhound … your dog, not so big now!"

"Nope," I said, trying to get over to the phone shack quickly to avoid a prolonged interaction. He was the one person in the village I didn't want to really get to know.

"I hear your dog has some wolf in him?"

"Yes, part Lab, shepherd, and wolf I was told."

"My dog can kill wolves. I don't worry about animals up at my place tearing up trash, messing with my cats anymore." He looked at me straight with a slight smile. Meddy, as big of a man that he was, began to struggle to hold the reins of this moose he was strolling with through town. Watching him, I slowed my pace, trying to determine as to whether I should speed up and make it to the porch of the phone shack, or slow down so he could get past me with that beast. So, I just stood there watching Meddy strain to hold the animal when it picked up its pace and prayed its interest was not in my direction. The inadequate leash Meddy used was meant for a dog three times smaller, and if it snapped, I wasn't sure if I could make it inside before it would reach me, if I became its intent. That was not to say that the dog would be vicious, but only a fool would take bets on that, especially with what I knew about the owner. He was mean, a bully, people seemed afraid of him, and he loved killing and starving, weak, unwanted dogs.

"Have a good day," I said and watched him continue down the road with that monster, on patrol.

The feud between my family and the neighbor next door began long before what became known as the shootout. The adults' first major battle was fought over a bush! I was about ten when what we called "The Bush War" started. It was a beautiful bush with white flowers bunched together, making one large round ball of flowers that peppered the whole bush along with green spade-shaped leaves. We were allowed to smell the white flowers when they bloomed along with the lilac, peonies, tea roses, and everything else Mom planted. But "we bet' not pick 'em" because that was for Mom to do. I asked her one day the name of those white flowers, and she smiled thoughtfully and said, "Call it, snow-on-the-mountain." She looked away with her arms folded tight and a faint smile across her face. I decided that either this was a name Mom made up or it was a name given to the bush by the old folk. Either way, that was Mom's bush and she knew it and every plant out there like the palm of her hand.

Snow-on-the-mountain sat right on the property line in the front yard, and when Mom had the chain link fence put in, the fence had to go through the bush. Most of the bush grew on our side, so when the fence people said that they had to trim some of Mom's bush to install the fence, we came that close to not getting the fence at all. She watched them shear one side of her bush and pain seemed to pass through her, but the fence was installed. The metal hatch links pressed against the wound of the bush like a bandage until it healed and grew past the poultice fence. Snow-on-the-mountain grew back beautifully and you couldn't tell it was ever cut. So, when the feud started, the neighbors were quick to cut the bush flat again on their side, right up to the fence, and that made Mom mad and the bush look terrible.

I could tell right off that Mom was not fond of Mr. George's new wife. Mom was friendly enough to neighbors and always extended a proper Southern welcome with a genuine willingness to help, but something went wrong in the moments they first spoke. It might have been the tone of the woman's voice, a lack of sincerity, or that Mom believed that she was stuck up. I didn't mind that because the new wife had two girls, one my age and the other my sister's age. She was different from Mom in almost every way. She was tall, thinner, a little younger, modern, and spoke with an office kind of proper voice that Mom practiced out loud to herself while cursing the woman out at the same time. They both were light-skinned, but my grandmother had longer hair, and I was always told this was a woman's crown of glory.

Arguments broke out over all kinds of things: Mr. George's stepdaughters tromping down our grass or being too loud and disrespectful when on their porch. When they got the second dog, things went to a whole 'nother level. They already had a small, yapping cocker spaniel before he got the Great Dane. When he decided to get the dog, it seemed right after my step-grandfather decided he needed a hunting dog. We had two female shepherds before my step-grandfather decided he would get his own dog. Now we had three dogs, and my step-grandfather's big, red male Lab mix named Rusty would dominate our yard and female dogs just like our step-grandfather did us. Like everything that my step-grandfather owned, we were not allowed to touch or play with it. My grandmother was a country girl and loved things that grew. She had a balanced attitude about animals, and cruelty to them was a big no-no in her book. My step-grandfather decided to add gunpowder to Rusty's food to make him tough, causing a big fight between Mom and him. She swore she was going to turn him in if he kept it up. "What's wrong with you, man, you gonna tear the dog's stomach up … and kill 'em. Tryin' ta make him mean … you ole fool? *Tryin' ta make him mean.* You'll make him mean alright, dead mean."

I think Mr. George, a dark short, muscular man that never smiled, had the same ideas for his Great Dane. I watched their girls play with the dog, and he seemed like a big playful horse. They threw balls and sticks. The Great Dane's favorite was tossing rocks in the air like a ball, while its sidekick, the cocker spaniel, ran yapping under its stilt legs. My grandmother warned us to stay away from their dog. I thought it was just her not wanting us to have fun or because of their feud until one day I witnessed why.

It was summer, late morning, when I heard yelling and a frenzy of dog barks from our yard and in the front of the house. These sounds were not new coming from next door or our yard, but we were expected to control the barking of our dogs by keeping them in the basement when things got too noisy. If their dogs slipped out the door when bringing in groceries or taking out trash, it could start a neighborhood symphony, especially if there was a passing stray. The orchestra was in session, and I assumed it was because their dogs slipped out since the racket was so loud.

This time it was different. The screams were blood-curdling. I ran to the front porch, calling my sisters as I headed towards the noise. Looking from the perch of our porch, the Great Dane had a small dog, the kind that wore bows in their hair and their feet moved fast across the ground like a centipede. It was clinched in the monster's mouth. The woman that owned the dog stood in the street screaming. We all were screaming, a high-pitched ringing sound that numbed your ears. I watched the thin leather leash still attached to the little dog whip around in the air like a streamer. The little dog in its mouth made no more sound, and the Great Dane trotted around with it for a moment before dropping it. There was dead silence for a minute, then the cocker spaniel that led the charge was dragged into the house. Everyone slowly moved towards the Great Dane and the small dog lying on the sidewalk; the air ignited with energy. The little dog got up and attempted to find safety in its owner. One of the girls grabbed the collar of the Great Dane, and almost at the same moment, the Great Dane ripped from her. It snatched the little dog up again by the neck, shaking and whipping it around violently, then stepped on its little body. The Great Dane pulled and split the little dog before carrying it off.

I don't remember seeing the Great Dane after that and don't know what happened to it. The events of that day changed how I saw animals and how I saw the people that had those animals. Not long after that day, a fight between my grandmother, step-grandfather, Mr. George, and his wife started over the barking of our dogs. The adults stood in their yards with the fence between them, snarling and snapping at each other about everything from bushes, to rude disrespectful kids, to barking dogs. We were not allowed to be outside in the middle of an adult argument, so when the neighbor's girls started adding their two cents, I knew that would not sit well with my grandmother. She believed that children should be seen, not heard, and never get into grown folk business. Mom came into the house fuming. "That hussy think she can run somethin' over here and can't even control the mouths of them little nasty girls of hers … tryin' ta tell me what I can do and not do in my yard … just evil, what kind of people just butcher somethin' that make their raggedy yard look better … ain't gotta a flower or nothin' growing in their yard, but want ta kill what's over here … wish I had of grown some real snow-on-the-mountain, that would have fixed they behind."

Mom ranted on while we were instructed to prepare dinner. When my sister went to put the dogs in because of the barking, Mom said, "No, leave 'em out there. They can bark all night long as far as I'm concerned … Think they can boo-up in my face and tell me what ta do, they got another thang comin'," Mom said, sitting in her chair simmering.

My siblings and I were sitting at the kitchen table, having our dinner when I got up to get water from the icebox. I was holding the glass water pitcher in my hand carefully and pushing the icebox door closed with my back when I noticed the dogs had stopped barking. There was a small window next to where the icebox sat. It opened to the small screened-in back porch where we sat and peeled bushel baskets of fruit for preserves or scaled fish almost every summer. I held the pitcher close to my center and could feel the cold water, and its movement sloshed back and forth while I peeked over the tiny window frame. I looked for the dogs in the blackness when I heard a whistling sound and a *tink, tink* sound like pebbles hitting glass or the metal siding of our house. The dogs must have gone to the basement to lie down, I thought. I listened longer for the sound when my grandmother with a rage of a bull ran into the kitchen and eyes locked on me.

"Get away from the window, get away now," she said, snatching the pitcher from me and waving at us all to get up and go into the back rooms. She was screaming at my step-grandfather, explaining indirectly what was happening all at once. "Have you lost your mind man! … You fools' shooting at the porch … I'm callin' the police if you don't stop it. You hear me? You can kill one of these kids …"

I found out that both men had been drinking and an argument started when Mr. George threatened to shoot our dogs if we didn't make them stop barking. All I could think was that Mom wouldn't let us lock them in the basement, and he wanted to kill them. So, Mr. George started shooting at our back porch, trying to hit the dogs, and my step-grandfather went upstairs and started shooting back at him. The poison that I saw between our families never ended until his new wife and her girls left Mr. George and didn't come back. His house was set on fire some years later by someone looking for revenge. He escaped with his life thanks to my brother-in-law breaking down the door and getting him out. I was fourteen then, and the house, well, it burned to the ground.

Chapter Fifteen

Anna was spending more time with me. We used that time for crocheting projects, sharing recipes, and indulging in harmless gossip. The Thanksgiving holiday was right around the corner, and I was grateful for the time I was able to have with her. She helped fulfill that need for family coming into the holiday season, along with Seth and Rawsh. The days were significantly darker to the tune of about six to seven hours of light a day, and the need for companionship was becoming crucial in fighting cabin fever. However, I think Anna's reasons for spending so much time with me lately went beyond her general kindness and desire to teach me crocheting. The holidays themselves brought an unwanted side effect of drinking and partying, and often some form of tragedy that went along with it. Some of the villagers didn't need any reason to party. The holidays, however, gave the entire village an excuse to let alcohol flow like a stream, and that was a painful reality for Anna.

Anna and her husband Haze were respected elders in the community. Haze was on the village council and Anna was a healthcare provider. She worked with the visiting doctor when he came to the village to do routine healthcare checks. The role of the regular healthcare provider carried a lot of responsibility. It would be difficult under normal circumstances to do this job. Having the responsibility for every man, woman, and child with the added complication of them being related to you in some kind of way seemed a very heavy mantle.

When the doctor came to do his healthcare visit, she assisted him. She was the voice that helped ensure that every child had their shots and all the elderly got their high blood pressure and cholesterol checked along with arthritis, insulin, and any other medication they needed. All emergencies in the village and transports to a hospital in town were arranged by Anna. She desired and bore the responsibility to educate her people on the effects of fetal alcohol syndrome and how to care for their babies. Sometimes I could tell it was all too much for Anna. The look on her face told a thousand stories. She also expressed some of those thoughts.

Village life was not only isolated, but insulated from the outside world as little and as much as they wanted it to be. I began to understand that the decision of who came in or went out, including drugs, alcohol, and opinions, would be in their control. That idea blew me away. It was a power my community didn't possess, but I pondered the thought a minute; *But could we?* I knew it was okay for me to see and listen to the village problems, but like my grandmother's adage, "I can talk about them, but you bet' not." At the end of the day, I was an outsider and could share no opinion. However, being an outsider and having an elder spend so much time with me socially wasn't winning me any popularity contest. Anna was a proud woman who loved her people, but was frustrated with alcoholic deaths and destruction, and I completely understood that from my own experiences. By just doing ordinary things like having tea, crocheting, or sharing stories, we relieved some of the pressure we felt.

Anna and Haze only had one child, a son in either Valdez or Cordova. I seldom saw Anna socializing. I believed it was because tea sometimes quickly turned into happy hour or a drunken domestic fight. However, she could be seen coming to my house or me going to her home regularly, and this created social tension with some of the women. I think it might have given the impression that she preferred my company over theirs. I knew that wasn't true.

There was this feeling when we spent time together that there was a barrier between us, however small. Of course, there was a large age difference between us. That might have explained it, but I'd been around older people my whole life, and it didn't feel like that was the problem. This veiled barrier existed despite how much we liked each other's company and shared so many things in common. It never left, so I accepted it. There were times I did wonder if I were being used by Anna, but not in a malicious way, maybe more passive-aggressively. So, she could use me to punish them, for not changing their ways, the way a teacher or parent points out the good behavior of a child to another saying, "See, why can't you be like them?" I hoped that the women would believe that Anna was just being nice to the Cheechako to avoid resentment. Yet with every passing social encounter, I began to feel the reality of the social discourse in the village. One day Anna and I stopped to talk on the road as her niece and another woman walked by.

"It wet … today, ah," the woman in her late thirties said in Anna's and my general direction with a slight smile on her round moon face. She never made eye contact as she walked towards us. "When you come visit, Aunty, haven't had visit from you in a long time. Have tea? Come see *piipiq* (baby) Sister miss you too … ah." Her politeness ended with a rhetorical statement, "Lot holiday parties, Ms. Schwartz Bring your husband!"

The women snickered with a glance towards each other but stopped when they turned back towards Anna. One of the other women cut the uncomfortable air. "Yeah! Come visit … 'lot of food …'" I wanted to go, hang out, listen to music, eat, drink, and dance like any other twenty-two-year-old, but I couldn't risk it. Getting a reputation for being a partier could cost Seth and me this job, or even worse being in Alaska.

Though their culture was less formal and people could and did just show up at one another's homes without an invitation, I didn't feel comfortable doing it. Seeing myself arriving at a stranger's door and saying, "Hey, just stopped to hang out, listen to some music … I'm here to see who's cookin' bear or moose meat and grab a beer." Plus, it didn't feel like a real invite with all the smirking and snickering going on.

Anna turned and said, "Have to go! Mrs. Schwartz, come by later, I have something for you, bring your blanket you working on, eh!" For Anna,

I think those projects gave legitimacy to tea and talks peppered with gossiping about teens or stupid drunken behavior that called her out of bed in the middle of the night. I could hear the pain in her voice when she talked about *the drink* and how it was maiming and killing her people. But these were her people, her family. Her husband Haze seldom said anything except to smile and greet me when I came to visit. He would just sit in his chair while we kibitzed among ourselves until it was time for her to tend to the needs of her husband or he'd go out for a brief time.

Watching them took me back to my great-grandparents. A place far off and distant in my memory as a young child, but I remember them. They had a small wood-frame house, not unlike Anna and Haze. I can see their home, neat and orderly with everything in its place. Every fragile whatnot and linen doily they stewarded for years was as pristine as its beginning.

My memory of my great-grandfather found him always in his chair, not unlike how I would find Haze. Little-bitty Grandpa, we all called him, would be dressed in a pale-colored, buttoned-up, short-sleeved shirt, dark pants, and suspenders. His black eyes, framed by his pale fair skin drooping over his once chiseled features, always stared straight ahead. My great-grandmother and great-aunt seemed to be regularly busy with the everyday needs of the house. I wondered what was behind that easy smile of Little-bitty Grandpa's face that appeared out of nowhere occasionally. Maybe there was nothing more to it than the smile of a senile old man or a kind of resignation that all men succumb to when there's no more laboring for them, no more women to beat or to womanize, and no more liquor to share among his fellow male kind. Haze sat quietly too, with a look of contentment or a look I was not yet trained to understand. Whatever the look, I knew we were all just doing what we could to get by.

I'd learned several new crochet stitches and even began to master knitting, which until that point had been a debacle. Despite myself, learning these two homemaker's arts I produced two and a half throws from Anna's tutorial. Anna had a gentle speech, sarcastic, but in the way that Alaskan Native people poked humorously at your shortcomings. Their sarcasm never seemed harsh or mean-spirited like what I'd experienced with white folks' sarcastic comments aimed at me.

"You learn that stitch good, you did the ho' blanket in it, eh? What do you call that stitch?" she said shyly, smiling.

I smiled with some trepidation and said, "It's the stitch you taught me the other day."

She laughed hard. "That's not my stitch, your stitch, eh. Take ho' thing out, I'll show you again. Don't say I teach you that, eh."

We laughed while I unraveled hours of my work.

"Anna, could you show me how to salt fish? I got a lot of salmon when the boat came in."

"You want salt fish, eh, what for?"

"My husband Seth likes pickled herring and I want to make some with salmon."

"You take fish and some rock salt ..." she began telling of the process, and before she finished, she could read in my face what I had not spoken in words. "I'll show you tomorrow," she said. I smiled and headed home.

We stood straight and tall, my siblings and I. Four brown, willowy saplings with one foot in the sitting room and the other stepping into the dining area, a formal dining room with a table that stretched across to the other side. The table was draped in an off-white linen tablecloth that floated satiny stitched roses and leaves, all buttery and pouring over the sides. The table looked as if it was a birthday cake with candles in the center and silver spoons nestled in each napkin placed to make a setting for six. Red and green poinsettia accompanied the candles to complete the Christmas centerpiece. Small delicate plates with a Christmas tree scene and diamond cut glass bowls trimmed in what I imagined was real gold were at all six place settings. Mrs. Lockhart had gotten the notion that she would give us kids a Christmas gift of ice cream at her high-rise luxury apartment. I guessed we wouldn't receive our usual token gift of cookies, coloring books, and old clothes cleared out of some attic. She would be too busy getting ready to leave for some beautiful place in Europe or

China to bother with finding gifts for her help's grandchildren. I didn't understand their relationship, she and my grandmother. My grandmother was always referring to Mrs. Lockhart as her second mother, but I don't think mothers and daughters act like they did: "Mary, I need you here to serve me and the ladies … Mary, I want the cupboards all cleared out … Mary, I need you to stay late. Mr. Lockhart has a few colleagues coming tonight," and always my grandmother had a, "Yes, ma'am," as her answer.

We sat waiting for the big event to take place and to be called to the table. I don't remember asking, but at some point, I was given permission to get up and look out the big picture window. The table was beautiful and promising, but being up so high and looking out from Mrs. Lockhart's high-rise apartment on the exclusive, old money Country Club Plaza was a once-in-a-lifetime moment. I was seven, and this was the highest I'd ever been. If I'd thought about my issue of motion sickness and height sensitivity, I wouldn't have looked out. My fear of heights was discovered early in my life when I used to try and follow my brother climbing trees or whenever I went swinging. Looking out the window, I could feel that uneasiness you get from being up high. Your feet feel like they're trying to balance on clouds and you can feel yourself swaying side to side. I was scared and cried out to my grandmother. She immediately reprimanded me in her low public voice and told me to sit down.

The loud whispers of oohs and aahs from my siblings drew me back to the window. What I saw made me forget that I might fall and crash into the tiny, barely visible gray sidewalk below. Instead, for those moments at the window, I was flying. The tops of trees were white with lights that twinkled like snow. Red, blue, green, and yellow lights trimmed the shops and buildings like winter flowers glinting in the sunshine. The cars and people moved quickly on the snowy roads and walkways, and I hovered above and traveled with them without attention or care. A giant Christmas tree flamed in colors. Wreaths and French horns dangled on light posts. I could see far off in the distance, outside of this magic plaza place. There were houses with Christmas lights, cars stopping and going, and streetlights flickering off and on. It was a fortressed maze that circled the Plaza. I looked past all of this into dark lands, and I wondered where our house was.

"Come and sit down," my grandmother said, and she gave us a look to be quiet and behave in the way we were trained. She pointed to where we were each to sit, and she stood by the table like a sculpture when Mrs. Lockhart entered and sat at the head of the table. I stared at my grandmother as she bent slightly towards the thin white woman with white hair and asked if she should serve now. The white-haired woman answered and called my grandmother by her other name, the one that's written somewhere on important papers, but was never said aloud. It was my grandmother's middle name, Mary, like Jesus's mother or the name Catholic people gave to their children. But it was not my grandmother's familiar name that everyone we knew called her, the same name shared by my father's eldest daughter.

All of it made me go crazy in my head; seeing my grandmother serving, remembering being sick and her leaving me and knowing my grandmother loved this white woman like a mother. It made me forget how I was supposed to act in front of white folks and the punishment that would surely come from forgetting my place. But that's what crazy looks like. Whatever was making me go against the norm I couldn't keep it from coming out, no matter what the consequences.

She began asking the typical adult standard questions about school: how we liked it, what were our favorite subjects, and how were our grades. That is when I had a fit of the crazies. It happened somewhere between the questions, my grandmother serving us ice cream and cookies, and my siblings saying, "Yes, ma'am," and "No, ma'am."

"LaVern, you haven't said how you're doing in school. Do you like your school?" She spoke softly and politely and then it happened.

"Yes."

That was it. The dam was bursting. Three little letters and I could feel my grandmother's strong farm hands reach into my little throat, and with just her thumb and forefinger pinch close my larynx. She did this mostly with her eyes and the raising out of her seat she had finally taken at the table to the left of Mrs. Lockhart.

"It's okay, Mary."

She did it again, called her Mary! But my grandmother sat back, and we continued to eat vanilla ice cream and canister Dutch butter cookies.

I knew them to be Dutch butter cookies because they showed up around this time at home almost every year. We would have them instead of the ones my grandmother made from scratch using the little tin cookie press for green, red, and white butter cookies. Mrs. Lockhart gently wiped her hands free of crumbs on her napkin, sat up straight, perfect, and continued her round of questioning disguised as a conversation with an even and soft voice while my grandmother cleared the table.

"Has your school gone on holiday yet?"

"No, ma'am, not until next week," one of my sisters answered.

"I'm sure you can't wait."

"Yes, ma'am."

They all responded with their polite ma'ams. I said nothing …

"How about you, LaVern? Aren't you excited about Christmas break?"

My sisters and brother all stared at me with big eyes and silence. I don't know why I did it. I couldn't make myself not do it. It wasn't like she did something mean to me like spit on me or say I was ugly. It just didn't feel right, this whole situation. I was mad deep inside and wasn't allowed to say that ever. I wasn't allowed feelings about what others said or could do to you, and now the feelings chose to slip out.

"Yes, I guess I am."

I said it, and there was nothing anyone could do. No! No, *ma'aming from me*. It's a strange feeling when you have what you thought was a victory, but when it's over and you walk away, it doesn't feel much like a victory at all. My grandmother had finished clearing and cleaning, and our coats were on to leave. We said thank you and how much we enjoyed ourselves.

I looked back at the window and saw none of the lights, buildings, or people, only the dark sky from where I stood. I didn't want to leave that view from the window, and I wished I hadn't gone crazy. I was myself again, and I was afraid to leave because I knew what was going to happen. The ice cream and cookies made me feel sick. I never saw that view again or Mrs. Lockhart.

She did not send cookies home that year, but on her return from a trip to China that Christmas, she sent satin pajamas and Chinese slippers for my brother, sisters, and me. I wore them until they had holes and my toes could no longer stretch out. One day I stuffed the toes of the shoes with cardboard, tied them with string to my feet, and forced myself up on the tips of my toes like a ballerina. I endured the pain. These things I did quietly in the corner of my room released only a flicker of the dream living inside me. I lived in a place where dreams belonged to thieves.

My grandmother told me, "Don't tell people what your dreams are because they'll steal them and you'll never see'em realized, but if you keep 'em quiet inside yourself, you'll never see'em grow either." I asked her if she ever had a dream and she told me she wanted to be a nurse. As soon as she answered, I realized she'd said her dream out loud and a thief would come and steal it. I gasped, holding my mouth.

She looked at me and said, "Go on out ta play if you finish doin' your chores, so I can get my work done. This food won't cook itself, and you'll be up in my face sayin' you're hungry."

I was walking out when I heard her talking to herself in that way she'd always did when something troubled her. "Always something needin' me ta feed 'em. If it ain't animals, it's people lookin' at me hungry … My God, my God, what I could have done!"

Thanksgiving was here, and Seth and I were to spend a quiet time with each other enjoying a meal of duck provided by a local hunter. There was always a variety of food being harvested from nature here in the village, and the people shared even with those that were considered outsiders. The table was set with homemade bread, cranberry sauce made from bog cranberries I'd gathered, stuffing made from saved stale bread the way Mom taught me, mashed potatoes, canned peas, and chicken gravy. The centerpiece was two small orange-glazed wild ducks. Seth's favorite thing in the whole world to eat was mandarin duck, and here, placed before him, was my gift of love. We sat down and began to serve ourselves, fluffy mounds of whipped buttery potatoes, sage, onion, and celery stuffing, both drenched in gravy, peas, cranberry sauce for me, and homemade jam for Seth. I carved the duck, the skin popped and cracked crisp, and the dark meat sweated with moisture.

I blessed the table and spoke of thankfulness. We started to smile at each other from ear to ear as if we just pulled off some great scheme or escaped a near-death experience. It was pure salivating anticipation and the gratitude for familiar pleasure. Together we lifted our knives and forks, cut into the duck's dark meat, and smiled one last time before devouring the first bite. I could taste the sweet tangy orange sauce swell the taste buds on the tip of my tongue, and almost immediately and simultaneously, I could hear Seth cry out as my mouth erupted with a taste my brain could not correlate and confirm between my eyes, taste buds, and knowledge of what mandarin duck was supposed to be.

"Ughhh! What is that!" Seth said, no longer smiling. I grabbed my napkin, gagging, and spit the duck out.

"Eeeew, I think it's spoiled," I said sniffing the meat on my plate. It smelled delicious, orangey, and inviting. Seth took another taste, this time detective-like and all senses on alert, and I instead dabbed my finger in the sweat of the meat. Almost synchronized, we said, "Fish!"

"Oh man, these ducks feed off of fish, not grain like the domestic kind we're used to." The teacher in Seth lit up. I couldn't process any of it except my meal was ruined. Thanksgiving that year ended up being just sides and no fowl at all.

I spent the rest of my time preparing for Christmas. Anna instructed me on salting some of the salmon. This came to about five or six silver salmon I filleted and salted or steaked and froze. Cleaning and cutting up the fish was most of the work. The rest was pretty simple. I got a clean five-gallon bucket and sprinkled the bottom with rock salt. I then layered the filleted salmon with skin side down against the salt. All pin bones had been removed and the fish was air drying in the refrigerator overnight for twenty-four hours. I added a second layer of fish to the bucket, flesh side to flesh side, always salting in between each layer of fish, keeping flesh to flesh and skin to skin until I filled the bucket. I had to leave about four or five inches at the top of the bucket for a plate to be used as a press along with a large beach rock. As it cured, the salt leached the water out of the fish and preserved it.

Once the fish was cured, I could start my next gift of love to my husband, and this time I was hoping for success. I knew how much he loved pickled herring, and Anna told me that pickled salmon was much better. So, with a basic pickling recipe from Anna, I began the process of making pickled salmon for my Jewish husband, taught to me by a sixty-something-year-old Alutiiq woman in Tatitlek, an Alaskan village. Even more fun was that I made bagels and chopped liver to boot, as my grandmother would say. We had a regular New York deli over the Christmas holiday. Seth had turned me on to pickled herring, and it was okay but I was not a big fan. I tasted my pickled salmon. I was now a fan of pickled fish, hoping he would like it the same.

Seth found us a Charlie Brown Christmas tree, and we decorated it with handmade ornaments. Strung cranberries, popcorn, and paper cutouts were used to adorn the house and tree. Christmas was my favorite holiday, and I wanted my first Alaskan Christmas with Seth to be as memorable as how I saw it in my childhood. That was likely my first mistake.

Seth was an ambivalent Jew, not religious and most of the time he would shirk off any real acknowledgment of his family's faith, but a holiday like Christmas would come around and he would say, "Hey, I'm a Jew, we don't celebrate Christmas, that's your guys' thing." I was starting to think his Jewish-ness got pulled out for convenience only. Though he did help me with making snowflake cutouts and some minor decorating, beyond that he was not inter-ested and had a somewhat "humbug" attitude, with the exception of food.

I was able to get small gifts of jam sent to my grandmother and a few other family members early enough to beat the mail calamity. Making a phone call around the holidays with one phone was a nightmare. It got particularly backed up not just from the grandmothers calling grandkids and children, but the endless ordering of supplies with an emphasis on booze. Bush planes rolled in like taxi trips to the liquor store in the hood, but these folks weren't playin'. I'm talking cases of alcohol coming off those planes, not just a fifth. When the invite came from Anna and O'Brennan's wife to celebrate Russian Christmas, my mood shifted. Russian Christmas fell on the day after my birthday, January seventh, and they celebrated for several days.

I was getting depressed and homesick. I missed the smells from home, my dad spending the day with us, Mom putting up the gold drapes, and the mixer sitting out on the counter to make a cake. I missed home even if it wouldn't be the same way I remembered it as a child. My sisters and brother stopped coming home after they got married and left. It stopped being the same when she put Mr. Allen, my step-grandfather out of the house when I was thirteen, even though that was worth it.

My best memories of Christmas were from only a couple of Christmases we had growing up, and I'd been trying to have Christmas like that ever since. For Seth and I, our first Christmas as a married couple was the exchange of handmade gifts. I gave him a crocheted scarf and pickled salmon, and Seth wrote me a love song. He plunked it out on his guitar for me, and it was beautiful. My first Alaskan Christmas was not like the Christmas of my past, but it had the promise to maybe be better.

16

Chapter Sixteen

I headed down the road from my house. The sound of my boots crunching on the packed three-wheeler snow numbed my ears to everything else around me. The temperature was about fourteen to fifteen degrees Fahrenheit, and my breath bellowed a cloud of exhaust up and out of my mouth as I continued briskly. I cupped my hands and tried to catch the warm internal steam that escaped my body. I sniffed the trapped vapor quickly, trying to check my breath for bad smells. The smelling of my breath seemed ridiculous when faced with the fact that I was about to be completely naked in front of a bunch of women I didn't know. I had been invited to a women's sweat, and with no reference except for some shadowy '60s television Western of Indian people having a sweat in teepees for the purpose of furthering the story of some white man, I had no idea what to think. I also thought about some of those high-life city movies where the white characters, wrapped in huge white towels after a steamy spa bath, sashayed around.

"Caw caw … caw caw caw." The sound bellowed from a tree behind the houses. One of the ravens landed near the road, speaking to me with his cawing, gurgling, throaty voice from the shadows of a broken house just off the road.

I jumped at the sound and spoke, "What do you want? Scaring the hell out of me … go away, I'm already late." The short distance to Ms. Elaine's sweat house didn't minimize the bombarding thoughts running through my mind. She was nice to me whenever I saw her. She worked at the school cleaning up, and we talked on occasion about cleaning and how she grew up in the village and where I grew up. She talked a little about the BIA, which stood for Bureau of Indian Affairs, schools, and the missionaries that taught her.

"They hit you lots then," she recalled. "They were mean to us kids." I could see the deep thought in her face when talking about back then. "Now school's different, they can do 'lot more than when we had school." She was an elder to me, around the same age as Anna, and I think shared more of the same traditional beliefs as well. She didn't like all the alcohol and felt the young people were more disrespectful. She said, "We were kid', we showed respec' to elders, they show us how to live, knew our ways." For me, it was the twenty-something-year-olds that looked at me sideways and suspiciously.

My mind twisted with every step I made closer to the sweat. I could hear the dark wings of the ravens and their caws following me. "I should've got a swimsuit?" I blurted out and continued the conversation in my head, and sometimes out loud. *Huh! Oh, man! Why didn't I think of that, damn it … that's dumb, they wouldn't wear swimsuits, right? Maybe they want to see if I got three boobs or something … What if this is their plan to get rid of me? Feed me to a bear than one of them'll take and marry my husband? Just go home already … What the hell do I talk about naked anyway? Alright, already! This is stupid …*

I arrived in front of the house and was about to turn around to leave when someone came out. Busted! I couldn't just leave now, they saw me. "You in time, they just go in. Right there …" She pointed. "You go in there … through the back. There's a place to undress then go in the sweat," the woman said. I opened a plywood-type door attached to a plywood fence, partially obscuring the yard and the back of the house. There was a small A-frame building to the left of me. The smell of wood burning floated back from the smokestack and singed my nose.

I knocked on the door, and a partially naked woman opened. "You don't have to knock, come in, no men around." They laughed shyly and smiled. "We run them off … You like sweat, bathe, ah? … We like it hot, first one we do this year now it's cold … Put your clothes there then come in quick."

They disappeared through another door while I took off my clothes, slowllly piece by piece, and hung them on the pegs made from birch tree limbs. This small outer room had wooden benches with space to slide your boots on plywood flooring. A naked light bulb hung above my head and offered no help with warmth. The walls and door were the only protection from freezing to death in the unheated changing room, and I could hear the wind whistle at me through the seams. The racing thoughts stopped as my nakedness was exposed to the frigid air. I now was ripping off my clothes and busted through the door the woman disappeared through minutes ago. The woodstove heat rushed to me and bathed my skin in dried stifling air that burned and pricked my cold flesh. Along my back, the cold air bit at my bare behind. Both the wood heat and cold air quickly swirled together and formed a mist that briefly blinded and disoriented me in the dark room.

"Close the door! The door! Ah! let all the heat out," voices yelled at me from somewhere in front and to the right of me. I closed the door and stood there a minute, trying to let my eyes adjust in the hot dark room where the only light came from the thin gaps in the door and frame and the glow that escaped from the old wood stove. Ms. Elaine's voice found me in the dark and called me to sit near her. I placed my towel on the bench and sat down next to her and the three other women that chatted softly to each other.

"Glad you come. Ah, heat good when it's cold like this," she said as my eyes had just begun to clear and I could see her. She was a tall woman, taller than me, about five foot nine, solid and wide. She wore her salt and pepper hair short and pinned back out of her face on one side. Her light sun-rich skin absorbed the orange glow of the fire and now seemed to illuminate the room more.

"You have these a lot? Have sweats I mean?" I asked.

"Not like we used to … We used to do this lots. I think maybe work too much now!" They all laughed.

Ms. Elaine continued, "You work at the school all the time now, ah?"

"No, I'm just helpin' out with the play the kids are doing. My husband asked me if I would help with the school's Christmas play, *Scrooge*."

"My son is one of the ghosts. Gee! He says his lines every day to me."

"My daughter too, I know all her parts, I should be in the play." They all laughed, and someone asked me what they had me doing with the kids.

"I'm helping them with set design. I'm drawing the background, and they are painting. Some of the kids help draw too."

"My son Lewis is a good drawer. He draws all the time."

"Lewis is your son? He is a great drawer and nice kid. He's helped me a lot. The kids that don't want to be in the play are learning other jobs like lighting, set design, and costume design. So, I've been helping with some of that too."

"He like doing the art parts, he tell me he learning lots."

"That's good, I'm glad."

Ms. Elaine got up and put more wood on the fire. This was the third time since I'd sat down.

"Elaine, it's getting nice and hot now, ah … feels good!" one of the women commented. "Yeah! Sweat out everything, ah … too much food … too much drink … sickness … husbands! Everything come out in the sweat." We all burst into laughter and the list kept getting longer for a few minutes. Ms. Elaine talked about how the elders sweat all the time to keep sickness away and to balance everything.

"We need this sweat, so we don't get sick." A barrel of water sat in the corner, Ms. Elaine dipped a pot in it and rinsed her body of the salty sweat and impurities she said came out of the body.

"Sweat help' you clear your mind too, and let' you see clearer." She dipped again and handed it to the rest of us to do the same. She pointed to small branches of cedar and whipped her body gently with them.

My pores opened, and I washed away the salty heaviness and began to feel lighter. Afterward, she splashed water onto large round stones she had been pulling from the wood stove and replaced those that had cooled several times back in. This made layers of thicker and thicker air that formed a heavy gray mist. I listened to the women's voices that now seemed farther away, like a dream trying to reach me. Ms. Elaine spoke about things I couldn't seem to comprehend, stories of animals, something about a bear and people and words in Aleut, or maybe I heard a song. The muffled sound of wings covered my ears like the ravens that ruffled feathers in the trees coming over here.

I sat quietly now, even the inside of my mind was now still, not caring whether I was participating in the conversation or in what they were saying or thinking. Somewhere between the steam, darkness, and sitting on the bench, watching the flicker of orange and yellow light through the gray haze, there became nothing but silence and peace. The voices became heat, and I was water, and we both rose as vapor. I stopped processing anything, I felt nothing and thought nothing. It seemed like hours but was likely minutes. Ms. Elaine finally spoke in a way that carried me back to my body.

"Russian Christmas coming, you have to come with us and take the star to the houses and sing Christmas Eve."

"When does that start?" I managed to say.

"January sixth and Russian Christmas is the seventh."

"Oh! My birthday is January sixth!"

"Your birthday, ah! Special blessings born that time. Holy day during advent, you know! It's the night that the star was seen by the three kings. Some Catholics celebrate Epiphany on your birthday the sixth, some the seventh. The Feast of the Three Kings. You have lot responsibility born on that birthday, my niece too, she born on that date too!" I could feel the mist taking me over again. "You might be getting too hot, ah! You should go out. When there's snow in wintertime, we like to go out and rub it all over and cool off, then come back in." *I'm not used to so much heat, maybe?* I thought, but my ancestors come from the hottest continent on earth. I can take the heat.

"We can sweat long time." They all laughed in a private way to themselves. "Maybe you should go out."

Someone said, "Put more wood on." I stood up and my legs wobbled under the weight of my small frame. I was overcooked, colorless vegetables.

"Ms. Elaine, I think I better go home now. Thank you for inviting me, thank you ladies. I'll see you at the school, Ms. Elaine?" I heard the words come from my mouth, but my focus was on willing my body to move. I didn't think I would make it to the door, but I followed the light that came from the naked light bulb, showing me the way out through the small crack in the door. I heard the voices of the women sending me off with good-byes and the sound of wood being added to the woodstove. I embraced the cold with gratitude, then the cold air slapped me and brought me back fully into my body. I pulled a gift of jam from my jacket pocket and left it on the bench for Ms. Elaine. This was the custom my grandmother taught me, to always come bearing a gift, and O'Brennan's wife explained this was expected amongst the people here too.

There were just a few days before the Christmas play *Scrooge* would be performed for the whole village, and I was recruited by my husband to do backdrops. Yet, one by one, I was losing participants after school whose jobs were to help me finish. Even the most talented artist of the group, Lewis, fell prey to the influences of the other teens, along with the distractions from the partying adults. A few of the kids, like Lewis and his immediate family, didn't drink. Lewis, a sweet boy of fourteen, was a wonderful illustrator, and I understood was quite the hunter as well, but he was said not to be the cleverest academically in the bunch. Depending on what cultural lens you were looking from, his hunting abilities would have been the stuff of genius. He wore pressed button-ups and khaki pants most of the time I saw him. His hair was cut neatly in a high and tight style, and his black-framed glasses made him look like someone out of the '50s. However, the greatest difference, unlike many of the other youth, was that he always looked well-rested. His straight-laced demeanor and willingness to follow the rules got him picked on by the other kids. Simply having a stable or more stable family environment versus those that did not was enough of a catalyst for bullying, even in my community.

Still the overall impact that alcoholism had on the village spared no one. Despite whatever differences, the village teens stuck together. If some of them wanted to go drink, even if some didn't, they all weathered it and went. If an opportunity to steal alcohol from their drunk parents presented itself, they said nothing. Even in the case of some of the violent or sexually inappropriate behavior that sometimes sent one or another of them sleeping at someone else's house, they went through it together. Whatever was happening to one, it was happening to them all. That was the life of teens.

The next few days I would be painting well into the evenings to finish the backdrops and whatever other art-related project was needed for the upcoming performance. It was exciting to be involved, to have something to do that took me outside the house. I couldn't wait to see the kids perform as well as see the set I helped create. Even though this was just a school play, the entire community would come out to see it with a Broadway show enthusiasm. Winters were cold and isolating, and everyone looked forward to coming together and being entertained by the youth. One key foundation to village life was the sense of community, which was made up of extended families that supported each other. I became acutely aware of how much the land played an integral part in their ability to stay together. The land made them a people and the people made the land home. Like a blanket, the land wove the people into its design. They could go from this place and return to it. The land would continue to provide for them, and in the end, reclaim them back to the earth, and each generation that came before or after would always know where they belonged.

The villagers generally all showed up for communal events like the school play. However, there were always exceptions like those that were too drunk to stumble there. Melvin, one of the more popular kids, described as the smart one by the educators, strangely enough, played Tiny Tim, the most fragile and vulnerable of the characters. The students mimicked this belief of his intelligence by being playfully antagonistic. It was not their way to boast loudly and arrogantly about their abilities. Instead, it was much more subtle with sarcasm and playful competition. Melvin was acknowledged by O'Brennan and my husband even as the one most likely to succeed. Of course, everyone else was placed in some category as well. There was Leanna, that was his cousin and girlfriend. She was quick-witted with a sharp tongue and a fiery temper, tall for her age, pretty, an average student, and was always showing she had little interest in school. Leanna's sidekicks included Sandra, a chunky, round-faced pretty girl that played the role of comic relief to Leanna, her best friend. There were the twins that had fetal alcohol syndrome, and they had the sole purpose of doing whatever Leanna told them to do and often appeared grumpy. There was also the kind, talented, and good-hearted Lewis that was treated like he was the proverbial dumb blond. That was the crew, and it pretty much covered most of the older group of kids.

The day of the performance was the student's last school activity before Christmas break. Seth was at the school already, and I got there early enough to help set up and do some last-minute gopher jobs. O'Brennan was rushing around in that slightly irritated manner he always seemed to have. The kids were going over their blocking and doing a last-minute run-through with Seth on the stage that O'Brennan and one of the local men had constructed. Student chairs were set up for audience seating, and with every prop in place and painted backdrop up, it was now time for the community to start arriving. People began to pile into their seats, and an audience hum filled the space. The sounds of the audience mixed with the sound of teenage laughter and squabbling behind the other classroom door, followed by a trail of hushing.

"Thanks for coming out. We're going to get started here in a minute. I want to thank all of those parents that helped out in various ways, and a special thanks to Ed for helping build the stage." Everyone began to clap. A loud bang of the door closing and a clanging of metal chair legs hitting in the back of the room made everyone jump and turn.

"Hey! What I do … Thank you." A drunk man stumbled to a seat to the sound of snickering and annoyed looks "When it start? I want see my kid."

"Geeee, sit!"

A collective shush covered the room, and O'Brennan continued, "Every one of our students worked hard, and even if you don't see your child, know that they chose their own jobs and all the jobs were crucial in bringing you this production of *Scrooge*. That being said, Meddy would like to have a word before we get started." The room became quiet except for the outburst from the drunk wanting to know when the entertainment would start or was it over.

"Excited to see your kids, ah? But have to see me first!" Meddy laughed, and the audience responded with uncomfortable sounds and movement. "Too many bear' at the garbage dump, they comin' in, too close to the village. Bear comin' round houses up top. So, everyone needs to get their trash put on the trailer because the truck not working. Mondays, Fred Totemoff will take the village four-wheeler and pull the trash further out on the point. He has to make lots of trips with the four-wheeler, but he's making only once a week Monday morning. Keep a lookout for bears, and don't keep trash outside your house."

Meddy started off the stage then stopped and added, "Anyone not get your trash out there on time will have to take it to the dump. And village four-wheeler can't be used." He sat back down next to his wife, a tall woman that fit him but looked to be white. A low murmuring could be heard. I looked over and saw Anna's face soft, but stern, and could hear her voice in my head saying "dum-dum."

"Ah! I miss it?" said the drunk. "Gee," someone turned and said. The drunk burped while leaning forward, elbows on his knees slipping off several times in his stupor. The play was a success as all school plays are, since they are packed with a biased audience of family and friends. Most of the kids remembered their lines and all stayed true to their personalities. Leanna got mad when someone missed their lines, barking annoyingly at them, and acted silly if she could not remember her own. Her best friend Sandra was ready to defend her every move, and the boys sat back laughing and making occasional immature comments. Everyone agreed it was wonderful.

Chapter Seventeen

My grandmother was what I would call a seer. A seer can peer into the spiritual world, and they are given glimpses of what is coming or what has already happened. I was told that I would be the next in the family line to have such abilities. When you're a seer, the spirit might come as a brush of wind out of nowhere across your body, and you're given something to know. Later you find out it happened or some truth. Sometimes things come in a dream, and the bed shakes and wakes you up, so you'll remember what you're supposed to know.

Some thought of my grandmother as a root woman. That is a woman that has special abilities in using roots, herbs and other objects to conjure spirits, but I know she used what she knew for healing. Others said she practiced Voodoo and Hoodoo; if that was the case then you'd think they would be careful about what they did and said around her. I think they were just superstitious and scared of what they didn't know. Could've been because she was married to a Louisiana man. He was always boasting about what he knew and bringing teas and ground-up roots that looked like dirt. Nobody knew what the stuff was, including Mom. The one thing we all did know, is that he was too stupid and lazy to practice anything that might take effort. Maybe it was because my grandmother grew things people hadn't seen before, knew almost every plant around us and how to use it. She also had dreams, visions, and told people what she saw. Often, her visions came true.

There was a power about my grandmother other than the stored-up anger that would come out. When she walked into a room, her presence would suck the air out. She was small in stature, but striking in looks and carried herself like nobility. She had Nigerian and English blood, and both were equally dominating factors in her personality. The English blood made her cold, stern, and an overbearing disciplinarian. The Nigerian part of her was fiercely strong, determined. She was devoted to family and demanded respect. Her pride never wavered even when survival required cleverness. That's the way I saw her; she could hurt you or heal you with her hands. Then terrify you with the spiritual things she knew. Nothing explains that more than what happened one Christmas.

The house was quiet, and the smell of roasting meat, baked sweets, and brown butter lingered as we fell into a deep sleep in our cramped, tiny room the three of us shared. It was Christmas Eve and would be the third night in a row that one of us awoke screaming from some uneasy spirit hanging around and terrorizing our dreams. This night did not start like the previous two nights that had unleashed the deadly shrieks of my sisters. Instead, it was quiet in our part of the house, but not for my grandmother. The night prior, along with the entire day, my grandmother sat in her chair meditating and praying. Calling out to Heaven, the ancestors, and all that she knew to be good to show her what had been tormenting us. She called to those that had been long gone to give her strength, and then she asked the unthinkable, that whatever it was to reveal itself.

That night when the house was dark and quiet, and Mom had just fallen to sleep, she was awoken by a scratching noise on the floor at the end of her bed. She lay there listening in her groggy state, trying to clear her thoughts. It led her to believe one of us had come into her room or the dog got up the stairs and crawled under her bed. "LaVern! That you ... what you doing up?" she called in the darkness, but nothing said a word. Laying back down, and satisfied that it must have been the furnace turning off or on, she began to doze. The sound began again but louder, like nails clawing through the oriental padded rug all the way to the wooden floor. "I hear you! Whatever in hell you are, but I ain't scared of you neither. You've been scarin' my children? Come on out and show yourself. You hear me?" she roared at the unknown thing.

As quickly as she spoke her words, the thing was just as quick to respond. It leaped on her chest and knocked her back to a lying position. Its torso was heavy and as wide as a man. It had almost no legs and no feet. The arms were disproportionately smaller and the hands were childlike, but with big, fat nubs for fingers. Its face was twisted, and her heart raced. Without a thought, she took her left arm and knocked it from her chest. She heard the hard thump of its body hitting the floor.

"Oh, my God!" The words fell out of her mouth. "Lord, Lord, lord … Oh! Jesus, what is it?" She lay there in the dark with light from the corner streetlamp casting itself on the wall. The swatch of light was from a broken blind at the head of her bed that permanently lay open. There was the sound of quick shuffling on the floor where she'd knocked the thing off. Out of the corner of her eye, she saw a dark form. She turned to examine what it was and discovered it was growing in size and blackness. The dark thing had shape and form, and it continued to grow taller and taller until it reached the ceiling and towered over her and the bed. My grandmother lay beneath it, weeping in fear. Prayers came from her lips like chants to all things holy, with closed eyes. When she opened her eyes again, moments later, the dark form had shrunk. Lifting itself and hovering over her, it moved towards the second window in the room. It was on the far side of the bed and in the shadows between the houses. It continued to shrink as she watched it pass through the window, getting smaller and smaller until it disappeared into a spot of dim light.

That morning we woke to the smell of coffee and Mom saying we won't be bothered again. I asked her why and she told me this story. My step-grandfather left around this time. I realized that dark spirits could be made to leave, but I also knew the fear I felt would never disappear that easily, not as long as there were bad people and other evil spirits waiting to hurt you.

Russian Christmas was explained like this: the villagers cleared out their pantry of food items, sometimes homemade treats and gifts were added, money would be wrapped tightly, and all these items were stuck to the floor or ceiling with tape. Then the visitors came to sing and spin the Russian Christmas star. Once all the songs had been sung and the star stopped spinning, like musical chairs, everyone dived towards the goods on the floor and tried to get as much as they could grab. This was a part of a tradition to share their wealth and abundance. Those that had more, as well as those that had little, would now share what they had, and the balance of wealth could be made equal. This was especially important during January in the dead of winter when resources were diminishing.

Seth and I went through our pantry and brought out a few cans of beans, peas, cranberry sauce, and tomatoes. I added several jars of jam and fresh bread I made, while Seth tied a small muslin bag filled with loose change. Since this would be our first time participating, we had concerns that what we'd put out might be either too much or could very well be too little, but we resigned ourselves to what it was. Until later, we wouldn't have known how little we contributed.

As the time neared, I couldn't help but feel a charge of excitement in the air. This was going to be a special Christmas Eve, I felt. At least, I'd hoped; after all, it was my birthday and Christmas Eve, according to the Russian Christmas calendar. The anticipation of people in our home on my birthday, singing and having fun, made me vibrate with excitement, but also with the concern that the one thing that has always meant so much to me would be a disaster. What if I didn't know some of the songs or made a mistake and offended someone? I knew they would be singing Christmas carols and not happy birthday to me. I knew they were celebrating the greatest birth ever, and I just happened to share it with Jesus because of a date on a calendar.

Caroling was a plus! It was something I'd dreamed of doing since I was a kid but never knew how someone got to do it. In my neighborhood,

I couldn't see myself walking up to doors singing "Silent Night." First of all, people would think you were crazy at best or they would just clown your ass. "You ain't Debbie Reynolds and you can't sing, get out my yard before you freeze there … didn't you get the memo? Black folk don't just stand around in the cold for fun." But I know it wasn't always like that. My grandmother told me stories of when she was growing up and folks would come around and sing, play the fiddle, or harmonica. They'd sing a song or two, then be invited in to warm up by the fire and have a hot drink and maybe fresh-popped corn, chestnuts, or roasted peanuts before they went on to the next house to share the spirit of Christmas and the gift of music with their neighbors. I listened to those stories and wanted to do that, spread joy. So, here it was, my chance and I could barely contain myself. The magic of Christmas and my birthday all rolled into one, and the northern location guaranteed a perfect birthday.

A rap came to the door, and I could hear the shuffling of feet, low voices, and the crunch of snow on the creaky floorboards of the porch. Seth opened the door and a few of the kids entered first. "Hey Mr. Schwartz, Merry Christmas … Merry Christmas, Mr. Schwartz … hey Mrs. Schwartz … Merry Christmas." They all pressed in, about ten to twelve people, with Ms. Elaine and a couple of the other older women, a few men, and the Star Keeper. Of course, several of Seth's older students and along with a few of the kids' mothers that had been friendly, at least enough to speak when passing, filled the space quickly. A prayer was said, and then the moment I was waiting for.

With mouth poised and lips licked, throat cleared, I tuned my ears to catch the first few familiar words, so I could chime in. They all began to sing, *Xo#@%0%#@^&'** … *What in God's name, noooo!* I thought in my head, *they were singing hymns, fricken' Russian Orthodox hymns. Ugh!* I just stood there lost, not knowing what to do, and in some weird attempt to connect I started moving my mouth to words I didn't even know or understand. *What an idiot!* The alternative would have been a look of total pissed-off-ness and misery on my face, seeing how I show everything on my face. I'm known for being a blurter and not always having a filter when it comes to my feelings. Seth looked on in silence and with little expression. He was most likely glad he had no idea what they were saying. The whole religious thing made him uncomfortable, but the promise of food at the other houses secured his commitment no matter what he had to listen to. The small-framed man that had brought in the forty-pound star began to spin it. The large, wood-framed, star-shaped object started slow then picked up speed quickly in his skillful hands. You couldn't help but notice it looked as if a bunch of stay home moms all dug out last year's Christmas decorations, put all the supplies in the middle of the floor, and along with their kids, went at the star gluing on everything. The star was less star-like because of all of the tinsel, bobbles, and the other various shiny objects attached to it. Yet it was mesmerizing when it spun. It was a spinning Christmas firework.

When the star stopped, the participants grabbed the homemade bread and jam up first, and several of the kids went for the money. Only one of the boys came up victorious and dangled it in the air. They then looked over what was left, like picking through bad fruit they chose to leave. Ms. Elaine said, "Eh, say happy birthday to Mrs. Schwartz." "Happy birthday" rang out every-where as Seth and I rushed to put on our coats and boots so that we might add to the group that was now moving to the next house. Ms. Elaine placed a small gift in my hand just before we stepped into the cold. I laid the gift on the end table beaming, guessing earrings or the like. For now, knowing that she thought of me enough to give me a gift was more important than what was in the wrapping. Anna's gift to me came earlier that day. It was a beautiful crocheted hat and smoked salmon, my favorite. I pulled myself away with a last look and a smile. I went out the door to follow the rest of the villagers.

The air was bitter, between negative five to ten degrees, and the wind carried an extra sting from the salty ocean. We traveled to the lower houses where most of the elders still lived before climbing the hill to where the new houses were being built. Every morning, right from the start, we woke to the hollow clang of lumber being stacked and the pounding of nails in the wood. Now you can hear only occasionally the muffled sound of labor coming from the hill in ghostly echoes off in the distance. Half of the houses were already completed, and the rest would be ready for move-in during the spring. We climbed to those that glowed with light and warmth. The wind and cold domi-nated the conversation and made light and cheerful banter scarce. "Hope they have hot drink ready! … Yay hope so … an' some fry bread!" They all giggled softly. Anna was with us now and telling me about the moose stew her niece makes. "Make you warm fast, eh!" Someone punctuated the sentiment. Octopus became another topic, brought up by one of the five men traveling with us. I hoped there would be octopus and it was made by Leanna's grandfather. The delicate disk that swam in a creamy cold pickled sauce was the best thing I had ever eaten. He sent it as a welcoming gift when we moved in. The only thing second to that octopus was crab. When the crab boats came in at the end of the season or if they had crab that wouldn't bring in the best price, the men would bring it to their family in the village. We got black garbage bags full of live crab, and we stayed up all night processing them for the freezer and eating bowls of crab meat with butter until we were almost sick. They talked of smoked fish and seal oil, salmon roe with cream cheese, and something called chiton which I didn't have a clue about. In spite of the cold and the long climb up the hill, I finally felt a part of them and all was right at that moment.

The stars in the sky were bright and scattered like spilled rice, and the sound of the ocean was always constant. The moon helped light our way, and the peace at that moment could not be bought. Like the cracking of ice or a snap of a frozen branch underfoot, the serenity was broken. The sound of drunken voices arguing at the bottom of the hill could be heard. We quieted our speech. The steep climb and cold wind, along with the desire for the light that glowed from the houses in front, gave us no more voice.

"Ehhh! What you doin' … No, stop! I said Idontwantto … give it back … to me! I'm goin' uphill to see my aunty." Everyone stopped, stood silent, as if in a snow globe that had been shaken and the snow was falling gently around the figurines. There was a deafening silence that exists inside such a thick glass until it drops and shatters, and that was what it did. I could hear her breath, hot and panting hard, as she ran up the hill towards us. I heard her breath when I could no longer hear my own or those that were around me. We all seemed to be holding our breath. The sudden stop was like an engine that just shut off. We all watched her climb the steep man-made hill that was covered in large cracked jagged rocks, snow, and ice.

With the speed of a great bird with massive wings and talons, he was there, a small but stout man in his late twenties. I didn't see him before or hear his voice at the bottom in the dark before she started climbing. He gripped her quick and strong, like an eagle. For all her struggle, she moved fast as a mouse or quick as a rabbit, scrambling to reach us. His hand closed his fingers around her tangled long black hair, pouring out over the white snow like used motor oil. She lay on her back now, screaming as she rode down the icy rugged rocks. His hand tightly gripped her hair while he stepped down each icy stair until they reached the bottom.

"Oh! My God! What is he doing … Hey!" I blurted then moved forward to the edge of the hill to go down and stop him. I felt a firm yet soft grab on my arm, pulling me back. When I looked around it was Anna. She softened her gaze and shook her head, almost unnoticeable, and my muscles relaxed. The young woman let out a screech that hung in the air as she cursed and kicked at him, only to have her feeble fight met with a blow. He hit her, and I bolted away from Anna. "What the hell!"

This time Seth stopped me on my descent down the hill, and I turned to the men in the group. "Aren't you going to do something? We can't just stand here!" Almost like zombies, they turned to the light. The voice of a man spoke low and clear. "Don't get involved, not your concern." I looked at Seth with helpless eyes, begging him to help me, waiting for something that wasn't there, wasn't in him. All I could hear was the word coward raging in my head, and all I could see was the glow of the houses, ablaze in red, as I held the tears of shame and anger back for my part in doing nothing. It was clear now, this was who we really were, who we were going to be as a couple, and I had missed it or refused to see it. The group started to move again up the hill; the crunch of our boots on the snow, now marching away, made a painful sound in my ears.

The last house on the top of the hill was where everyone congregated. It was the biggest and most likely wealthiest home in the village. This was not the only big house up there. Meddy's house was one of them, but it was the last one the star went to. There was food that covered every counter and extra tables set up to hold it all. Fifty- and hundred-dollar bills were taped with clear box tape to the floor and ceiling. Large gifts and small toys, jewelry, and more covered the floor. When the songs began, the voices in the room rang out like a choir in a great cathedral, but with a touch of giddiness. As the star spun,

Leanna, with some of the other teens and a few of the young adult women, urged me to participate in the dive for the bounty. I had been forewarned well in advance not to go for any of the money. It was highly suggested not to go for anything at all, but that was up to us. I was now twenty-three, in a house that was bright and cheerful, where the cold dark night we'd just escaped could not follow. Being invited required me to not be rude and standoffish, as my grandmother would warn me against. The kid in me was mesmerized by the lights, glitter, joy-filled sounds, and laughter. So, when the star stopped and everyone dove I was pulled in by the bodies around me and the hand of Leanna. Hands and feet went everywhere, grabbing and pawing.

I grabbed what I could feel amongst the entangled bodies on the floor, but from a squatted position. Whenever I felt something to grab, I was struck on my hand with something sharp. I would quickly release it and try reaching in another direction. A strike came to my hand again. I saw the twins and some of the other students up on shoulders trying to get the money from the ceiling. I saw a small box with a Christmas necklace that no one was going for with arms full and shirts stuffed. I reached for it, and like the sharp prong of a fork, something dug into my arm, the pain going down the length of my forearm. I released the box without knowing who or how they got me except the laughter from Leanna when our eyes met. Things continued to be torn from my hands, a kick to my knee, or a boot to my head, and the laughter hovered sinisterly above me.

It came like a click or flash, that thing that is always there inside of me, it was now almost fully present. I felt it getting stronger every time someone's fingernails dug into my flesh or the jab of an elbow. I thought the next time some unseen hand took hold of me, I would grab their fingers and twist violently until they let go. I pushed bodies and arms, trying to stand up off the ground, away from the clawing pile. As I was getting up, a powerful hand swiped at my arms, knocking the small box and some canned goods back onto the floor. I went home that night battered and bruised, emotionally and physically. As I walked down the hill past the place where the girl tried to climb up to me, I did it with my arms full, carrying a bag full of food and gifts that the host of the house gave us. I felt cold and numb, both from the air outside and from something very familiar inside.

Chapter Eighteen

I laid in bed late until ten a.m. and listened to the wind circle the house and blow ice kisses through the cracks. January had fallen quiet now, and February was there for hibernation. It was profoundly still, and nothing was planned. Not a single event to go to, a tea invite, or a trek over an unexplored hill awaited my exploration. I could not hear the cries of crows or seagulls, even if they were calling me from some nearby tree or from the dock that hung over the sea. They were not heard, because I was busy listening from my bed to the sound of my dog moving, then plunking his heavy body down several times in boredom, waiting for me.

For weeks after Russian Christmas, I enjoyed the buzz that the holidays brought. I would get up reasonably early, motivated to complete household chores, making homemade gifts and pouring myself into various projects. With the radio turned up high after dialing from sound to no sound and back to sound, I'd find a pop song or two I liked between the static and country music, but never R&B, which I loved. So, instead, I'd pop in a cassette of the Isley Brothers and think of "Summer Breeze," or jam to the Spinners, "Working My Way Back to You," and Joni Mitchell playing my wedding song, "Shadow and Light." Now it was February, I slept late and played a lot of "Shadow and Light." When I caught the news, it was always about murder and crimes and all the Black people accused of them. They were all found guilty. So, I stopped listening to the news. Instead, I fought with Seth about what the news said and what it didn't say, but it didn't matter because they're all guilty anyway. And I couldn't do a damn thing about it. I couldn't do a damn thing …

Three o'clock in the morning and I couldn't sleep. I thought about what to cook, what I needed to order, or whether it would be too windy and cold to go for a long walk.

Eleven o'clock, *I meant to get up earlier and … do what, walk in the frigid cold? I have to take Rawsh out; it's been four hours since Seth let him out. I look a mess, I hate the way I look. My hair has grown out and it's in its ugly stage … Who gives a shit? Nobody cares how I look … cares about me. I don't care how I look.* Rawsh came in and laid his front paws and head on my leg. He must have heard my tears fall.

It's three forty-five a.m. and it starts again. Many more to go …

In late February, I was asked to teach. It came with great surprise and real fear. The fear was of making a debacle of the job because I had no training and didn't want to make a fool of myself. Worse than this happening was that Seth's friends would hear of my failure and sing their song, *we told you so*, in his ear. I would teach two thirteen-year-old girl twins, and the subject was the art of home economics. The twins' age might have been enough of a challenge. I had to ask myself, *What thirteen-year-old girl listens and doesn't think everything is stupid?* Then there was the fact that the twins had fetal alcohol syndrome and anger issues. I had no training to deal with either, but I knew plenty about anger. I guess my domestic skills qualified me to teach them how to cook and sew, but how this detour would help them read or write was beyond me. I felt like the girls were getting the short end of this deal, but I would do my best.

I remembered when I had my first encounter with the twins at our house during Russian Christmas. The twins, along with Leanna and her sidekick, came to our house with the star and other carolers briefly. Before the singing began, one of the twins, with a scowl on her face, stomped out the house, and the snickering from Leanna and sidekick followed after. It was clear that the manipulation and bullying by Leanna were a part of the dynamic of their relationship. She returned later with her sister by her side. Together they were one and felt stronger against Leanna. The twins followed the group to the remaining houses. It was there that I realized the social rank and file. There were the elders, Meddy, drunks and kids, outsiders, and then me.

By the second week, the girls' short attention span, irritability, and disruptive behavior were becoming much easier to address in this environment. Working with them one on one gave them the attention they craved and met the necessity of going at their pace with patience. Based on my personality, I was not exactly fitted with patience, or so I thought, but I had learned that my tolerance for those that were vulnerable was my kryptonite.

I was mostly frustrated with the fact that the twins' family spoiled them to the point that they were destructive. They were allowed unchecked behavior at home and school discipline had limitations, especially in a village. Because the education system had screwed up so badly with the abuse of Native children in the past, the village council now had control. Yet the kind of destruction of culture that had happened to Native people since the Europeans made contact in the 1700s had also planted many seeds of self-destruction, alcohol being one of the greatest.

The alcohol in the village was the destructive substance, and guilt was one of its by-products that was undermining the twins' lives. Their parents' guilt allowed them to make excuses for the twins' bad behavior. Everyone seemed to have low expectations for them. I couldn't help but feel that eventually all this, if continued, would create a place for the twins in a bottle of booze.

The first week was awful. The girls would just get up and leave impulsively if they didn't want to do something, like clean up after themselves. They would scream or become frustrated and throw something and let me know they didn't have to do anything. They would tell me they were allowed to go home when they wanted to. I knew that they could learn and had something in them that could be reached because when they were happy and having fun, you could see it. They loved joking around and trying to make me laugh.

Laura was the oldest of the two and displayed most of the temper tantrum problems. Her sister would respond in kind to whatever she did. Once when I was teaching them to sew Laura stuck her finger, and you would have thought they both were stabbed with a dagger. It took everything I had to contain the situation and keep the girls from bolting or completely tearing up the place. Success came in small things, like a first aid kit used to teach them self-care and how to care for one another. Eventually, they accomplished cleaning up after themselves and completing a project. The best change was them speaking to me and a hug or two on their terms.

I went to the school later that week to turn in the last of the progress notes for the twins' three-week home economics class elective. Thinking about the experience, I was surprised from the start that someone like Anna or one of the older women had not been asked since they likely had more skill. On the other hand, I might have been more suited, not being a part of the village and not being related to them. I wouldn't face the same pressure, scrutiny, or conflict that someone from here might if they said or did something the parents didn't like. After all, I was expendable and could be fired or put out of the village with little feelings about it and preserve family ties. The project had ended, and it was neither a failure nor an absolute success. There was not enough time to expect more than that. What the girls needed was consistency, time, and someone that wouldn't reward them for bad behavior, and they deserved as much. They could be sweet, kind, and loving, but the one thing we were out of was time. Things would go back to the way they were, and they could count on getting their way with nothing to show for it in the long run.

My second job came right around break-up, which was at the end of March and the beginning of April. Break-up happens when the inlets and rivers start to warm and the ice breaks apart, which allows for inlets to be passable again. The village council negotiated for the houses being built to include the hiring of local villagers. The project would require at least thirty percent of the hire to be qualified Natives. Of the ten houses being built, nine of them were completed and the tenth was nearing completion. The construction company had now posted a notice, wanting to hire women to clean the new houses and the pay would be twenty dollars an hour. Seth, after seeing the notice, said in his very Seth-ish way, "You know how to clean, and at twenty dollars an hour, I can stay home."

I was ecstatic about the prospect of making money and having another job so soon after teaching the girls ended. I would be making three times more money than I ever made in my life, but the reality was that they might not hire me because I wasn't a villager. I went up to the trailer and got an application along with several of the other women in the village. One of them asked if I was there to apply for the house cleaning job. When I said yes, the village woman said very politely that the company was just hiring local women. She said it in that passive-aggressive way I'd heard white women speak down to me and others like me. It was in her tone and the phony smile she gave. What she was really saying is we have all the power.

As I turned in the twins' final progress reports, O'Brennan asked me if I applied for the cleaning job for the new houses. I told him that I picked up the application, but some of the women said that they were only hiring locals. O'Brennan turned slightly pink in his normally pale face. "That's up to the construction company, who they hire. They do have an agreement with the village council to hire a certain amount of locals, but they still can hire anyone they want, especially if they can't fill all the positions ... You should put in the application and I suggest you do it today."

I went home, got the application, took it to the construction trailer, and left it with the guy inside. I watched the houses now with real interest and anxiety, wondering if I would get a job. I saw people coming and going more frequently up on the hill and my hopes began to fade. All I could think about was leaving my house every morning and going to a job, feeling my days had a purpose. I loved working with the girls, but that was over. But the following week, there was an envelope with my name on it when I went to check on my mail at the phone shack.

"I got work!" I blurted and ran out quickly to tell Seth the good news. On the way to school, I couldn't help but think about what I could do with the money. Paying my grandmother back would be first on the list, buying something I wanted without asking if I could, and most of all showing Seth's friends and family that I'm not some gold digger or lazy. Seth read the letter and noticed they were only paying me seventeen dollars an hour when the post said twenty dollars. O'Brennan chimed in, "They have to pay the Natives twenty dollars but everyone else gets paid whatever they want! You got work at least." Yes, I thought with the sour ball of unfairness that had a permanent place in the back of my throat. A smile then formed and my face bloomed with the gratitude that I would have work.

The houses were big and roomy compared to the small bungalow-style houses below that many of the elders didn't want to leave. There were high white ceilings and windows that made the rooms bright in the daylight sun and cheery even when it was going down. Beautiful dark wood cabinets circled the kitchen and long counters looked out to the living area. When I arrived at my first assigned house, according to the schedule at nine a.m., there were already two women there cleaning.

"Oh! Someone's here already ... the schedule said nine. Were we supposed to be here earlier?" I asked.

"No," they said, continuing working in the living room, wiping down walls. I could feel the nervousness moving in with the holding of my breath.

"Oh, okay, should I start on the other side and do walls there?"

"Finished already," she said quickly.

Here we go, I thought, *they're going to make this difficult ... just keep trying, ask again nicely.* "Ok, maybe, I'll just start in the kitchen then."

"The kitchen, already clean, don't go in. We started at six in the morning."

"If I knew you were starting so early, I could have been here at six. I was just going by the schedule. It said nine to nine thirty. Sorry, no one told me the time changed." There was total silence, and I stood there awkwardly, totally ignored and not knowing what to do.

"Since you're mostly done in here, maybe I can start in the bathrooms and bedrooms?"

No response. My anxiety began to take over standing there and my body was starting to tremble. "I was told I would be on Kathy's team cleaning?"

They both snickered slightly.

"My sister is helping me. She knows how to clean my way." She spoke with a sharp tone that was tempered only by what was an attempt to cover with a smile but looked more like a grimace.

"I understand, but they assigned me to …"

"Go talk to them! This my house, I can finish my house with who I want, my way!"

I could feel my whole body tremble violently and they could see it. I didn't want to give her the satisfaction of knowing how upset I was. I reached down to pick up my things. My water slipped from my hand when I went to grab the bucket of cleaning supplies. The bucket tipped over with a loud clanging sound as I tried to set it right. All of this was followed by my water bottle falling again. "Damn it."

I stomped down the hill with my rubber boots making a popping sound against my legs that created a comforting rhythm. I went straight to the trailer and told the stocky, tall white man at the desk what happened. He looked at me like I was crazy and said, "Well, what do you want me to do? It's her house. If she wants to clean it herself, that's up to her." I stood there looking at him, looking at me, looking at him in total disbelief. I thought, *What kind of crazy is this? You hired me!*

I was about to leave when a gray-haired white man came from a side office and said something to the big guy, and he called me back over to the desk. "Go up to the third house over from where you were and see if they need help there, when you're done with that one, you can move on to the next one. Make sure you fill out your timesheet every day and drop it off here." I don't know what the old white guy's reason for helping me out, but at that moment, I was glad.

I went to the third house and told the women working there that the office sent me to help clean. They invited me in and directed me to help them get the dust from the sheetrock of the walls and the kitchen cabinets. I immediately went to the kitchen while they worked in the living room, wiping walls, ceilings, and cleaning windows. I wrapped a broom in a soft cloth and began dusting the ceiling and walls down. Finished cleaning all the woodwork, I went through and polished all the cabinets. The two women talked and laughed together the whole time, and I decided since they were not trying to include me it might be best to stay quiet and just work. We went on this way for most of the day with the exception of my going down to the trailer for various supplies. When three p.m. came, the one woman whose house it was said, "Need to get home, cook, before my kid get' home school soon!" I had overheard it was her house earlier. "Get your things," she said to me. "I like to be here early, like six okay, so I get 'lot done!" We left and that was that, my first day at my new job.

The next several days were much the same, getting dust off the ceiling, then washing them down, polishing the wooden baseboards, cleaning and washing all light fixtures, window seals, crevices and corners, twice. That was how it went for a week, and they only warmed up to my presence a few days before we finished. One woman even shared some fish salad with me over lunch towards the end.

Monday morning rolled in, and it was a bright and sunny day. I headed up to the house where I assumed the women would be to collect supplies for the next house. When I entered, to my surprise, they were cleaning as I had found them the first time.

"Good morning! Did something happen? I thought we were supposed to go to the next house. I just came to get our supplies?"

"I want to finish cleaning my house," she said.

"Oh. Okay! What needs to be done?" I said, puzzled. The woman in the kitchen climbed up the step stool and began to polish the cabinets. "Oh! I did those already, three times." I was a bit annoyed and confused.

"I like, take my time, do it good. I like my house clean, the way I like it." This sounded very familiar.

"So, what can I do," I asked.

"Clean the bathroom … wherever you want." I headed to the bathroom loaded down with cleaning supplies only to be blinded by the shine on the porcelain. The silver finish of the hardware was polished and not so much as a water spot. I turned on the faucet frustrated and baffled. I hated having to redo a thing if I knew I did it right the first time. I scrubbed the tub, sink, and toilet and wiped down the walls. On my hands and knees, I cleaned the floor, backing myself out the door so, not to make a track. It was perfect, just as before. I packed up my gear and left the woman in the living room still wiping the same damn spot. I dropped everything off, and I quit. One week and one day, my great job was a great disappointment.

I found out later what the women were doing. Cleaning one spot forever was intentional. They wanted to milk the construction company for all it was worth, so they dragged their heels to rack up as many hours as they could to make as much as they could before the job ran out in the two weeks allotted. I was relieved to know it wasn't about me at all. Maybe it was about me a little since they never let me in on what they were doing. I had to be honest with myself. If they had told me, I wouldn't have had the constitution for stalling or pretending to work. It just wasn't in me. I'd rather go home than stand around and do nothing, no matter what the pay.

19

Chapter Nineteen

Spring was truly around the corner. The air felt different, and the sun shone brighter. Even on rainy days, it felt as if it was raining with a different purpose because it was April versus September. Rawsh and I spent our day strolling along the beach on bright and sunny days. I had not seen Meddy's dog since my encounter near the phone shack when he pranced him up and down the road intimidatingly. It crossed my mind that maybe the dog was never Meddy's in the first place, instead he borrowed a dog to prove to me "his" was bigger than mine. I hoped that this dog didn't meet some nefarious fate as other dogs had while in Meddy's charge.

The day was perfect, cool but bright. I could hear a plane flying over. I watched it overhead, coming closer and lining up to land on the runway. Planes were not a regular sound you heard flying in the area. Sometimes you could see jets in the distance, so tiny they were like fleas on the back of a dog. Planes came here only occasionally to bring in supplies. Residents tried to coordinate orders or important appointments, like seeing a doctor, because the cost of a plane was so expensive. Lifting my face to the sun with closed eyes, I walked blindly for several steps, but I could still hear the plane. The red blood vessels of my eyelids and yellow rays of the sun flooded my closed orbs. This was a challenge I gave myself, to see if I would be afraid, panic, and open my eyes. Maybe this time I wouldn't and I'd use my instincts instead, stay the course and not walk into the sea or smack into the side of jagged rocks. The hum of the plane vibrated in the distance to my left and the ocean smacked the shore on my right. When I opened my eyes, I saw nothing but bright blotchy red, yellow, and white light, and I teetered off balance. Waiting before I moved, I blinked to clear my sight and stood perfectly still for my body to ground itself. As my eyes began to focus I sought to locate the plane in the distance.

I watched the plane above me through a blinding high noon sun. I couldn't read the identifying words on the side until it came in lower along the tree line and landed on the runway. It was a state trooper! I figured a drunken fight had gotten out of hand and it was decided they needed to be taken out of the village so things could cool down. It was spring or near enough, and contrary to the common belief that there are more suicides in the dark and cold winters, studies showed that the numbers were higher in the spring. I always wondered if the sheer energy it takes to bare-knuckle it through the dark and cold waiting for spring makes it just too overwhelming when it arrives. Whatever makes people compelled to wait till spring to end their life, maybe it also has an effect on people that sends them out of control in general. Whatever the reason the troopers were here, it must be serious enough to call them. The news about the reason would spread soon enough.

Anna and I hadn't gotten to gather much lately. I was working every day at the school, and she was extra busy with winter and spring illnesses along with accidents and God knows what else. Seth and I were becoming more and more like ships passing in the night in spite of my finally having a job. All of it made me sad, and the more I tried to talk about it, the worse it seemed to make things. Between his drinking or smoking with the locals I caught wind of there were very few things in his behavior that pointed to him doing better. I felt outside of everything and that included our marriage. No one seemed to care how I was doing with the exception of my grandmother. She always seemed to know when something was wrong from just the sound of my voice, but I never told her what was happening or being said about me. Yet I think she sensed what it was from the way she encouraged me. "You're strong, LaVern. You'll be alright. You just remember what I taught you, and don't worry about what people say, they talk because they just have to say something!"

I felt like a failure. I found myself wanting to go home, back to a place I had no friends and I never felt I belonged. Seth and I agreed that we would go for part of the summer as soon as school was out, and now I couldn't wait. The strong need I had to go back felt foreign, but it proved that no matter how bad home might be, the place you know is better than the place you don't know.

I headed over to the school to clean about four p.m. and everyone was all abuzz about the troopers arresting one of the locals. I knew not to be nosey and go asking questions. I had to just wait and let the information come to me. At this point, the kids were speculating and hadn't talked to their parents. Finally, Seth filled me in on what O'Brennan had told him.

The man that came to the house looking for Seth and sat staring at me while I made tea had been arrested. Sometime in February, his mother and him were drinking and partying. He was using drugs and alcohol. Some of the locals told the trooper they had been partying for a few days. At some point, she said he grabbed her and started pushing her around. The fifty-something-year-old mother started yelling at him, cursing him out, and that led to pushing and shoving. He hit her and started beating her up before he raped her. She was still in the hospital.

I didn't know how to process what he was telling me. I couldn't breathe for a moment. Seth touched my arm and asked if I was okay. His hand, where he touched me, felt like acid melting my skin, and it ran down my arm then all over my body. I pulled away and asked if she was going to be okay. He said yes, but how can she be? How could you ever be? I was mad, but I said nothing. I thought about how this man was in my house. I thought about the situation Seth put me in and how bad it could have gone. I burned like fire at all of the situations I'd been in and those responsible for protecting me that didn't. I just wanted to scream the building down, scream in their faces, but I said nothing. I grabbed the trash can and went outside.

The plane lifted back into the sky, clearing the trees, then the village. This time when I looked up at the plane, I was not blinded by the sun. This time I caught its image unencumbered by the sun. I could read the words clearly on the side. Yet it was the large shadow it cast, a wave it made over the trees and houses, that left me without the warmth of its first appearance and wondering what could happen next. No one spoke of the situation. She never came back to the village, but I heard rumors that she was somewhere in Cordova or Valdez with a sister.

20

Chapter Twenty

The gratitude I had for my job and the sense of independence and worth working gave me was amazing. But, as wonderful as it was, I began to understand why Ms. Elaine gave up the job so easily. School was winding down, and there was a lot of extra work that went along with closing out the school for the summer that had nothing to do with the general cleaning. I helped with inventory and junk removal. I cleaned out light fixtures, shelves, books in disrepair, closets, as well as the basic everyday stuff that had to be done like cleaning bathrooms, sweeping and mopping floors, and emptying trash cans. This was what I was doing when Seth came back into the school after he'd already gone home for the evening.

"Hey, are you busy?" he said, and I thought, *Really?* as I continued to push the bits of paper and pencil eraser with the rest of the trash across the floor in front of him.

"Yessss! What's up?"

"I picked up the mail."

"Oh! Okay, did I get anything? Did Mom send me a letter?"

"No, just a Lands' End catalog."

"Okay, just take it home. You take Rawsh out yet?" I emptied the trash cans into a plastic bag while Seth just sat there looking at me. "What! Did you take Rawsh out?"

"Yeah, but I need to tell you something … don't get upset!"

Now I was upset, my mind immediately thinking he let Rawsh roll in some stink or worse.

"What Seth? What's wrong? Rawsh alright?" I said, no longer working. I stared at him, leaning on the broom.

"Just promise you're not going to go crazy."

"What is wrong with you? Just say it already. You're making me mad."

"Alright, alright … I was in the phone shack picking up the mail, I had Rawsh outside … he was just lying there waiting for me. Meddy came in …" I could feel myself immediately get tense, I took a deep breath, then held it.

"What about him!"

"I just want you to know, I took care of it." he fumbled around with his words as I grew more impatient.

"Took care of what, Seth? Just tell me what's going on!"

"Alright, alright already, just calm down and don't be yelling! So, like I said I was in the phone shack, and Meddy came in and started talking to me about his cats …"

"His cats!" I said.

"Yeah! Just wait, so he said that he had some cats killed and dogs have been coming up around his house chasing his other cats."

"Yeah, okay, why is he telling you?" I asked, taking regular breaths now.

"So, he asked me, are we letting Rawsh out at night?"

"And what did you say?"

"I said no, that if Rawsh goes out, we take him out with us, he's not out by himself."

"Well, I'm sorry about his cat dying, but I know Rawsh didn't kill it. He's just a big puppy. If anything he probably thought he could play with the cat, if he did that. He knows good and well, he's never seen Rawsh out alone. I'm not thinking about that man." I start straightening the desk and stacking a few chairs on top, moving on with my work.

"Well, I have something else to tell you."

"Now what!"

"Meddy said if he found any more dead cats or saw that dog of ours, he just might come up missing."

"What the hell does that mean? He's threatening to kill my dog? Really! Where's that big beast he has? I notice he's gotten rid of it. It probably killed the cat or a half dozen other animals out there, including the bear that was roaming around here. He just keeps trying to find a reason to hurt my dog."

"Well, I told him if my dog came up missing, I'm going to sue him." Seth made the statement as if it was resolved, neatly put away, and all parties were in agreement. More importantly, Seth was acting like Meddy would be quaking in his boots. Whatever restraint I had up to this point in trying to respect or understand cultural differences, I was done. This was not about ethnic differences, this was just one more privileged asshole and bully.

"Was he still in the phone shack when you left?"

"Yea! Com' on, don't do this, I knew I shouldn't have told you … Like I said he knows I'll sue his ass."

"I hate cowards, and he's a coward. He wants to kill my dog? Then he should be a man and grow a pair and own it, but he's not. He likes to take innocent dogs to the point and kill them and talk bullshit about if my dog comes up missing."

"Hey! Can't talk like that in the school, someone might hear you."

"You're right!" I grabbed my jacket and hat and headed out the door.

"Oh! Crap." I heard Seth's voice trail after me, but he did not follow. It was bright, sunny, but crisp outside as I marched down the dirt road trembling with anger. I could hear the cry of the gulls before I could even see the dock. Then, as God or the Devil would have it, I saw who I thought was Meddy coming towards me at the opposite end of the road before the docks. I calmed myself and practiced over and over again what I was going to say, *Meddy, I'm sorry about your cat, but I assure you it was not my dog … I understand Meddy you lost a cat … So Meddy, maybe that bear killed your cat.* I was going to be diplomatic and just tell him my dog wasn't much more than a puppy, and plus he was with us all the time. By the time I was about four or five yards from the dock, Meddy had already reached it and was turning to go down. I called out to him and, he stopped and waited until we met in the crossroads. I didn't notice the other man that was coming up from the dock to meet Meddy.

"Hey Meddy, so, I just spoke with Seth, and he told me that you think Rawsh has been up on the hill and killed your cat." I was trying to just keep to the facts.

"Yeah! I said I had a cat killed and I saw him on the hill. You need to keep your dog away from my house." He spoke in a firm and assertive tone, then looked over to his friend that chuckled, and he smiled. *Just speak clear and calm, get to the point,* I coached myself.

"So, I know that he wouldn't hurt your cat. The one time he was on the hill he was with me walking around. Rawsh is always with me or my husband when he goes out. Matter of fact that day, he went up to a cat, tried to play with it, the dumb dog. The woman I got him from raised him with cats and they played together. I watched him running around back and forth, trying to get the cat to chase him until the cat scratched him across his nose, and all he did was run over to me," I laughed to myself, thinking about it.

"That dog come 'round my house, something might happen to him," he said, still smiling with his friend, laughing like a schoolboy. His friend was a thinner, shorter, strawberry blond, white man covered with grease. It wasn't until right then I became aware of him and that there was a boat at the end of the dock, with tools laid out from where it was being repaired. It wasn't until then that I noticed that the cries of the seagulls, which had been so deafening minutes ago, seemed completely mute now, yet I could see ten or twenty of them gliding about, over the dock. That feeling of something behind me was pressing in the center of my back and was moving, no, running up my spine, sharp, cold, hard, and it spread over my scalp like a cold shiver and went into my brain.

"You want to kill my dog? The door's open, go down there take him out, and kill him you fuckin' coward! What is this bullshit about, 'he might come up missing?' Just be a man and grow some balls and take him out of the house and kill him asshole!"

The thin straw man began to move away from us. Meddy's mouth moved, probably saying something like, "Who do you think you're talking to? I can do what I want, this is my village," and then he said something that was clear: "Go back to the ghetto!"

"Go back to the ghetto? Where the hell do you think you are? You think that white people don't see you the same? This ain't nothing but a ghetto to them, you idiot!" I don't know why I didn't see the large wrench come from his pocket to his hand, but I saw how he gripped it and shook it around and how he towered over me, blocking out the sun.

"Somebody better get her," he said.

We both looked around, and his friend had now backed down towards the boat. The curtain of the house we stood next to suddenly closed. The icy grip on my brain was now red-hot.

"So, what? You want to hit me with that, you fuckin' coward? Go ahead, I dare you. Everyone around here is scared of you, but I'm not, you bully. You want to kill my dog, go get him, and when you do, you better watch your back because I'm comin' for you. You want to know when? I'm going to shoot you if you shoot my dog."

He raised the massive wrench higher and pulled back at his waist slightly. The fire in my mind became white, blazing white, and I started to jump up to scream in his face and poke my finger at him. Screaming over and over again, "You coward, be a man and own it. You want to kill my dog. I'm not afraid of you." I could hear his voice trail off as he backed down the hill to the dock where his friend had disappeared too.

The birds returned with their cries that were quieter and came only in rhythm to the lapping of the waves. I stood there a minute trying to pull myself together, put everything back, but I was sure it wasn't going back. I felt different deep down in myself but I couldn't get to that feeling yet. I was shaking, and I just had to get off the road and make it inside my house. I took the first couple of steps towards the house and I could feel my legs wobble like when I came out of the sweat at Ms. Elaine's.

I was still mad, mad enough to stretch my arms out and run down the road with superpower strength and rip apart whatever I came into contact with. I walked as fast as I could. I could hear my own heart pounding in my ears telling me to slow down, but I couldn't even if it meant my heart would burst. I could feel the fatigue in my muscles as they slowed without my permission and the hot sweat became cold. I thought for a second who was watching me, what they would think, and just for that second, I allowed it to exist. I stepped hard on those feelings of shame and ground them into pulp with every mad step I took the rest of the way home.

I walked into the house, and Rawsh met me at the door. Falling to my knees, I hugged and petted my dog, crying softly with him and telling him what a good boy he was. He returned the compliment by licking the tears from my face. I realized that I had spent this whole time trying to not be the mistake or the reason that made it fall apart. Not realizing it had nothing to do with what I did or didn't do. Some decisions are already made, and some just need to be allowed to fall apart. Hugging Rawsh, I headed outside to go back to work. The day had been sunny and crisp like the day the troopers flew in. However, no two days are the same. This one was very different, and I could feel that. I walked along the road, and everything was very quiet, not even the seagulls with their deafening cries made much noise. I saw them on the dock as I passed them, perched quietly, with the exception of a few gliding in with soft calls. I walked past the house where Meddy and I argued. I saw the curtain was pulled slightly open again, and I waved without looking for a response. It felt good, this walk back to work, and I thought about what I needed to finish in the school and nothing else.

Chapter Twenty-One

Waking up felt different since the argument with Meddy. It wasn't that the routine had changed that much. It was pretty much the same: waking up, getting dressed, taking Rawsh out, eating breakfast, cleaning, cooking, and going to work. The difference was in how I felt. It was like my skin was different. I don't mean the color of my skin like I wasn't Black anymore. It was more like it had stretched, and I had grown bigger. The first day after the fight, when I woke up I noticed my body took up most of the bed. I had to stretch from one side to the other to feel like there was enough room. When I stood up, I felt taller, and not just in the morning, but all day. When I was walking down the road, one of the villagers I'd thought was taller than me passed by. I spoke and they didn't respond, which was not what I found fascinating; I realized that I was much taller than them. It was weird. I could see right over their head, and it made me smile.

Rawsh came in and laid his face and paws across my chest, licking me to get up like he always did. Instead of a quick rub on the head and heading to the bathroom, I sent him for his favorite toy and we played tug of war until he pulled me out of the bed, and then I headed to get dressed. It wasn't just how tall I felt. It was how rich the colors looked all around me. The sky was bluer, the trees were a deeper green, and my brown skin was richer than any of the brown colors around me. I looked like good soil. Even though I could literally see a transformation happening in me, it was not lost on me the other things that were happening in my surroundings.

Ever since the troopers took that man that raped his mother away, everything had started losing color. It was like the gray cloudy days of spring washed away the colors of the earth into the sea. The people seemed drained too, and they just sloshed around like the wet bog around us—saturated. Most of the people that were always distant with me, but at least showed the courtesy of a smile or slight nod, wouldn't even acknowledge me now in passing since my fight with Meddy. Those that were friendly still waved or spoke but moved away quickly so as not to be seen having a conversation.

There was a young Native woman about twenty-eight, and she belonged to one of the lower forty-eight tribes. Whenever I saw her, she'd always talked with me. She married a local guy, and she'd shared how hard the people were on outsiders and that included her too. I remember how her husband had killed the bear that kept coming around the houses in the village. There it was laid out after they had skinned it. The bear's color was as brown and rich as my own, but with all of its insides gone. Yet its teeth and claws still embodied the bear's spirit of fearlessness. I could tell right off how different she was from the people here. Her speech wasn't an Alaskan Native accent. She always looked me straight in the eyes when she spoke to me, and her smile felt warm and reflected less mistrust. Most of all she didn't hesitate to talk to me. Even her hair was different from the long straight river of black oil that most of the Native Alaskan women had. Her hair was very long, and it went way past her hips, but the texture of her hair was wavy and kind of kinky, which reminded me of people I knew, like my great auntie. I saw her outside the phone shack. She said that her husband and her were leaving for their place, a cabin deep in the bush. They had been staying with her mother-in-law and helping her out for the winter because she had been sick. She then spoke softer and said, "It's time to leave, starting to get too crazy." She told me to take care of myself, walked away, and I never saw her again.

In spite of my newly discovered stature, it was growing harder and harder to deal with the level of ostracizing I experienced. I wasn't even seeing

Anna much other than in passing. This left me unsure of the reasons, whether she was really busy or she felt like I deserved the way I was being treated. No matter what she or anyone else thought, I didn't regret anything I said, because I'd meant it. I only wished I could have found my voice sooner and said them to others as well. It wasn't that I couldn't be apologetic for the bad language, I could. If I had anything I was sorry about, it would have been the bad language. That was something my grandmother would not have approved. At the end of the day, it was difficult for me to feel all that bad even for that. He was a bully, and I just did what everybody else wanted to do, but didn't.

Seth and I didn't talk much about what happened between Meddy and me. The one exception was when Seth came home one day, and said, "I don't know if I'm going to be asked to come back and teach next year." He did not look at me, but he had a tone that felt slightly accusatory. I could feel that old nagging pain of guilt and shame twist in my stomach, and then with a breath, it was extinguished. "Did O'Brennan tell you that or did Mr. Worsham say something to you? I'll talk to them if you want because you had nothing to do with it. What did they say about what happened between me and Meddy?"

"Eh, nothing, I don't want to talk about it," he said, moving away from me.

"Did you ask … why? I'll call Mr. Worsham and talk with him. I want to know if it was because of me. I can't understand why my argument with Meddy would affect your job. At least I can apologize for losing my temper."

I searched his eyes, but he simply responded, "I don't want you to talk to them, just drop it, don't worry about it. I decided I'm not going to teach here another year anyway, it's too much crazy stuff. I'm applying to other districts." He spoke, never looking at me.

"Could it be you just didn't want to know. Because you know it's not just about what I did? Maybe it's not about me having some stupid argument with Meddy in the first place? It probably has more to do with the mess you've been doing the whole time? I'm not as stupid as you and your friends might think! I know you've been drinking and smoking with the locals even though you promised you'd stop. You're happy to play it off like it's all been because of me … and what do you mean you're going to apply somewhere else? So when did you plan to say something? Seth, you don't get to make every decision for our lives."

He just looked at me and said nothing as I kept spewing how mad and fed up I was. Right as I was feeling my power and using my voice, he turned to walk out the door and said to me, "It's my career, I can do what I want." The fact was, he was right. I needed to figure out what I was supposed to do with my life.

It was May, and only one more month remained before the school closed for the summer. You could feel the nervous energy in the air, and all of the students fed off of it and each other like candy. I, like all the other adults at the school, was trying to stay the course till the end of the year. I had been spending a lot of time at the school working. A great deal of my time was now spent doing end-of-the-year cleaning jobs. It was helpful during this time to have something to keep me focused, and my mind off of my life. I saw Anna very little, and other than to get dinner on, take Rawsh out for a walk, shower, and sleep, I worked as much as I could.

I've never thought of myself as especially moral or even immoral. I think that a person can be pushed to choose between right or wrong. Depending on what you choose, you may go against what is the standard and acceptable behavior. Sometimes we can be pressed and squeezed so much, we find our morals become less a decision and more of a reaction. Since the age of ten, the one thing I decided for sure was that I hated secrets. Secrets to me were one of those moral traps that people set to control you or steal your life away. I hated people keeping secrets from me, and I didn't keep many secrets of my own.

A few days after Seth dropped on me his decision to apply for a new teaching assignment without including me in the conversation, I told him I had decided to go home at the end of the month. We had originally planned to go home together at the end of June when school was out or possibly tramp around other parts of Alaska before going back to Kansas City. I knew I wasn't going to make it that long. I needed space from him, his secrets, and everything that had happened. Time to just figure out what and who I was now. I gave O'Brennan my two-week notice and the money I made would be used to pay for my way home.

In spite of the fact that home was not always a safe place for me, the reality was there was no place else to go. I also was aware that I was different because of this journey that took me so far north. There was something that was clear to me now. Though I knew nothing of the world and was nothing to the world, the world was as much mine to know as it was anyone else's. I could take that home in me and leave again if I chose. I realized I saw and did things that most of the people I knew had never experienced or ever would. Things and people of the past die a slow death, and because of those things, I was left wondering if they would see what I was beginning to see in myself. Or was it possible I would be another trinket or souvenir brought back to my family, and they would place me on the whatnot shelf to collect dust? I wasn't sure, but at home, I would return to the land of my people.

My desire was also that Seth might find value in me again, in the way he saw me before I knew his family and friends. I feared I was to him at best what his father believed I was, a curiosity. Worse, I would have been his latest Peace Corps project that was meant to save the world while really it was meant to punish a father and mother that had abandoned him his entire life. Maybe the truth was we were just two orphans that found each other for a while.

The stress was stifling, and thinking past my need to just get home, answering my own and others' questions about whether Seth and I were breaking up was way too much to think about. He and I fought constantly about my decision to leave early. The fact that I needed Seth to purchase the plane ticket because I didn't have a credit card caused him to believe he had leverage over me. He stated confidently one evening, while I was packing some things, "How are you going to pay for your ticket? I'm not paying for it."

I could feel the smug stench coming off him the same way I'd heard from his friends. I reminded him that I was working, I had enough to cover the ticket, and I didn't need his money. Furious, he came back at me for not being fair and responsible. I thought, *Seriously, irresponsible?* His concerns seemed to be less about missing me and more about missing what I did for him.

He started in, "I'm working until the end of the school year. How am I supposed to get everything packed up and out of here? The landlords are saying we have to be out on the day school ends. Plus, food? I don't know what half of this stuff is in here. I don't even know what to do with most of it. I'm just saying, there's no TV dinners in here!" It was always easy for me to give in, especially if I felt responsible.

"You have a master's degree. I'm sure you'll figure it out, and as far as you not helping me with the ticket, you can either help me or I'll ask someone else. If I have to, I'll ask O'Brennan." I walked out of the room.

My ticket arrived in the mail and a bush plane was arranged for me to be picked up. I'd organized as much as I could with boxes labeled as keep, give away, or dump. In reality, we had very little because the furnishings and most of the cookware belonged to the landlords. Small things I cared about were packed to go with me, and other things too difficult to take on the plane, I had already mailed. I had one bag, Rawsh and his kennel, a half-filled bucket of salted fish, and a box of frozen crab, double boxed, frozen solid with freezer packs. This would be my gift to my family, so they could have a small piece of Alaska. I prepared as many premade dinners as I could for Seth, and there were enough breakfast foods and peanut butter for lunch. I knew he wouldn't starve. He in turn made all of my arrangements and seemed to come to grips with my going home. He would meet me in Kansas City, as planned, when school was out.

However, I didn't find out until after I'd left that Seth's plan was not to head back to me right away. He headed instead to see one of the friends, Robert, before he returned to Kansas City. Like our journey to Alaska had been filled with great uncertainty, it seemed our journey forward would prove to be just as challenging. Yet, for me, the journey to find oneself hinged everything in life. This was now my most important journey to travel.

A few days before I was to leave for Kansas City with Rawsh, O'Brennan and Lisa invited me over for a proper goodbye. We talked and laughed over a light lunch while school was still in session. Lisa gave me a small gift wrapped in a cloth to open later, then headed back to class with neither of us making promises to stay in touch, but we'd embraced warmly. O'Brennan pulled me aside. *Oh no,* I thought, *another one of his warnings.*

"You know, Meddy came over that night after your argument to talk to me about what happened," he said with a smile I rarely saw. I was now a bit uncomfortable and not looking forward to hearing whatever was going to be said, "He was scared shitless." I looked at him and had to check to see if my mouth was open. *Did I hear O'Brennan get so loose with his language and say Meddy was scared?*

"What! Really? He didn't seem all that scared to me. He was waving that wrench around like he was in charge and wanted to beat the hell out of me."

"I'm telling you, this man came over that night, banging on the door. I thought something serious had happened, a house was on fire the way he was acting. He kept looking around and talking low like any minute someone was about to jump out. So, I said 'What's up, Meddy, is everything alright? Did someone get hurt?' Meddy started telling me about the argument. When he was done that man looked like he was scared for his life. I knew you scared the mess out of him. I wanted to laugh so bad. It took everything I had to keep a straight face. I've never seen him act this afraid of anybody."

I couldn't think of anything I did or said that made Meddy so afraid other than he'd never had anyone stand up to him before. O'Brennan started laughing and imitating Meddy, "Eh! You think she'd really shoot me?' I looked as serious as I could, glanced around the room like somebody might be listening, and said 'Meddy … Man, if I were you, I'd be real careful and watch your back … you never know!'" At this point, O'Brennan was laughing so hard and he had me laughing so much that I almost forgot where I was. We said our goodbyes, and he politely said to let him know if I needed anything. He surprised me with a hug and thanked me for the gift of seeing Meddy get what he deserved, being the big man that was scared to death of a little Black woman. The thought of what O'Brennan said gave me mixed feelings about O'Brennan's perception of me and possibly Black people, along with the pleasure I felt when thinking about Meddy.

The day came for me to leave, and I had no expectation of anyone seeing Rawsh and me off. Some of the students came by the house one evening and said goodbye. I received big hugs from the twins when I was heading out of school. The plane was there early that morning, around seven a.m. Seth and I headed to the runway with Rawsh, a couple of boxes, a duffle bag, and Rawsh's kennel that had been brought up earlier. We were there for only a couple of minutes while we waited for the plane. It was awkward as we made small talk and Rawsh ran around as long as he could before having to be kenneled. I looked over the land and took a deep breath to hold it inside when I saw Anna and Ms. Elaine. They were coming up the hill along with one of the women from the sweat lodge, coming to see me off. The O'Brennans had said their goodbyes and stayed at school to run classes while Seth was with me. My heart leaped as I threw my arms around Anna in an uncustomary way. A raven flew in a tree nearby and called loudly, but I ignored it for my friends.

"Damn them! Make my friend leave … not right he does this, ass!" Anna said.

The plane landed, all my belongings were loaded, and the last embraces were packed away. I held Seth the longest, which for him was also uncustomary. Saying goodbyes were never something I did well. For a moment, I wasn't sure I was doing the right thing. A part of me wanted to burst into tears and say, *I made a mistake, I was wrong, everything's great,* but even if I cried a river, everything else would have been a lie. I looked over my shoulder and now three ravens were perched in the same tree, but the roar of the plane muffled their cries and the voiceless open mouths of the people waving. As the plane took off, I couldn't help but feel profound gratitude to see that I was wrong, and someone did care for me enough to say goodbye and think of me as a friend in the shadow of so many that did not.

The plane lifted, and I looked down from the passenger seat at the faces that bore witness to my being there in their village and in their lives, if for only a season. This was the place and the people that were a part of the change in my life, and I had no regrets. I focused straight in front of me, looking up at a clear blue sky, and I looked out the window at the people waving, the blue dome of the church, my husband, the sea, and dock swarming with seagulls screeching a morning song and whispering their goodbye. It was all perfect.

The End

Images

My grandmother ("Mom"), step-grandfather, brother, two older sisters, and I pose by our Christmas tree. I hated the pink wool skirt I was wearing.

Me and my second-oldest sister playing with Chatty Cathy dolls we got for Christmas.

Mom (my grandmother) and Mr. Allen (my step-grandfather) in my childhood home on Bellefontaine, in her bedroom, between 1965–1968.

Uncle Dee as a younger man. Approx. early twenties.

My sister, Janice at ten years old, with my grandmother Purnie Mary Stovall-Hill in 1955.

A portrait of Mrs. Lockhart.

Front living room of Bellefontaine in 1982, days before leaving for Alaska. Grandma Purnie ("Mom") and Seth's cousin (on the right) are pictured.

My mother, my father and I at my high school graduation in 1978.

Seth, Rob, and Reuben (from left to right) after arriving in KCMO to meet Mom (my grandmother) at her home on 4044 Bellefontaine, days before our wedding.

Seth and I on our wedding day outside the Community Christian Church (aka the Frank Lloyd Wright Building) on May 22, 1982.

The Badlands in South Dakota in 1982.

Road going into Fairbanks from the ALCAN (Alaska–Canadian) Highway.

Seth posing by the entrance to Anchor Inn in Whittier, in 1982. I ate lots of pumpkin pie here.

Photo of the 14-story Begich Towers (built for the army) in Whittier in 1982. Everything under one roof; it has apartments, a grocer, school, and more.

Photo of Columbia Glacier in 1982.

O'Brennan and his wife, Lisa, near the Columbia Glacier.

The husband of the woman pictured killed this bear.

Seth and Rawsh searching the Aspen Forest on Copper Mountain, between 1982–1983.

Rawsh and I on the beach in Tatitlek.

The village burial grounds behind which is "the point" Meddy frequently visited, 1982.

The "Scrooge and Marley" school play. I created the backdrops and several costumes.

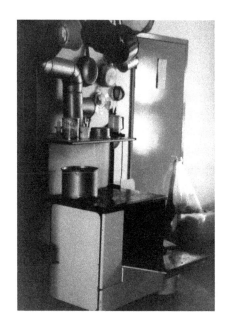

The oil-burning stove in our house in Tatitlek, used for food and warmth, 1982.

A young boy spinning the Russian Orthodox star during Russian Christmas.

The older houses of Tatitlek village with Copper Mountain behind.

Melvin posing in front of the Russian Orthodox church, between 1982–1983.

Leanna, on the left, and Sandra on Tatitlek's dock. Copper Mountain can be seen in the distance.

Author's Note:

In 1983, just weeks after I left the village of Tatitlek, word reached me that the young man my husband taught and we called "the handsome one" died from a self-inflicted gunshot wound to the head. He was no more than fourteen years old.

Melvin's death was instrumental in what happened next in the village of Tatitlek. The village council made a decision to ban drugs and alcohol coming into the village, to go dry. They made a decision to save lives.